MARGIN
OF
VICTORY

MARGIN OF VICTORY

Five Battles that Changed the Face of Modern War

Douglas Macgregor

Naval Institute Press
Annapolis, Maryland

Naval Institute Press
291 Wood Road
Annapolis, MD 21402

First Naval Institute Press paperback edition published in 2023.
ISBN: 978-1-68247-690-1 (paperback)
ISBN: 978-1-61251-997-5 (eBook)

The Library of Congress has catalogued the hardcover edition as follows:
Names: Macgregor, Douglas A., author.
Title: Margin of victory : five battles that changed the face of modern war / Douglas Macgregor.
Other titles: Five battles that changed the face of modern war
Description: Annapolis, Maryland : Naval Institute Press, [2016] | Includes bibliographical references and index.
Identifiers: LCCN 2015046174 (print) | LCCN 2015046307 (ebook) | ISBN 9781612519968 (alk. paper) | ISBN 9781612519975 (epub) | ISBN 9781612519975 (mobi) | ISBN 9781612519975 (ePDF)
Subjects: LCSH: Battles--History--20th century. | Military history, Modern--20th century.
Classification: LCC D431 .M26 2016 (print) | LCC D431 (ebook) | DDC 355.4--dc23
LC record available at http://lccn.loc.gov/2015046174

♾ Print editions meet the requirements of ANSI/NISO z39.48-1992 (Permanence of Paper).
Printed in the United States of America.

31 30 29 28 27 26 25 24 23   9 8 7 6 5 4 3 2

Maps created by Charles Grear.

In memory of General Glenn K. Otis, USA (Ret.),
1929–2013

Contents

Illustrations

MAPS

TABLES

FIGURES

Foreword

There is nothing readers seem to like more than a book that discusses great battles, major campaigns, or turning points, but a number of factors set *Margin of Victory* apart from the pack. That's what makes Douglas Macgregor's book a great read.

First, we have the battles themselves, each one a turning point in the history of the twentieth century. We have the British Expeditionary Force (BEF) desperately holding the line at Mons; the Imperial Japanese Army grinding it out at Shanghai against an outclassed but numerically superior Chinese army; the Red Army smashing an entire German army group in a rapid and seemingly effortless blow; the Israel Defense Forces (IDF) getting surprised early by an Egyptian thrust across the Suez Canal in 1973; and, finally, an irresistible U.S. armored juggernaut tearing through Saddam Hussein's Republican Guards in 1991 as if they were not even there.

Beyond serving as a tour d'horizon for twentieth-century operational-level warfare, however, *Margin of Victory* does something all too rare in the world of "great battle books"—it actually manages to link its battles thematically. If one thread ties together all of these fights, it is Macgregor's warning that change is constant, but it is the reaction to change that really matters.

The British, for example, would not have had a BEF deployed at Mons at all if a few clear heads (above all that of Secretary of State for War Sir Richard Haldane) had not recognized the changed realities of industrial-age warfare and carried out a series of far-reaching reforms from 1906 to 1912, including the establishment of a general staff, the formation of an elite strike force backed by a large trained reserve, and an emphasis on soldier education. Haldane's pre-war military reform prepared Britain (just barely) to fight and win the war. If the BEF had not been at Mons to hold up the Germans for a crucial few days, the German First Army of General Alexander von Kluck might have had an open shot into the left and rear of the entire French battle array—with incalculable consequences.

The Japanese, by contrast, failed to change enough. Well into the 1930s, they were still clinging to phalanx-like "square divisions" (four regiments) that might have been ideal for the attritional nature of trench warfare but were far too unwieldy for swift maneuver. In a broader sense, they continued to rely on massed manpower when they might have downsized the force and used the savings to invest in higher-tech weapons such as tanks and aircraft.

The result was, as Macgregor recounts in some detail, a bloodbath, a struggle of attrition at Shanghai and the "grinding mill of flesh and blood" at Luodian. As they bogged down well short of their objective, the Japanese did have to introduce tanks and aircraft—pretty much their entire arsenal at the time—in order to grind forward and drive the Chinese defenders out of Shanghai. The lesson of the criticality of mobile armored firepower and its integration with the striking power of the air force and navy went unlearned, however, and it was a relatively unreconstructed Japanese army that took on even more powerful adversaries in 1941, sacrificing wave after wave of brave but undersupplied infantry against superior Western matériel.

The destruction of Army Group Center (Operation Bagration), by contrast, is a tale of two reforms: the Germans dramatically increasing their tactical fighting power at the point of impact and the Soviets deepening the process on the operational and strategic levels—and 1944 would demonstrate dramatically which side had become more effective. From the reading here, it is almost possible to drum up sympathy for the Wehrmacht—relatively de-motorized, undersupplied, indifferently led (at least on the army group level), sitting in that vast, vulnerable bulge east of Minsk, waiting to be destroyed. The Germans learned the meaning of "full-spectrum dominance" in a way they never imagined.

Likewise, 1973 is a complex story of military reform on the Egyptian side prior to Operation Badr, and on the Israeli side in the midst of the fighting, when it looked like all was lost. The Egyptians had spent a great deal of time contemplating the debacle of the physical and moral collapse of a vast mechanized army in a matter of days in 1967, and they had drawn up a careful, cautious operational plan based as much on their weaknesses at maneuver warfare as on any particular set of strengths.

The Israelis, meanwhile, had not given much thought to the Egyptians at all. Why bother? They were hardly going to do anything rash like start a war. The IDF high command kept thinking that—right until those high-powered water cannon blasted a series of holes in the high earthen berm on the Israeli side of the Suez Canal and enemy infantry and tanks began pouring into the Sinai. It was a shock that still reverberates across the Middle East. Macgregor analyzes the IDF's pain but also takes the reader carefully through the process by which the Israelis recovered their equilibrium. They reformed themselves on the fly, using infantry to dig the Egyptians out of the irrigation ditches of the Chinese Farm, for example, and then launched their armored counterstroke. A canal is a two-way crossing, after all!

Finally, there is the victory at 73 Easting, the signal moment of the coalition triumph in Operation Desert Storm. The outcome of thoroughgoing (and expensive) military reform during the Ronald Reagan presidency, Macgregor argues, was nearly thrown away before it happened (by timid leadership in the field) and then squandered altogether (by equally timid leadership in Washington). The result was the need for an encore, a repeat performance, as it were, in 2003: Operation Iraqi Freedom. Macgregor knows something about this battle: he was an officer of the 2nd Armored Cavalry Regiment and played a key role in the fighting, an action recounted in depth in his 2009 book *Warrior's Rage: The Great Tank Battle of 73 Easting.*

While *Margin of Victory* might have stopped there, it is the concluding chapter that truly sets this book apart from so many others on the scene. Here Macgregor transitions from a mere campaign history to a fervent policy recommendation for military reform. I can say with confidence that there are very few authors in the world who write as effectively or knowledgeably on this topic as he does. In previous books such as *Breaking the Phalanx* (1997) and *Transformation under Fire* (2003), he warned that an industrial-age military relying upon size and brute force needs to slim down and become leaner, more agile, and more scalable. Increased intelligence, surveillance, and reconnaissance and strike capabilities are here to stay, he has been arguing, and have changed warfare dramatically and fundamentally. Yet our armed forces and defense establishment still organize themselves very much like the year is 1945 rather than 2016. Read what he has to say here and see if you agree.

In the end, of course, Carl von Clausewitz was right. "In war," the Prussian sage once wrote, "everything is very simple, but the simplest thing is difficult." All the more reason, then, for Americans to read this thought-provoking book. The "margin of victory" is always slim, and the walk from the victory lane to the losers' club is all too short.

Robert M. Citino
U.S. Army War College
Carlisle, Pennsylvania, February 2014

Acknowledgments

This book would not have been written at all were it not for the assistance and support of many good people. First and foremost, I am indebted to Dr. John T. Kuehn, the William A. Stofft Professor at the U.S. Army Command and General Staff College, Fort Leavenworth, Kansas. John not only advised me on chapter 2, but he also corralled poor unsuspecting colleagues into reading my chapters. One of those was Dr. Nicholas Murray, associate professor of history at the U.S. Army Command and General Staff College. Dr. Murray provided excellent insights and suggestions for chapter 1. I also want to acknowledge the assistance of Dr. Jeff L. Groh, colonel, USA (Ret.), professor of information and technology in warfare at the U.S. Army War College, and of Louise Arnold-Friend, reference librarian at the U.S. Army Military History Institute at Carlisle Barracks, Pennsylvania, for their assistance with chapter 1.

Special thanks go to Dr. Jake Kipp, director of the Foreign Military Studies Office at Fort Leavenworth, Kansas, and to Dr. James S. Corum, dean of the Baltic Defense College, Tartu, Estonia, for their exceptionally perceptive comments on chapter 3. Particularly warm thanks go to Dr. Eado Hecht, who teaches at the Israel Defense Forces Command and General Staff College as well as at Bar Ilan University. Dr. Hecht's broader insights into Israel's 1973 wartime experience were of inestimable value.

Dr. Eitan Shamir of the Department of Political Studies at Bar Ilan University was also kind enough to suffer through early drafts of all the chapters. Lt. Gen. Dave Deptula, USAF (Ret.), and Adm. Mark "Lobster" Fitzgerald, USN (Ret.), contributed important insights to the conclusions and encouraged me throughout the project. I am also indebted to Frank Prautzsch, president of Velocity Technology Partners, LLC, and Lt. Col. Tim Miller, USAF (Ret.), for their advice on technology and logistics. Steve Daskal, defense analyst and retired USAF Reserve officer, indulged me by reading and commenting on numerous aspects of the book. Steve's comments were always comprehensive and astute.

Most of all, I am indebted to Mr. Young Kim, my colleague, friend, and research assistant who read all of the chapters repeatedly and prepared the illustrations, tables, and maps. I count myself fortunate to have Young's friendship and expertise in my life. However, for the errors and omissions in this volume, I alone am responsible.

Finally, this book is dedicated to Gen. Glenn K. Otis, USA (Ret.), who left this life in 2013. General Otis led from the front in every aspect of military life. He set a brilliant example of integrity and professional competence that continues to inspire me. I sincerely hope that from his new vantage point in the realm beyond, he is pleased with my treatment of a subject about which he taught me so much—the greatest tragedy of man's existence, war.

MARGIN
OF
VICTORY

INTRODUCTION

In 1925, a member of the U.S. Senate complained to President Calvin Coolidge that a colleague had told him to go to hell. Coolidge consoled the senator, saying, "I looked up the law, Senator, and you don't have to go."[1] This book argues that the United States also does not have to march into hell, as many of the great powers whose stories are recounted in this book did.

Hell is real. It can be defined in three words: defeat in war. Based on my experience in the turret of a tank leading 1,100 men into battle across Iraq in 1991 to my position as the director of the Joint Operations Center during the Kosovo air campaign in 1999, I can assure the reader that the United States wants to avoid hell at all costs.

Margin of Victory is about avoiding hell. The battles and wars described in this volume were chosen with that view in mind. Americans can cultivate a new twenty-first-century margin of victory and avoid the hell that consumed untold millions in the last century. Each chapter is a clarion call for the United States to recognize that wars are decided in the decades before they begin, not by the sudden appearance of a new, technological "silver bullet" or the presence of a few strong personalities in the senior ranks during a single battle.[2] How effectively national political and military leaders adjust the framework of organization, technology, and human capital to relentless change in society, technology, and world affairs determines whether the nation-state prevails or perishes in defeat.

These points explain why *Margin of Victory* focuses on wars that Carl von Clausewitz called "absolute wars" or wars of decision. Clausewitz was the first to distinguish *wars of decision* from *wars of choice* and *wars of observation*. Wars of decision are interstate conflicts that affect the vital strategic interests, if not the very survival, of the nation-state.[3] They are fought with all the means of violence at the disposal of government and society to preserve the nation-state and to destroy its enemies. Nation-states fight wars of decision with the expectation of eventual conflict termination based on the attainment of a defined political-military end state.

The United States' participation in two wars of decision, World War I and World War II, is instructive. Both conflicts fundamentally changed the world's international political and economic systems. A comparison of the map of the world in 1939 and the postwar landscape of 1945 tells the story. The devastation caused by strategic bombing, the dramatic drop in the standard of living of the survivors, and the loss of vast territories to the victors paint a grim picture of postwar Germany and Japan.[4] Wars of decision are wars the United States cannot afford to lose.[5]

The interventions launched after the terrorist attacks of September 11, 2001, were wars of choice: open-ended conflicts fought without a clearly defined attainable political-military end state.[6] The conduct of patrols, raids, and checkpoints from heavily protected and comfortable forward operating bases in Iraq and Afghanistan was closer in character to British and French colonial police actions in Africa, the Middle East, and India than to history's wars of decision.[7]

Today, there is a critical need to reorient American civilian and professional military thinking about warfare toward the potential for future wars of decision.[8] Thankfully, such wars, like financial collapses or "black swans," are infrequent. In his book *Currency Wars*, James Rickards uses the example of a forest fire caused by lightning to explain the real meaning of a black swan event.[9] Whether a fire destroys a single tree or a million acres, it is usually caused by a single bolt of lightning. The same bolt of lightning can strike with little or no effect, or it can cause a catastrophic fire. The outcome depends on a range of variables that are difficult if not impossible to predict. Wars of decision are similar. They are the massive forest fires no one expects, but they inevitably occur.

Wars of decision usually occur fifty to one hundred years apart. The two world wars in the twentieth century were exceptions in that they occurred in rapid succession. In both world wars, great powers in Europe and Asia fought for several years before the United States joined the fight. This gave Americans the opportunity to build up their military might—to train, organize, and equip millions of Soldiers, Airmen, Sailors, and Marines without interruption. However, when the United States did join the fight, the human cost was still enormous. World War I cost the United States 318,000 casualties in only 110 days of combat.[10]

World War II was worse. From 6 June to 7 December 1944, U.S. Army ground forces in France and Belgium sustained 90,000 battlefield casualties per month, or 3,000 casualties a day, against 20 percent of the German army—an army that fought without any tactical air support.[11] Of course, compared with the human and material losses taken by the Europeans, Soviets, Chinese, and Japanese, American losses were modest. As a result, the United States emerged from World War II relatively undamaged in a position of unprecedented economic dominance.

In the twenty-first century, Americans should not expect this experience to be repeated. The post–Cold War world and the international institutions that supported it are crumbling.[12] The great powers that once stood between the United States and its potential opponents are now reduced in number to two: Germany and Japan. To date, only Japan has rebuilt a fraction of its former power. Germany is an economic but not a military powerhouse. How much longer the North Atlantic Treaty Organization will maintain its cohesion is difficult to predict. The trend lines, however, are impossible to miss: Recent events in eastern Ukraine, Mesopotamia, and the western Pacific suggest the potential for major future wars in some of the same regions where wars of decision incubated in the past.[13]

Precisely how the forces of social and economic change in today's international system will shape future competition for access to the global commons—the resource domains that exist beyond the political authority of any one nation-state, including the high seas, the atmosphere, Antarctica, and outer space—is impossible to forecast. Americans cannot predict the international forces that, in ten or fifteen years, might test the nation's resolve to defend its vital strategic interests.[14] Today's strategic partner could easily be tomorrow's opponent, and a former foe could be a future ally.[15]

The only prediction Americans can make with confidence is that a future war of decision is coming. Deterring or, if necessary, fighting and winning such a war will demand the capability for offensive military action that combines technology and human potential in new and innovative ways.[16] Of course, devising new conceptual and organizational frameworks to create a profound strategic advantage is not an easy task, particularly given the expansive and sometimes confusing direction of U.S. national military strategy.[17]

On one hand, that strategy makes a good case that future aerospace and maritime forces will have to deliver powerful, disabling strikes through dense enemy air and missile defenses.[18] On the other hand, future military force structures and institutions are more opaque. Washington's emphasis on reductions in the numbers of troops—those in uniform who actually deploy and fight—obscures the hard truth that open-ended downsizing makes existing military establishments smaller without making them more capable.[19] There is almost no awareness in the executive or legislative branch that without prudent reform and reorganization, the downsized military establishment will end up on the road to extinction in the next war of decision.

Bad news is never welcome in Washington, DC, but sometimes it is necessary. The truth is that the last fourteen years have severely eroded the United States' military-technological edge and operational flexibility—particularly those of the U.S. Army ground forces.[20] If today's Army were hit and hit hard, if American soldiers faced an air defense threat, rocket artillery, cruise missiles, or a capable armored ground force, these troops and their commanders would be shocked, even paralyzed.[21] Occupations ruin armies.

Margin of Victory seeks a way out of this dilemma by illuminating how other great powers navigated through the harsh and difficult military equivalent of the process Joseph Schumpeter called "creative destruction."[22] The battle described in each chapter is a tale of how strategy, technology, and military organization continually interact with each other in the broader context of national culture, history, and human capital to produce success or failure.[23]

To some readers, the battles and wars of the twentieth century may seem distant, but these conflicts still affect us, influence our lives, and have much to teach us, especially now. Washington's current attitudes toward military power in general, and the U.S. Army in particular, are reminiscent of the attitudes in both political parties before the outbreak of the Korean conflict in 1950. In a speech delivered on 31 August 1947 in Lincoln, Nebraska, Gen. Jacob Devers, then–commanding general of U.S. Army ground forces, talked about these attitudes and the onset of the Cold War.[24]

Devers warned his audience that the Harry S. Truman administration was relying too much on nuclear deterrence and that the Regular Army was too small and too dispersed around the world on occupation duty to fight a war.[25] Tragically, Devers' prescient warning was disregarded. In 1947, the American public was still celebrating the World War II victories of armies that no longer existed, and politicians were distracted by more important issues at home.

In Washington's haste to harvest modest savings, the readiness to sacrifice a strong, existing armed force (what the concluding chapter of this book calls "forces-in-being") is back in vogue. No one in Congress, the White House, or the Pentagon grasps the critical need to win the "first fight."[26] Put differently, Washington is walking the path to hell.

The world has changed dramatically since 1950. In the twenty-first century, if Americans lose the first fight, they may not have the luxury of fighting a second time. Potential opponents understand that if military force is applied suddenly and with extreme violence, Washington is likely to be paralyzed.[27]

If the U.S. Army cannot rapidly respond in a crisis with superior lethality to a Russian military buildup, the loss of the Baltic littoral or western Ukraine to Russian armored forces would be difficult if not impossible to reverse. The United States would confront the choice of conducting a humiliating withdrawal or fighting a costly war to redeem its honor.[28] American military failure in one region would undoubtedly encourage further aggression in others. It has happened before.[29] No amount of American aerospace and maritime power short of a nuclear strike that no one wants will rescue the United States and its allies from this strategic dilemma. The solution is a powerful, standing, professional U.S. Army.

For those readers who think the Marine Corps' light infantry–centric force structure can substitute for a powerful standing army, the battle narratives in *Margin of Victory* offer a sobering reminder that they cannot. In the maritime domain of the strategic periphery, the Marines are unmatched. But fighting in Europe or the greater Middle East or on the Asian mainland demands powerful Army ground forces, which must consist of robust mobile armored forces with significant theater air defense and missile defenses and ground-based strike and sustainment capabilities. These modern Army forces must fight as part of an integrated, joint force structure.[30]

With these points in mind, the central question that *Margin of Victory* poses in the final chapter is: What body of military leaders and supporting military mechanism can develop these forces and ensure unity of effort on the strategic and operational levels? The popular (but incorrect) assumption is that the right answers will arise from the chaos of competing service interests, partisan politics, and institutional rivalry.

America's future margin of victory depends on whether Americans are willing to subject their national military institutions to serious, unbiased reform—not cosmetic alteration, but fundamental change. Reform today, as in the past, must address the military's need to cope with weapons of new lethality and the nation's demand for economy. The national military strategy and the armed forces the American people need to fight and win in the future will only come from new thinking, new organizations for combat, and new institutions of U.S. national security. When the aforementioned process of self-assessment fails, the margin of victory narrows quickly. The result is always the same: defeat.

Change inside military establishments before and during war is always painful because adjustments to warfighting organizations and modernization threaten more people and institutions than we can count. Inevitably, in this struggle for badly needed changes in thinking, organization, structure, technology, and leadership, the enemy is not external. The enemy is us.

CHAPTER 1

MISSION IMPOSSIBLE

The Battle of Mons, 1914

There is an inclination among historians to depict the outbreak of World War I as inevitable, to assume that Great Britain had little choice but to intervene on the side of France and Russia in a regional European war against Germany and Austria-Hungary. The truth is more interesting. On 1 August 1914, the day Germany mobilized for war, the leading members of Britain's Liberal government had different ideas. Most of the cabinet was opposed to war with Germany. Sir Edward Grey, Britain's foreign secretary, and Sir Winston Churchill, the First Lord of the Admiralty, were the noteworthy exceptions.[1]

Prime Minister Herbert Henry Asquith, known as "H. H.," together with John Viscount Morley, John Burns, and David Lloyd George—the tenacious Welshman who would eventually become Britain's wartime prime minister—opposed war with Germany. Morley and Burns regarded British participation in a war with Germany as tantamount to an international crime. All feared the strategic consequences of fighting on the continent. Lloyd George was particularly disturbed at the prospect of war with Germany. In a letter to a friend he confided his feelings: "I am filled with horror at the prospect [of war]. I am even more horrified that I should ever appear to have a share in it, but I must bear my share of the ghastly burden though it scorches my flesh to do so."[2]

Lloyd George's fears aside, the eventual decision to fight was not the product of some long, complex decisionmaking process inside the cabinet. The British public's support for war with Germany—together with Asquith's political calculus that if he did not push for war, his government would be replaced by another that would—drove the anti-war party, namely Morley and Burns, to resign from the government.[3] On 4 August 1914, Britain declared war on Germany and Austria-Hungary.

Herbert Kitchener, the legendary figure who avenged the murder of General Charles "Chinese" Gordon and reconquered the Sudan, was recalled from Egypt and appointed minister of war. His first duty was to brief the cabinet on his thinking about Britain's conduct of the war. Kitchener's message regarding the time, money, and human resources fighting and winning the war would entail shocked his audience. He told Prime Minister Asquith and his ministers in the bluntest possible terms that Britain would have to raise an army of more than a million men and ready the nation for a war that would last at least three years. Kitchener's words fell like hammer blows on Asquith and his ministers.[4]

Churchill was noted for reminding cabinet ministers time and again that the Royal Navy was the only force that could lose the war to Germany in an afternoon, a belief reinforced by the mistaken assumption that Germany would opt to fight at sea on strategic terms that favored Britain.[5] Thus, the ministers found it difficult to accept the argument that the Royal Navy's great power at sea could not possibly decide the outcome of a continental war that would be fought primarily on land by Britain's small professional army.[6]

For most of their history, the English-speaking peoples of the British Isles had not needed a large army. In contrast to Russia, Germany, Austria, and France, Britain's frontiers were the narrow seas and vast oceans of the world. Britain's margin of victory was its enormous navy guided by a prudent foreign policy that saw no strategic value in alliances with continental European powers, which would contribute nothing to the defense of the British Isles, let alone Britain's all-important overseas empire. Thus, Britain's historic margin of victory may have been narrow, but it was wide enough at sea to make a large standing army seem like a needless expense.

Until Kitchener made his presentation, Britain's leaders did not seriously consider that their comparatively small professional army would have to fight for more than a few months. The Royal Navy's capability to blockade Germany was real and impressive, but in retrospect, the British cabinet saw German power and interests through a narrowly focused lens that magnified British strengths but also obscured Germany's greatest strategic asset, the Imperial German Army.[7]

Fortunately for the British Empire, Sir Richard Haldane was appointed as secretary of state for war in December 1905. Within the spending constraints of a national defense budget that enshrined naval supremacy as Britain's permanent margin of victory, Haldane fought for a strong regular British army designed for mobile, offensive warfare in Europe or Asia.

Though frequently frustrated by a government obsessed with economy, the Royal Navy, and a political culture shaped by the English-speaking peoples' lingering suspicion of large, standing armies, Haldane resolved to transform a British army optimized for irregular warfare—the suppression of rebellious tribes and peoples throughout Britain's far-flung empire—into a far more lethal professional military establishment. Despite the enormous obstacles arrayed against him, Haldane's program of army reform and reorganization built the foundation for a professional ground force capable of fighting an industrial-age European power: the 160,000-man, 7-division British Expeditionary Force (BEF).

Haldane conceived of the BEF as "a force that might make the difference between initial victory and initial defeat."[8] That is precisely what happened. To everyone's surprise, the BEF turned out to be a force that punched far above its weight in the crucial opening weeks of the war. When the soldiers of the First German Army pressed down the road from Brussels to Mons on 22 August 1914, the Germans discovered that 2 British army corps of 80,000 men were waiting for them along the Mons-Condé canal, a development they had not foreseen.

HALDANE: PRELUDE TO WAR

In 1879, Germany's "Iron Chancellor," Prince Otto von Bismarck, was asked what he would do if the British army landed on Germany's North Sea coast. Bismarck answered, "I would have it arrested."[9] Given the British army's imperial focus on irregular warfare, Bismarck's response was not an exaggeration.

After 1815, the British army's leadership focused almost exclusively on battles with technologically backward, even primitive, non-European opponents. British colonial warfare was not a complex affair. In battles with tribal opponents at Ulundi, Kandahar, and Omdurman, the application of overwhelming firepower substituted for tactics and strategy.

Bismarck's sarcasm, however, concealed a larger strategic appreciation for the enormous potential of Britain's global naval power to influence the peace of Europe.[10] Until his death in 1898, Bismarck argued, "The preservation of Anglo-German goodwill is, after all, the most important thing. I see England as an old and traditional ally."[11]

Because of the sea and British control of it, Churchill adopted a similar view of imperial Germany; its powerful army posed no threat to Britain. In fact, as a Liberal candidate for office in 1908, he reassured voters in Manchester and Dundee that the very notion of a German threat to British interests was a figment of Tory imagination.[12] Churchill reasoned that Russia and France, not Germany, were the anti–status quo states with strategic aims antithetical to British interests.

In the tragic aftermath of two world wars, Churchill's attitude may seem strange, but at the time, his views were quite reasonable. Throughout the eighteenth and nineteenth centuries, Britain's Royal Navy prepared to fight the fleet of a single enemy: France. After its lost war with Prussia in 1870–71, France was anything but stable. During the five-year span from 1881 to 1886, ten French governments rose and fell. In 1898, France and Britain nearly went to war at Fashoda, a Sudanese desert town on the Nile River where the countries' forces confronted each other in conflict over control of the upper Nile.[13]

A less thoughtful man in Haldane's position might have fixed his strategic gaze on France or tsarist Russia, a nation that frequently threatened British control of India, with the goal of creating a military establishment ideally suited to the challenge of warfare in the Baltic littoral, northwest India, or northern France. Fortunately, Haldane was more circumspect. He knew he did not have the luxury in 1905 of knowing precisely which power or alliance of powers Britain might eventually confront in war. Though in time Britain moved closer to the Franco-Russian entente, Haldane viewed his task in 1905 more broadly: to build a British Expeditionary Force that could be strategically decisive wherever it came ashore to fight.

Haldane, a Scottish lawyer turned politician with a formidable intellect that rested on the foundation of British and German graduate studies in law and philosophy, seemed an unlikely choice for secretary of state for war. Yet he turned out to be the best man for the job. He cultivated political support for his reform agenda with conciliatory gestures and reasoned arguments. Haldane sought out and listened to people with original ideas and concepts. In an act of supreme political sagacity, he made the leader of the opposition in Parliament, Sir Arthur Balfour, his confidante, and he skillfully kept the army's generals out of politics.[14]

Haldane carefully read the postwar findings of several royal commissions that examined the army's performance in South Africa against the Boers.[15] He was, therefore, keenly aware of the British generals' glaring incompetence in a war with an opponent that never numbered more than 70,000. He also knew that ending the war on British terms had required 500,000 British and colonial troops and cost 22,000 British lives, as well as the astronomical sum of £227 million (roughly $500 billion in adjusted dollars).

Despite the appalling record in South Africa, Haldane discovered there was no enthusiasm in the army's senior ranks for reforms of any kind. In 1905, Field Marshal Sir Evelyn Wood, a decorated combat veteran and former quartermaster general of the British army, told Colonel Gerald Ellison,

Haldane's military secretary, "If you organize the British army, you will ruin it."[16] Wood's views typified thinking inside an army where the men at the top were contemptuous of serious professional study and intellectual development. Many were children of the upper classes, men who worshipped the vigorous outdoor life and believed firmly in the myth of the gifted amateur.[17]

Moreover, the British public's historic apathy toward the army, the government's determination to reduce defense expenditures after the Boer War fiasco, and the general disinterest in the army's potential strategic value to Britain meant Haldane could not expect much support for the replacement of senior officers who obstructed change. These societal conditions were unfortunate because some of Haldane's reforms would eventually suffer decline and repeal by the reactionary military bureaucracy in the hands of Kitchener and his generals when the Great War began.[18] But in 1905, Haldane could do little to anticipate or stop this development.

Against this strategic backdrop, Haldane focused first on "software," or first-order questions (thinking carefully about strategy and organization and contemplating likely contingencies), and then on hardware (technology and equipment). To Haldane, thinking through the problem meant assembling a small group of talented and intelligent people from inside and outside of the War Office to help him answer the first-order questions: Whom do we fight? Where do we fight? And how do we fight?

Today, officers in the U.S. Armed Forces would describe Haldane's action as the formation of a *disruptive innovation cell*. Contemporary American and British chiefs of service frequently go through the motions of creating advisory groups on force design and strategy, but ultimately nothing really changes. A major reason for this failure is that true innovation is inherently disruptive and cannot be institutionalized. Put differently, "Armies don't innovate. People innovate."[19] Haldane seems to have intuitively grasped this reality.

To get the job done, Haldane provided his innovation cell with sufficient funding, authority, and, most important, the contemporary equivalent of "executive top cover," which extended to the prime minister and King Edward VII. For help in pushing through his reforms, Haldane also turned to a longtime friend, prominent British historian and Liberal politician Reginald Baliol Brett, 2nd Viscount Esher. Inside the Liberal government, Esher personally approved War Office appointments and worked behind the scenes to both support Haldane's reforms and cultivate Anglo-French cooperation.

Colonel Gerald Ellison, the man who became Haldane's military secretary, strongly influenced Haldane's reform package. Other key military figures included General Sir William Nicholson, an irascible, eccentric officer whom Haldane described as having a "big brain," and Major General Sir Douglas Haig, the inarticulate but socially well connected cavalry officer who would later become director of military training.[20] When Haldane sought to create a separate administrative branch to assist the army general staff with matters of modern finance and logistics, Haldane sought the advice of the famous director of the London School of Economics, H. J. Mackinder.[21]

Unlike most of Britain's generals who read and studied very little about their profession, Haldane thoroughly researched the works of Prussia's leading military intellectuals: Carl von Clausewitz, Paul Bronsart von Schellendorf, and Colmar von der Goltz.[22] Haldane also listened to the counsel of his advisory group, most of whom were familiar with the British works on military affairs of Colonel G. F. R. Henderson and General Sir Frederick Maurice. The results of his efforts were impressive. A detailed examination of Haldane's large and complex reform package is beyond the scope of this book, but the essential features included the following:

> ‣ The establishment of a general staff. Like much of Haldane's reform package, this originally Prussian idea was not new, but Haldane extended the concept from the confines of the British War Office to the whole army. To Haldane, the British General Staff was a brain trust— Haldane placed immense faith in such groups—that would, he hoped, in future wars supervise and conduct operations.[23] Haldane also demanded that corps, division, and brigade staffs become permanent structures rather than temporary arrangements as was the case before the Boer War.

> ‣ The creation of an elite strike force of six infantry divisions and a cavalry division, all designed for rapid deployment as part of the BEF. To support the BEF's training and preparation for rapid deployment, Haldane returned most of Britain's regiments to Great Britain. In addition, he created an "all-volunteer" professional force with a new training cycle: individual instruction in the winter; squadron, company, and battery training in the spring; regimental, battalion, and brigade training in the summer; and divisional or interdivisional exercises and army maneuvers in late summer.[24]

> ‣ The formation of a trained reserve of fourteen territorial divisions of volunteers including fourteen mounted yeomanry brigades. Haldane's reforms created a reserve system from which drafts could be drawn for

the expeditionary force. Sadly, in 1914 Kitchener cast aside Haldane's reserve mobilization system in favor of his own volunteer system. This change dramatically slowed and complicated the process of building up Britain's continental army, but Haldane's reserve system was restored after the war.

> The creation of Britain's first officers' training corps at schools and universities across Britain. Haldane insisted that the educated men of the middle class become the mid-grade officers of the new army.

> The raising of individual soldiers' education levels. As a student of German culture and history, Haldane knew that in 1866, Prussian army chief of staff Helmuth von Moltke credited Prussia's educational system and its teachers with the victory in Prussia's six-week war with Austria.[25] Haldane wanted to emulate this achievement with improvements to the technical training and preparation of soldiers for service and for subsequent civilian life.[26]

To summarize, Haldane maximized "military capability at cost." He forged a new professional army, perhaps the best in Britain's history. In the words of J. F. C. Fuller, who served in Haldane's BEF, "Now we became Europe-conscious, and as we did so these values crept in and compelled our Government to consider what part we were to play in a European war, and how we could most economically prepare to play it."[27]

Yet for all of its virtues, the new British army was hardly revolutionary. Even though the British government implemented a subsidy scheme for motor vehicles to ensure there would be a supply of roughly similar vehicles at the start of a future conflict, the BEF had only 827 cars or trucks and 15 motorcycles when it deployed to France.[28] British and European armies still relied on the horse, and most infantrymen moved on foot.[29]

With the expansion of Franco-British military cooperation toward the end of Haldane's term in the War Office, British and French generals concluded that a future war with Germany would be a short, decisive war of movement.[30] Not surprisingly, the generals placed a premium on lighter, mobile artillery designed to break up massed formations of attacking German troops in the opening phase of such a war.

Because British generals did not anticipate the need for heavy artillery to smash concrete fortifications, the BEF contained nothing to compare with the destructiveness of the heavy artillery (420-millimeter howitzers) that the Germans would employ in 1914 to smash through Belgium's twelve fortresses of Liege. That said, Haldane did strongly support the introduction of the short Lee-Enfield rifle, a lethal firearm with a range of eight hundred yards and a flat trajectory that proved very effective throughout World War I.

An error for which Haldane and his successors in the War Office must bear some responsibility was their collective failure to adequately prepare Britain's armaments industry for potential mobilization in a future war.[31] This omission meant that ammunition stocks would be inadequate in 1914. The other area in which Britain was woefully underprepared was modern optics. In 1914, Britain produced only about 10 percent of its peacetime requirements, with about 60 percent coming from Germany.[32] Further complicating Haldane's army transformation and modernization was Britain's economic crisis in the aftermath of the Boer War, which meant that austere British defense budgets were the decisive factor in Haldane's army reforms and British national military strategy.

As a priority in army reform, this concern for economy influenced all strategic and military planning. Haldane always viewed the British army he loved in a larger strategic context, which he explained to French president Georges Clemenceau in April 1908: "No country had ever been able to bear the burden of maintaining a very large navy and a very large army. I said that for myself I was determined that the bulk of our strength should be concentrated on the preservation of our naval superiority, and on developing as far as possible its organization. . . . If we maintained a large and costly Army at home, down would go the resources and money which we could pour into the Navy, and that I would not stand for."[33]

Clemenceau did not agree with Haldane, but the French were primarily a continental power with little understanding of Britain's maritime interests. In practice, this meant that far from identifying a potential opponent and simply organizing and arming British ground forces to defeat that enemy, Haldane set a mandatory financial limit and insisted that, if more effectively organized and equipped, the British army would fulfill the strategic requirements. Thus, British interest in maritime dominance and desire for economy rather than French national security were together the sine qua non of Haldane's army reform.[34]

In 1912, Sir Richard Haldane left his post as minister of war and assumed his new duties as lord chancellor, the cabinet member responsible for the efficient functioning and independence of the courts. Although the British Expeditionary Force would see action before many of Haldane's other reforms had struck deep roots, the force's cross-channel mobilization in August 1914 occurred with a degree of precision and efficiency unthinkable 15 years earlier when British army forces deployed to South Africa. On one day of the mobilization—the busiest—80 trains off-loaded troops and equipment at Southampton's docks. Before the 5-day deployment ended, an average of 13 ships departed daily for France carrying over 50,000 tons of troops, equipment, and supplies.[35]

Kitchener was pleased with the deployment of Haldane's BEF, but he had his own ideas about mobilization and decided to discard Haldane's plans and policies.[36] His decision meant that future British armies would take much longer to mobilize, train, and prepare before they could be committed to battle in France.

MONS: THE BATTLE BEGINS

On 22 August 1914, 5 divisions of the BEF, a force of 80,000 men, moved into positions in southeast Belgium along a 25-mile front. Mons, a town just 80 miles from Brussels, was at the center of the line. The weather was beautiful, warm, and sunny. The setting was deceptively peaceful. Even the French Walloons who populated Mons and its surroundings were reportedly relaxed about the British soldiers camped in their vicinity. Given that Europe had not experienced a large-scale war since the Franco-Prussian War in 1871, like most Europeans in 1914, the Belgian people were oblivious to the storm that was about to break upon them.

Three weeks earlier, Kitchener, Britain's newly appointed war minister, had no thought of committing the BEF to defend so far forward in Belgium. In fact, on 5 August, Kitchener urged the concentration of the BEF at Amiens, France, where he thought it could deliver a vigorous counterstrike once the true axis of the German advance was known. Field Marshal Lord Roberts, a former commander of the British army, disagreed. Roberts wanted to deploy the BEF to Antwerp, behind the advancing German armies, where it could cooperate closely with the Belgian army.

Prime Minister Asquith overruled both recommendations. Nevertheless, the wily Kitchener was able to secure the prime minister's permission to retain two of the BEF's six divisions in France, a decision that would prove prescient. Thus, when the BEF marched into Belgium, it consisted of two corps, each with two infantry divisions, plus five brigades of cavalry. Each infantry division had three brigades, each with four battalions armed with two Vickers machine guns apiece.[37]

Kitchener did not reveal his reasons for holding back the two infantry divisions. He may have assumed the Belgian army would be unable to hold its ground against the Germans. If this was the case, he may have worried that if the BEF advanced too far into Belgium, it might be cut off or would have to retreat and abandon much of its equipment and supplies. If he was correct, Amiens was simply too far from the leading edge of the French armies already facing the Germans.

Unfortunately, Kitchener left no detailed record of his thinking. Whatever his specific reasons were, he ordered Field Marshal Sir John French, the BEF commander, to move his force of approximately 80,000 men to Maubeuge on the French-Belgian border, a fortress town on the main road to Mons and Brussels.

The BEF commander was a familiar figure in British military affairs. French began military life in the Royal Navy but later transferred to the army for health reasons. The gregarious, hot-tempered French was first and foremost a cavalry officer—a true believer in the efficacy of the sword and lance with the uncanny ability to inspire men, something he demonstrated during his service in South Africa, the Sudan, and India. A year after becoming chief of the new Imperial General Staff, French was promoted to the rank of field marshal. From the beginning of his tenure as BEF commander, however, many British senior military and political leaders questioned his grasp of strategy and tactics. Some British observers even regarded him as weak-willed.[38]

Sir Douglas Haig commanded the BEF's I Corps, which comprised the 1st and 2nd Infantry Divisions. Haig's prewar career benefited from his close friendship with French, thanks to which Haig was permitted to enter the British Staff College in 1896 despite having repeatedly failed the entrance exam. Haig saw action in the Omdurman campaign of 1897–98. Like most of his cavalry contemporaries, he also served in the Second Boer War of 1899–1902, where he worked closely with French.

Haig's wife Dorothy Maud Haig was an important political asset to him. As the daughter of wealthy British aristocrat Hussey, Cresigny Vivian, 3rd Baron Vivian, Dorothy was a lady-in-waiting at the court of King Edward VII. Thanks to her position at court, Haig enjoyed "behind-the-scenes" access to the king, who continued to influence senior appointments in the British army and navy.[39] The combinations of friendships and connections rather than any demonstrated competence, character, or intelligence seem to have elevated Haig to the senior ranks of the British army.

Sir Horace Smith-Dorrien was assigned to command II Corps when its designated commander, the highly regarded Sir James Grierson, suddenly died of a heart aneurism on 17 August. II Corps, which would bear the brunt of the fighting, comprised the 3rd and 5th Infantry Divisions and was reinforced with 3 brigades of artillery. Smith-Dorrien was an apolitical officer with a solid reputation in the army for integrity and courage. He gained notoriety as one of only 50 officers and soldiers who survived the destruction of 1,300 British troops by Zulu tribesmen at the Battle of Isandlwana in January 1879. Smith-Dorrien's military exploits inside the empire were, thus, no less distinguished than Haig's. However, unlike Haig, Smith-Dorrien's relationship with French was marked by mutual dislike and distrust, which would complicate Smith-Dorrien's operational wartime task.

On 22 August, General Charles Lanrezac, commander of the French Fifth Army, was conducting a difficult retreat under pressure from the advancing German armies on the BEF's immediate right. In this hour of crisis, he asked Field Marshal French to hold the line of the Mons-Condé canal for twenty-four hours. His goal was to prevent the advancing German First Army from threatening the French Fifth Army's left flank.

French had been instructed by Kitchener to "cooperate with the French, but not to take orders from them."[40] When French complied with his ally's request, he was in his headquarters near Le Cateau, twenty-six miles from the forward edge of the battle. Neither French nor his corps commanders were aware that the French Fifth Army had already been driven back ten miles from its initial defensive positions around Namur.

In fact, by the time the first British troops reached Mons on the afternoon of 22 August, the French Fifth Army on the BEF's right flank was fighting the German Second and Third Armies less than twenty-five miles away, near Charleroi, the town where Napoleon spent the night of 15 June 1815 on his journey to Waterloo. The German First Army, temporarily under command of the Second Army commander, was simultaneously moving southwest instead of due west. If the First Army had followed its original axis of advance, it might well have surprised and annihilated the unsuspecting BEF centered on Mons, with serious consequences for the Anglo-French alliance. As it turned out, the First Army's requirement to adjust its movement in order to closely support the Second Army's advance ensured that the First Army would collide head-on with the BEF II Corps at Mons. The action drew General Alexander von Kluck and his First Army away from his original assigned axis of advance.

General von Kluck was a man who obeyed orders even if he disliked them. He aligned his movement with the Second Army, but he also kept one eye on the First Army's original purpose in Count Alfred von Schlieffen's plan of attack: to make the main attack with the powerful First Army to the north of Paris.[41]

In his book *The March on Paris and the Battle of the Marne, 1914*, General von Kluck says that on 20 August, both he and the Second Army commander, General Karl von Bülow, were told by German army headquarters in Louvain, Belgium, that the BEF was still disembarking in Lille, France, far south of Belgium.[42] This intelligence was wrong, but it reflected the German expectation that the British army was unchanged from its condition at the time of the Boer War.

Mons lies in Belgium's French-speaking region of Wallonia. In 1914, Mons was a prosperous (though rather dreary) commercial center of roughly 28,000 people. Its position along the Mons-Condé canal meant that the opening battle of World War I would be, at least, partially urban in character. Smith-Dorrien describes the importance of Mons to the II Corps defense in his autobiography:

> The morning of the 22nd saw us moving, and some twelve to fifteen miles took us to the line of the Canal, where in accordance with orders we took up a line of outposts extending from Pommeroeul (five miles east of Condé) round the north side of Mons to Nimy and thence to Givry, twenty-one miles in all. The 3rd Division went into billets round Mons in the area of Nimy-Ghlin—Frameries-Spiennes, and were there by 1 p.m., whilst the 5th Division rather later occupied the Canal on their left from Jemappes to Pommeroeul. Sir Douglas Haig's I Corps, which had moved on our right, took up a position facing north-east, prolonging our line by some seven miles, i.e. about a quarter of the B.E.F. front. As we were facing north except on the east of Mons, where we faced north-east, it will be appreciated that the British line formed a considerable salient with the town of Mons at the apex.[43]

Smith-Dorrien's description highlights the difficult position his corps was assigned to defend. In fact, Mons was open to fire from the north, east, and west. Smith-Dorrien saw the problem but still spread his forces thinly across his front—a dangerous move, since there was no time to adequately prepare the British reserve to lunge forward to blunt potential German penetrations.[44]

It should be noted, however, that Smith-Dorrien was reassured by the most recent intelligence suggesting the German forces to his front were not particularly strong. This perception was definitely shared by his commander, Sir John French. According to Smith-Dorrien, French had actually expressed his intention to resume forward movement toward the advancing Germans on 23 August.[45]

How could these two officers have been so misinformed? One obvious reason is that the front in August 1914 was very fluid. Telephone lines had not been installed, and aircraft were not yet truly integrated into British intelligence collection. In addition, the substantial cavalry formations at the BEF's disposal had not been sent forward of the canal in strength to reconnoiter, gain, and maintain contact with the advancing Germans.[46] The British cavalry skirmished with German troops on 21 and 22 August, then broke contact and retired.[47] In armies that relied on telephone wires, signal flags, and messengers, this break in contact with the Germans created an information deficit that plagued the British command structure and its intelligence officers throughout the campaign.

With a dearth of hard intelligence at his disposal and limited time to reconnoiter the new ground II Corps was assigned to defend, Smith-Dorrien made some assumptions about how and where the Germans would strike. Since he committed ten thousand British troops in and around Mons, he clearly assigned primary importance to the defense of the town and II Corps' connectivity to Haig's I Corps. The plan of battle Smith-Dorrien adopted is illustrative (see map 1).

On the right, Smith-Dorrien deployed the 3rd Division with its 8th Brigade in close contact with Haig's I Corps. This was a "doctrinally correct" decision, since 3rd Division's defensive positions stretched from a prominent hill called Bois la Haut, just southeast of Mons, to Obourg, northeast of Mons. Without maintaining close contact with I Corps, an effective defense was impossible. Smith-Dorrien assigned the 9th Infantry Brigade to man the outpost line on the canal to the bridge of Mariette, a distance of roughly six miles. The 7th Brigade was designated as the division reserve and was concentrated around Ciply, two miles south of Mons.

On the left, II Corps' 5th Division covered a much wider, more open area along the canal with 13th Brigade defending the three miles to Les Herbieres. The 14th Brigade covered the rest of the distance along the canal to the

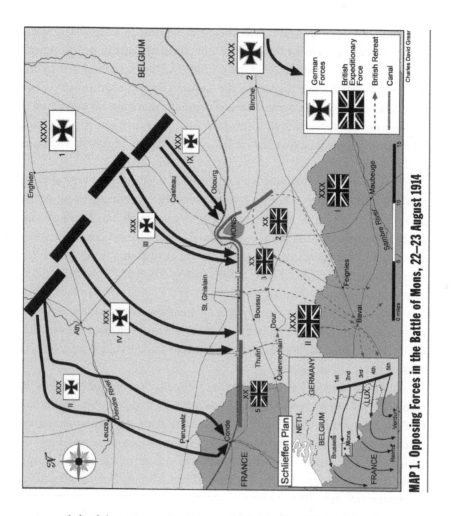

MAP 1. Opposing Forces in the Battle of Mons, 22–23 August 1914

extreme left of the corps at Pommeroeul bridge. The 15th Brigade was designated the divisional reserve and was concentrated around Dour.

"Defend" is probably the wrong term for the posture of the two divisions
under Smith-Dorrien's command. It is more realistic to say that I Corps'
defensive positions more closely resembled a hasty defense or a security zone
with outposts consisting of platoon or company strongpoints. For instance,
British infantry battalions created firing positions inside the town of Mons
and along the canal, but battalions were by no means entrenched on the scale
they would be later in the war. The urban terrain also fragmented the hasty
defense. The corps' disposition, therefore, reflected both the compartmental-
ized terrain that included houses, farms, and industrial buildings, as well as
the limited time Smith-Dorrien and his officers had to select and prepare their

positions on 22 August. Compounding these difficulties was the British army practice of issuing written orders, even in the heat of battle, which perilously slowed the decisionmaking cycle at the tactical and operational levels.[48]

According to Smith-Dorrien, II Corps' artillery was scattered across the countryside in less than ideal positions to effectively engage an attacking enemy. Guns were positioned to optimize direct fire engagements. At this point in the war, the British army had not yet learned how to concentrate and mass the destructive power of indirect fire.

The canal, which runs perfectly straight on an east-west line between Condé and Mons and then loops north and east, dominated II Corps' operation. In 1914, the canal was on average seven feet deep and sixty-four feet wide—perhaps not deep and wide enough to delay a determined enemy for long, but useful enough in a hasty defense.[49] An order to blow the bridges over the canal along the 5th Division front was issued during the afternoon of 23 August, but all of the bridges (with the exception of the lattice girder bridge over lock number four) in Smith-Dorrien's sector would not be blown until the morning of 24 August, long after German attacks had penetrated the British lines at several points along the canal.[50]

At 6 a.m., when French met with his corps commanders to provide his operational intent, the German artillery bombardment of the British lines around Mons was already well under way. According to Smith-Dorrien, French "told us be prepared to move forward, or fight where we were, but to get ready for the latter by strengthening our outposts and preparing the bridges over the canal for demolition."[51]

The word "outpost" most likely did not mean the same thing to Smith-Dorrien as it did to French. French's use of the word, which in the parlance of the cavalry suggests a temporary occupation, meant that he may have expected Smith-Dorrien to disengage his force after a short fight and retire to subsequent fighting positions. For the infantry, however, "outpost" may have been interpreted as an outlying post without necessarily suggesting temporary occupation in the form of a picket line. To the infantry officers commanding in II Corps, strengthening of the outpost line would force the enemy to deploy much earlier and serve to disrupt any forward move by the enemy without necessarily implying a rapid disengagement and withdrawal. The British experience against the Boers in South Africa, subsequently reinforced in 1905 by reports of the Russo-Japanese War, promoted the idea that a few well-trained British infantrymen, unsupported by artillery in direct fire, could defeat large numbers of attacking forces.[52] Subsequent fighting in the division area would suggest this was the more likely interpretation of French's instructions.

Fighting on 23 August eventually occurred in and around Mons where Dorrien-Smith had expected it. German cavalry appeared from Obourg in the east and moved toward the bridge facing Ville Pommeroeul in the west on the extreme left flank of II Corps. Contact on II Corps' left was relatively light. However, in the Mons salient and on Bois la Haut to the southeast, fighting was intense, as Smith-Dorrien anticipated it would be. Whenever the German artillery stopped firing, German troops assembled to storm the British positions. At first, British rifle fire drove the Germans back to their starting positions. The Germans quickly reorganized and repeated the attempt, normally on a new line of attack, only to be driven back yet again.[53]

Accurate British rifle fire definitely made a difference. The British army's prewar training program emphasized and rewarded rapid, accurate fire.[54] Translated into action, the average British soldier was reportedly able to hit a man-sized target fifteen times a minute at a range of at least three hundred yards with his Lee-Enfield rifle.[55] It may also be the case that in the early phase of the Battle of Mons, the attacking German troops were more densely packed so they could communicate in new and unfamiliar terrain. Yet it is worth noting that when the hasty attacks failed, the Germans rapidly adjusted their tactics.

The German army employed aircraft with a tactical system of colored smoke signals to identify and mark targets.[56] German aircraft soon arrived overhead, and the appearance of colored smoke nearby scattered the British defenders. Accurate, devastating artillery fire followed.[57] Like the British army, the German army also trained for mobile warfare, but the Germans viewed firepower, particularly artillery fire, as the real key to mobility in battle.

Thirty to forty minutes after the first hasty attacks failed, the German guns reengaged the British lines with greater precision and ferocity. Infantry reinforcements arrived, and the German attacks recommenced. This time, when the guns ceased firing, the German infantry moved forward in rushes supported by machine gun fire until they either overwhelmed the British defenders or discovered the British had withdrawn to new positions.[58]

These methodical and determined German attacks through the streets and alleys of Mons utilized artillery in direct fire to obliterate British positions, especially machine gun positions, inside buildings or behind barricades and sandbags. Given the inability of the British defenders to effectively employ their own artillery in the dense, urban terrain, the British infantry could not withstand these tactics for long.

British infantry fought back against the German attacks in and around Mons' houses and slag heaps. Losses on both sides were heavy. By noon, however, only six hours after the German guns began firing, nearly two German divisions had advanced to the canal in brutal house-to-house fighting. By early afternoon on 23 August, German troops crossed the canal at Jemappes, an action that made 3rd Division's defensive line in the Mons salient untenable. In several places along the front, the Germans were already south of the canal.[59]

While the German 18th Division attacked the Mons salient, the 17th Division had pushed forward, crossing the undefended canal to the right of the Middlesex Regiment. As the German infantry swung round towards Mons, they threatened the exposed right flank of the 3rd British Division. The 1st Gordon Highlanders and 2nd Royal Scots who protected the right flank were stretched thinly over 4 miles, angled back toward I Corps and facing the villages of St. Symphoien and Villers St. Ghislain.[60]

Given the weight of the German attack and the effectiveness of German tactics, by 1 p.m. on 23 August, the British were holding on by their fingernails. In fighting at the Nimy bridge in the center of the Mons salient, British lieutenant Maurice Dease of the Northumberland Fusiliers took control of the machine gun on the bridge after everyone in his section had been killed or wounded. Dease continued to fire despite receiving several mortal wounds by German gunfire. Another British fusilier, Private Sidney Godley, ran forward to man the fusiliers' last operational machine gun, but he was eventually overrun and captured by attacking German troops. Both men were awarded Victoria Crosses.[61]

In a phenomenal act of courage, German private August Niemeyer swam across the canal under intense British fire and brought back a boat so that his patrol could cross. The German patrol then crossed the canal and engaged the defending British soldiers. Then, Niemeyer set the swing mechanism in motion that moved the bridge back into position across the canal and reopened the bridge to road traffic. In its closed position, the Nimy swing bridge allowed traffic to cross the canal. When a water vessel needed to pass, motors rotated the bridge horizontally about its pivot point out of the way. The British troops rotated the Nimy bridge away from the banks but did not disable the mechanism. As a result, even after Niemeyer was killed, German troops were able to charge across and secure the bridge.[62] By 1:40 p.m., the British infantry was falling back under fire from the Germans advancing through Mons to Ciply.[63] Had the machine guns been placed at an angle in a protected position from which they could have swept the bridge, the British might have held it much longer.

But more important, the order from Smith-Dorrien left the decision to his subordinate commanders regarding when the bridges and boats within their zones should be blown. Though by no means atypical for British commanders, Smith-Dorrien's rather casual approach to the matter made the early loss of the canal to the attacking Germans a virtual certainty.[64] At 3 p.m., Smith-Dorrien decided it was time to withdraw his force to new defensive positions. He ordered the hard-pressed 3rd Division to leave the salient and fall back to positions just south of Mons. The 3rd Division's move necessitated a similar retirement by the 5th Division. Before midnight on 23 August, both divisions of II Corps were in a hasty defense along a line running through the villages of Montroeul, Boussu, Wasmes, Pâturages, and Frameries.[65]

Around 7 p.m. on 23 August, the situation on Smith-Dorrien's right in and around Mons was serious enough for Smith-Dorrien to ask Haig for assistance. As Haig's troops had hardly been engaged at all (I Corps sustained only forty casualties), Haig agreed to send his 5th Infantry Brigade to plug the growing gap in Smith-Dorrien's right flank. Fortunately, II Corps' 9th Infantry Brigade managed to restore the line before I Corps' assistance was needed, but the renewed German attack on II Corps' right signaled real danger. Three German infantry divisions were reportedly assembling for a major attack on 24 August.[66]

Smith-Dorrien and his 3rd Division commander, Major General Hubert Hamilton, did not know it, but farther to the east units of the German IX Corps were also crossing the canal in force, threatening to drive a wedge between the BEF and the French. The withdrawal of the French Fifth Army left the BEF's right flank wide open. What no one in the BEF knew was that all 4 French armies, not just the Fifth, were in a headlong retreat to the west. The French armies' combined strength had been reduced by 200,000 casualties, including 75,000 dead.[67] A German soldier who witnessed the French retreat described the scene:

> When we reached the ridge of those heights (above the Meuse) we were able to witness a horrifying sight with our naked eyes. The roads which the retreating enemy was using could be easily surveyed. In close marching formations the French were drawing off. The heaviest of our artillery was pounding the

retreating columns, and shell after shell after shell fell among the French infantry and other troops. Hundreds of French soldiers were literally torn to pieces. One could see the bodies and limbs being tossed in the air and being caught in the trees bordering the roads.[68]

Even with I Corp's assistance on the right flank, by nightfall all of Smith-Dorrien's infantry battalions were still retiring under pressure from advancing German troops. Smith-Dorrien had no corps reserve of sufficient strength to counter a German breakthrough anywhere along the II Corps front. Without a timely and rapid withdrawal under the cover of darkness, the 3rd Division might not survive at all. At midnight on 23 August, Smith-Dorrien waited impatiently for new instructions from the BEF commander.

Though Smith-Dorrien was not aware of it, Sir John French had decided at 11 p.m. on 23 August to completely withdraw the BEF to a line based on the town of Bavai. The reason for the delay in the receipt of French's order to Smith-Dorrien was that it had to be delivered by car driven in the dark over a distance of twenty-five miles. Thanks to landline communications with BEF General Headquarters (GHQ) at Le Cateau, Haig received the order at least three hours earlier and began disengaging his corps from its positions at 2 o'clock in the morning. Smith-Dorrien did not receive the order until dawn on 24 August, but he had reached the same conclusion much earlier in the day.

To the astonishment of both corps commanders, French left the planning and execution of the withdrawal entirely in their hands. Complicating matters, French commander in chief General Joseph Joffre directed French to keep the BEF west of the fortress of Maubeuge, restricting the number of roads available to the BEF. The BEF's retreat was just beginning—it would last for 2 weeks and cover more than 250 miles.

Smith-Dorrien did not wait for orders. He drove straight to Haig's command post and obtained Haig's agreement that I Corps would cover the retirement of the 3rd Division as it moved toward Sars-la-Bruyere. When 3rd Division began its withdrawal, Smith-Dorrien notified Haig that the 5th Division would displace to a new line running from Blaugies to Montignies-sur-Roc.[69]

French's decision to hold the line at Mons for 24 hours had achieved the aim of slowing the German advance, but losses in II Corps, particularly in the 3rd Division, were heavy. Total British casualties at Mons were 1,638 men killed or wounded. German losses were between 1,900 and 2,000, but of course, the Germans were attacking.[70] The British infantry performed beyond expectation against a much larger, more lethal German force. But the success was temporary. In the failing light of the early evening, German engineers were erecting pontoon bridges where the existing bridges had been destroyed. The German attack continued westward, wheeling around Smith-Dorrien's troops "like a closing door hinged on Mons itself."[71]

Von Kluck described his feelings about the fight for Mons: "After the severe opposition offered by the British Army in the two days' battle of Mons–St. Ghislain, a further and even stronger defence of Valenciennes-Bavai-Maubeuge was expected."[72] The BEF's successful disengagement from Mons meant the First Army commander would pursue the BEF, drawing the First Army farther away from the original and more dangerous axis of its westward advance to the north of Paris.

LE CATEAU AND THE RETREAT TO THE MARNE

When it was suggested to Helmuth von Moltke, the Prussian army chief of staff who conducted Prussia's series of victorious campaigns against Denmark, Austria, and France between 1863 and 1871, that he was now the greatest commander since Napoleon, he responded, "No. For I have never conducted a retreat."[73] Von Moltke knew what he was talking about.

Retreats involve far more detailed planning than simply picking routes on maps and ordering forces to move on them. Orders must reach fighting units early enough to permit advance parties to identify and mark the routes of withdrawal. Supply columns carrying the wounded, ammunition, food, and water must withdraw first to set up behind the new defensive lines. Cavalry must deploy to ensure the roads are not blocked. If anything goes wrong, the losses taken during retreats frequently exceed those of normal combat.

The withdrawal of II Corps at 5:15 a.m. on 24 August began with German heavy artillery fire falling on British positions along the corps' seventeen-mile front. The Germans were now attacking everywhere. At 6 a.m., the 3rd Division began its retirement. Smith-Dorrien designated the 5th Brigade of the 2nd Division to act as rearguard. The 5th Brigade had seen relatively light action on 23 August and was in sufficiently good shape to execute the mission.

Unfortunately, Major General Sir Charles Fergusson, the 5th Division commander, did not get the word to withdraw his troops until 11 o'clock in the morning. Like many British commanders along the I Corps front, Fergusson knew if he was to survive, he would have to get away before his line of retreat was cut off.[74] He did not wait for orders; when they arrived, the 5th Division was already falling back. The brigades of the 5th Division were under heavy artillery fire from German troops that were attempting to outflank them through the gap left by the retreat of the 3rd Division.[75]

German infantry had been advancing toward Condé since early morning in an attempt to move around the BEF's left flank. This would put II Corps' 5th Division and the BEF cavalry division at serious risk of envelopment. The French army's 84th Division left Condé at 2 a.m., and the 19th Infantry Brigade, an independent formation receiving its orders directly from BEF GHQ, began moving toward Elouges at roughly the same time.

General Edmund Allenby, commander of the BEF cavalry division, was aware of both the French withdrawal and the German troop movements and decided to withdraw his cavalry from positions in the rear of the 19th Brigade. Seeing Allenby's cavalry preparing to leave, Sir Charles Fergusson asked Allenby for assistance, without which, Fergusson said, he could not disengage from his defensive positions without serious losses.

Allenby understood the seriousness of Fergusson's predicament and complied with the request. Allenby acted quickly to position the BEF cavalry division around Elouges. The cavalry's arrival in this area offered immediate protection to the 5th Division's left flank from attacks by German troops moving south from Condé. As the 19th Brigade reached Baisieux, General Allenby took command of it and added it to the forces already supporting the 5th Division.

A major battle now developed around Elouges between several British cavalry formations and the advancing Germans. According to Smith-Dorrien, a seesaw fight ensued in which the 15th Brigade lost over 1,100 men, or one-third of its fighting strength. Fortunately, the combined cavalry and infantry flank guard action did succeed in protecting II Corps' exposed flank.[76] Yet again, these events occurred without Smith-Dorrien's knowledge, but he always understood that waiting for orders could potentially be fatal.

However, Smith-Dorrien's acceptance of the need to act without orders was not pervasive at lower levels in the BEF. Battalion commanders were sometimes directed by their brigade or division commanders to "hold at all costs"; sometimes they received no orders at all. When these conditions arose, disasters unfolded quickly. By the time battalion commanders realized the futility of defending against the German onslaught, their units were decimated. The stand of the Cheshire Light Infantry exemplified the problem; it was defiant but pointless. Only one officer eventually received any orders to retire. In the meantime, the 1st Battalion of the Cheshire Light Infantry was

surrounded, isolated, and destroyed. Out of one thousand soldiers in the battalion, just two officers and two hundred men survived.[77]

As the fighting retreat in II Corps continued on 24 August, Haig withdrew the 5th Infantry Brigade from its position without informing II Corps.
This was the same unit that Haig dispatched on 23 August to Smith-Dorrien
to shore up II Corps' defenses. For some reason, Haig decided to reclaim his
unit at 9 a.m. despite II Corps' far greater need for it. Worse, he did so without informing Smith-Dorrien about his intentions. Haig's divisions, which
had seen less action than Smith-Dorrien's corps, moved off in good order, but
not without the loss of equipment and ammunition. By midnight, I Corps
moved the 1st Division into Feignies and La Longueville and the 2nd Division into Bavai.[78]

In II Corps, the 3rd Division was now on the left flank, with the 5th Division on its right. Smith-Dorrien decided it was necessary to shift the divisions
across the sector. The 5th Division was still engaged in sporadic action against
the Germans near Bavai and St. Waast, but the 3rd Division could withdraw
under far less pressure over a greater distance to the left flank. This meant the
exhausted 5th Division, once it managed to disengage from the enemy, would
cover a shorter distance to its final position on 24 August.

Under the best of circumstances, moving 2 division-sized formations is
difficult. It is always dangerous to maneuver under the guns of the enemy. It is
a real tribute to the leadership and planning of the II Corps commander and
his staff that the operation came off as successfully as it did. Smith-Dorrien's
divisions got away, but not without paying a heavy price: British casualties
on 24 August were 2,606 killed and wounded, 700 more than on 23 August.[79]

Exhaustion and fear were beginning to have an effect on the retreating
British troops. Every soldier in the BEF hoped the new line of defense planned
along the Valenciennes-Maubeuge road would provide a respite from the
fighting. It did not. The German pursuit was relentless. The BEF was forced
to continue its retreat south on 25 August in parallel with the French armies.
This line of retreat squeezed the BEF into a small space between the forest
of Mormal and the suburbs of Maubeuge. Separated by the dense forest of
Mormal, I Corps withdrew to Landrecies. Simultaneously, II Corps retreated
in the direction of Le Cateau. Although it went almost unnoticed at the time,
the physical separation of the two corps in an environment of sporadic communications would profoundly influence the subsequent course of the retreat.

In the early afternoon of 25 August, Haig established his new headquarters in Landrecies just south of the forest of Mormal. Like his soldiers, Haig

needed rest; he had contracted the stomach flu and was quite ill. Unknown to Haig, his headquarters lay in the path of a German infantry regiment tasked with the mission of seizing a nearby bridge over the Sambre River. A battle developed with the 4th British Guards Brigade that lasted through the evening into the early morning hours of 26 August.[80] This battle would hold Haig's attention through most of 26 August when II Corps badly needed his assistance.

Elsewhere on 25 August, the Germans caught up with the BEF's cavalry rearguard, and a gap was opened between the BEF's rear and flank guards. The situation was perilous. The rear of the 2nd French Army Corps was then also completing its passage through the town of Solesmes inside a narrow defile.

Once again, battlefield commanders with courage and initiative saved the retreating British troops. General Allenby later reported that the 7th Brigade commander instantly collected the troops nearby, including a brigade of artillery. He then led them to a position from which they could cover the rear of the British column entering the defile. The 7th Brigade commander's scratch force stopped the German advance cold and maintained the defense under heavy fire until the British column withdrew in safety and darkness fell.[81] This was one of many costly and desperate rear guard actions that characterized the fighting during the retreat to the Marne.

By 6 p.m. on 25 August, Smith-Dorrien reported that II Corps' cumulative losses amounted to nearly 3,900, or about 17 percent of the corps' infantry strength.[82] On learning that French had come from BEF GHQ to his advanced headquarters at Bavai, Smith-Dorrien decided to track him down, describe the condition of II Corps and its current location, and ask for instructions. According to Smith-Dorrien, French replied that he (Smith-Dorrien) could do as he liked, but that Haig intended to start withdrawing at 5 a.m. on 26 August.[83]

How Smith-Dorrien, exhausted from a difficult withdrawal under enemy fire, felt at this point is unknown, but French's rather cavalier response must have enraged him. Haig always seemed to receive information and orders promptly. Now Haig was withdrawing, and he (Smith-Dorrien) could do as he wished. Smith-Dorrien must have been a man of extraordinary self-control. He concluded his remarks to French with the warning that without definite orders, there was a real risk of repeating the 24 August disaster, when orders were issued too late.

As if suddenly alerted to the danger, French changed his attitude and asked Smith-Dorrien what he proposed to do. Smith-Dorrien sensed he could now make his case, and he did not hold back. He wanted to get his transport, reserve ammunition, and supply columns on the road to Le Cateau soon after midnight, immediately followed by the troops. The idea was to ensure that I Corps' rear guard would be in position south of the Valenciennes-Jenlain-Bavai road by 5 o'clock in the morning.[84]

Field Marshal French approved, but not without reminding Smith-Dorrien that Haig could still do as he intended. At 8:25 p.m., French's chief of staff issued the order in accordance with Smith-Dorrien's wishes, and the BEF was instructed to concentrate at Le Cateau. French's statement regarding Haig's intentions was odd, since Smith-Dorrien heard nothing from Haig or from BEF GHQ regarding I Corps on 25 August.

As the BEF retreated and casualties mounted, Smith-Dorrien thought unity of effort between the two corps was vital. Based on French's order to concentrate at Le Cateau, Smith-Dorrien reasoned that I Corps would join him in the Le Cateau position on 26 August. This assumption would prove false, but Smith-Dorrien did not doubt it at the time.

When II Corps' columns arrived in Le Cateau shortly after midnight on 26 August, the skies poured buckets of rain on II Corps' soldiers. They had had no rest or respite from enemy fire since the morning of 23 August. The exhausted soldiers spread out across the town of Le Cateau and among the farms on its outskirts. Whether Smith-Dorrien realized it or not, his infantry formations were not busily entrenching themselves. Rather, thousands of British infantrymen were either on the march or lying on the open ground in a state of complete exhaustion. It should be noted that half of the BEF's troops were reservists, and although they had served in the British army for years before joining the reserves, they were now part-time soldiers unaccustomed to long, demanding forced marches.

Much of II Corps' supporting artillery, signal units, engineers, ammunition, and cavalry were also scattered across the countryside. There were no phone lines. Orders would have to be sent via messengers who needed hours to inform the battalions and brigades of any decision Smith-Dorrien reached about whether to halt or continue the retreat. A coherent defense seemed impossible.

Smith-Dorrien decided it was impossible to resume the retreat. The combination of rain, exhaustion, and confusion resulting from the retreat in darkness suggested to him that it was now imperative to stand and fight. His goal was "to strike the enemy hard and, after he had done so, continue the retreat."[85]

General Allenby saw things differently. He urged Smith-Dorrien to get his exhausted divisions away before daylight on 26 August.[86] Smith-Dorrien was no fool; he listened to Allenby. There were good reasons to move his force farther south and west toward Cambrai. Smith-Dorrien suspected that several German corps-sized units were converging on his position. However, in Smith-Dorrien's judgment, a retreat in the face of overwhelming force might prove more lethal than a pitched battle. He also continued to believe that Haig's I Corps would join him in time to present a formidable challenge to the German advance.

Having decided to stand and fight, Smith-Dorrien asked Allenby to add his cavalry division along with the 19th Infantry Brigade, then under Allenby's command, to II Corps. Allenby acquiesced and positioned his troops accordingly. Meanwhile, the BEF's 4th Infantry Division that arrived from England on 24 August established a defensive position on II Corps' left flank. The additional forces at Smith-Dorrien's disposal undoubtedly strengthened his resolve to defend the positions in and around Le Cateau.

Tragically, Haig does not seem to have made the effort to inform Smith-Dorrien that I Corps was still tied down in a fight of its own several miles to the east. When Smith-Dorrien finally discovered at 3 a.m. that Haig would not come to his aid at sunup, he realized that II Corps' right flank was wide open and unprotected.

By the time French's written instructions reached Smith-Dorrien at 9 a.m. on 26 August, they were meaningless. French's orders lacked clarity and even sounded contradictory: "If you can hold your ground the situation appears likely to improve. 4th Division must cooperate. French troops are taking offensive on right of I Corps. Although you are given a free hand as to method this telegram is not intended to convey the impression that I am not anxious for you to carry out the retirement and you must make every endeavor to do so."[87]

The battle of Le Cateau began on the morning of 26 August when the German First Army launched an attack with the elements of 6 German divisions (see map 2). It must have been hell on earth for the BEF's II Corps. Sixty-eight thousand British troops with approximately 400 guns faced General von Kluck's First Army, a force of 160,000 men and 550 guns. In the early morning hours when the initial ranging shots from German artillery exploded near British positions in and around Le Cateau, Smith-Dorrien's orders to stand and fight still had not reached many of II Corps' units. Some received no orders at all.[88] Others prepared to resume the retreat and began marching southwest. Lieutenant Rory MacLeod of the Royal Field Artillery described the scene at Le Cateau on the morning of 26 August:

> It was a very misty morning. You couldn't see much. In front of our battery we had a nice little ridge, but the difficulty was there that we couldn't clear the crest at 1,500 yards and the infantry [British] were along the top of it. . . . Then, the mists cleared further and we see a place called Rambourlieux Farm on our left flank completely looking down the line of our guns. . . . More and more German batteries came into position and more and more shell fire came on us—very heavy indeed. Then, some aeroplanes came over and dropped what looked like stream-ers of silver paper and very soon an intense fire was opened all along the line of guns . . . gun after gun went out of action—the 11th Battery suffered terribly.[89]

Smith-Dorrien's troops sought cover wherever they could find it, includ-ing behind stone walls in open fields or inside the town. In Le Cateau, as in Mons, German soldiers rapidly infiltrated, fighting from house to house and from alley to alley. British rifle fire exacted a price on the advancing Germans, but German artillery once again devastated the defending British troops; its accuracy and lethality were unmatched by British guns. The Germans sys-tematically beat down British resistance before attacking the unentrenched soldiers in their hasty defensive positions.[90]

By early afternoon, the British infantry could take no more. In his monu-mental history of the First World War, J. E. Edmonds noted that after six hours of intense fighting, the British position at Le Cateau was close to the breaking point.[91] II Corps' flanks began to crumble under relentless German attack, and I Corps was still far from Le Cateau. Still unaware that Haig's troops were not coming, Smith-Dorrien saw no alternative but to give ground and retreat. He ordered his remaining units to withdraw southwest toward St. Quentin.

Smith-Dorrien's decision to break off the fight and withdraw came just in time. His force narrowly escaped the envelopment he anticipated the night before thanks to the unexpected arrival of a French cavalry corps on the British left flank. The cavalry secured the flank long enough for II Corps to withdraw.

Smith-Dorrien's decision to halt and fight the Germans at Le Cateau was a dangerous choice, made more so by French's failure to inform him that Haig's corps was actually retreating away from Le Cateau. Several battalion-sized

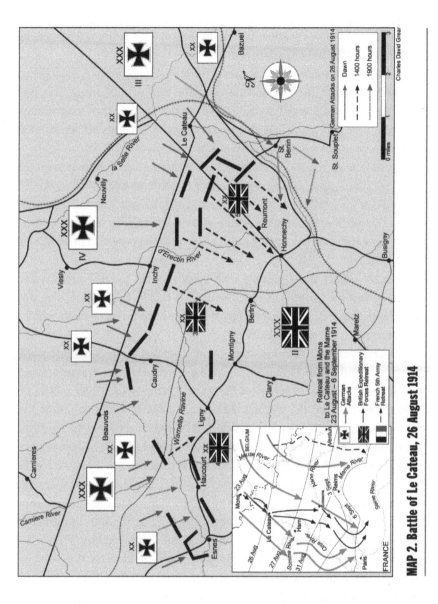

MAP 2. Battle of Le Cateau, 26 August 1914

formations determined to cover the withdrawal of their surviving comrades disintegrated under the crushing German assaults. Others surrendered when German infantry overran their positions. Of the 68,000 British troops engaged in the fighting in and around Le Cateau on 26 August, roughly 12 percent of the forces (8,482 men) were lost. Of this number, about 2,600 were taken prisoner. In addition, 38 guns were lost.[92] A German officer who fought against the BEF recorded, "We fought against a tough enemy. In some positions he had fought to the last man, without giving up. And as soon as he disengaged, he withdrew in calm and organized fashion."[93]

It is also noteworthy that von Kluck, the First Army commander, deduced that he had fought the preponderance of the BEF at Le Cateau. This was never the case, but it may have caused von Kluck to pause just long enough for Smith-Dorrien to disengage his surviving units. II Corps' strong stand at Le Cateau no doubt contributed to von Kluck's illusion.[94]

At Le Cateau, von Kluck's troops failed as they had at Mons to prevent the BEF from disengaging and retreating out of reach. Evidence for the weakened condition of the First Army can also be found in von Kluck's repeated requests on 26, 27, and 28 August for the release of the German reserve corps in Brussels to replenish the First Army's ranks along with the provision of additional heavy artillery.[95]

On 29 August, Joffre pleaded with French to halt the BEF's retreat and turn it against the Germans. French refused. What the British troops needed now, French argued, was ten days out of the line to rest, reequip, and wait for reinforcements, not another battle.[96]

The exasperated BEF commander pointed out that the force had lost nearly 15,000 men and 80 guns in a week of fighting retreat. He was not exaggerating. Heroic British rearguard actions at Étreux on 27 August (and later at Néry on 1 September) slowed the German advance, but the actions also resulted in heavy losses for the BEF that the French could not easily replace. Distinguished British historian Nigel Hamilton provides a snapshot of what happened next: "The debacle at Mons had broken Sir John French's nerve. By a miracle he had evaded the claws of the German Army—and, like [Lord John] Gort [the BEF commander in 1940] three decades later, he wanted now to separate the BEF from their seemingly doomed allies, leaving the line altogether to 'refit.' Only Kitchener's trip to Paris on 1 September stopped him."[97]

When Kitchener arrived at the British embassy in Paris on 31 August, he wore his blue field marshal's uniform, an unusual step for a British minister of war. It was an act that the highly sensitive French interpreted as an insult calculated to reinforce Kitchener's superiority over him. Perhaps it was, but Kitchener's task was to aid the French armies in their desperate struggle with the Germans, and he was not inclined to tolerate opposition.

Behind closed doors, Kitchener argued vehemently with French, insisting the BEF had to stay and fight it out. Eventually the two emerged from their meeting and announced that the BEF would return to the fight. In Kitchener's words, the BEF would conform "to the movements of the French Army."[98] A week later, on the final day of the Marne counteroffensive, the BEF fought shoulder to shoulder with the French, at the cost of another 13,000 British casualties.

AFTER THE GREAT RETREAT

At Mons and during the retreat to the Marne, the BEF achieved the strategic objective of preventing the French Fifth Army from being outflanked.[99] Unable to compel the BEF to stand and fight, the superior German forces of First Army did not destroy it. Von Kluck summed up his account of the Great Retreat: "In spite of the great efforts of the First Army, the British had escaped the repeated attempts to envelop them. They continued their retreat southwards."[100]

At Le Cateau, Smith-Dorrien's II Corps slowed the German advance, albeit at an enormous cost in British lives. In each of the British battalions that fought in the great battles of the Marne and Ypres by November 1914, there scarcely remained more than a handful of officers and soldiers from the BEF that landed in August. In the words of J. E. Edmonds, "The old British Army was gone past recall, leaving but a remnant to carry on the training of the new armies."[101]

The near-constant exposure to enemy fire transformed large numbers of British soldiers and officers into psychiatric casualties. Exact numbers are not known, but it is an understatement to suggest that the soldiers who survived the retreat were both physically and mentally exhausted. Amazingly, however, the confidence, discipline, courage, and valor of the average British soldier were seldom, if ever, really shaken. Field Marshal Earl Wavell's observation that "the British soldier . . . will not easily withdraw confidence from his leaders, even if they fail to win success" was demonstrated during the long and arduous retreat and again when the counterattack began on 5 September. [102]

Looking back on the bloody battles of August 1914, the BEF's greatest achievement may have been to survive at all. At the outbreak of World War I, the Imperial German Army's six million men were superbly trained and equipped, perhaps the most lethal killing machine in human history. In *The Rise and Fall of the Great Powers*, Paul Kennedy characterized Germany's Imperial General Staff as "an array of intelligent, probing staff officers who readjusted to the new conditions of combat faster than those in any other army, and who by 1916 had rethought the nature of both defensive and offensive warfare."[103]

When viewed in this context, the BEF's resolute performance in the opening weeks of World War I must be seen as nothing less than extraordinary. Officers in the BEF had studied and planned retreats at the British Staff College that were very similar to the retreat from Mons. For example, the 4th Division trained in 1913 to disengage and retreat during peacetime maneuvers. Historian Brian Bond recounts the similarity of the BEF's 1913 maneuvers with the battle of Le Cateau, observing, "As in the battle, the 4th Division out-marched its pursuer and turned in good order to meet them."[104]

Von Kluck's inability to pin down and decisively engage and destroy the BEF is a tribute to the British officers and soldiers who fought their way from Mons to the Marne. However, there were serious problems with the BEF's performance that were, in many respects, inextricably intertwined with British national culture and experience.

In contemporary terms, the BEF was an army built to "do more with less," a product of constrained defense budgets. In the time-honored English-speaking (British, Canadian, Australian, New Zealand, and American) preference for technology-/capital-intensive navies (and, eventually, air forces) in defense outlays, the British army was a distant second to the Royal Navy. For the BEF to be most effective in action, its national military leadership had to capitalize on both technological innovation and effective strategic employment, and this meant the use of the BEF under favorable strategic conditions, such as close cooperation with the Royal Navy.

In hindsight, Lord Roberts' argument for employment through Antwerp deserved more study than it received. Operations in and around Antwerp offered the BEF the opportunity to cooperate with 120,000 Belgian troops while diverting German troops and heavy artillery from attacking the fortress at Maubeuge and conceivably buying valuable time for the retreating French armies to reposition farther north and west to neutralize the German right hook. Command of the sea and control of the 13-mile-long waterway connecting Antwerp to the sea meant that when the time came for the BEF to withdraw, it could do so at far lower cost in terms of men and matériel.[105] Unfortunately, the BEF was committed too far from the coast to benefit from British naval supremacy, and technological innovation was largely missing from the BEF's force design and modernization programs.

Like the first battles in the early period of any war, the fight for Mons and the long retreat that followed revealed many tactical weaknesses in the BEF's training, organization, and equipment. When Allenby's cavalry formations were employed as mounted riflemen (a tactic he personally had employed during the Boer War), they were effective.[106] On the other hand, the BEF cavalry's performance as a reconnaissance force tasked with the discovery and collection of information was weak, leaving the British commanders on the battlefield in the dark about German movements and intentions.[107]

The BEF's artillery was successful in direct fire when it could be employed for that purpose, but it would take many months of fighting the Germans in Flanders before the BEF organized and employed indirect fire effectively. This deficiency was identified during the Boer War, but the British artillery fiercely resisted measures to fix it.[108] As a result, the BEF command structure was not able to exploit the artillery's potential in close support of defending or retreating British infantry.

Though Smith-Dorrien and his division commanders issued orders to blow the canal bridges, II Corps' failure to do so early was inexcusable. Depriving the Germans of the bridges even for a much longer period would have presented the British defenders with the opportunity to direct artillery and machine gun fire onto the assembling German forces. Disengaging from their hasty defensive positions in and around Mons would have been less hazardous for the British.

French's vague and convoluted orders, the absence of routine lateral coordination across the front, and an acute insensitivity to the devastating effects of artillery and machine gun fire were unforgiveable. French's failures on the operational level were even worse. He made no effort to shift any of his forces to the decisive points during the fighting, particularly when it was obvious quite early in the fighting at Mons that II Corps was the main target for the advancing Germans. His failure to achieve unity of effort across the BEF suggests that Haldane's reforms had not moved him or his generals psychologically or professionally very far from colonial to continental warfare.[109]

Military culture—the totality of behavior patterns, beliefs, and values—always plays a major role in victory as well as in defeat. In the British army, initiative and imagination were the prerogatives of generals and no one else.[110] The British generals never comprehended the Prussian-German concept of mission command, a philosophy of leadership that cultivated subordinates with the ability to independently exploit opportunities by empowering them to take initiative and exercise judgment in the pursuit of their assigned mission.[111]

Given these observations, it seems reasonable to conclude that Sir Richard Haldane's reforms were still too recent to thoroughly prepare the BEF and its leadership for a war in 1914 with the Imperial German Army. When the retreat from Mons ended and the static war of bullet, spade, and barbed wire began, Kitchener exclaimed, "I don't know what is to be done—this is not war!"[112]

New facts in war should lead to changes in strategy and tactics. New facts should also prompt senior commanders to reexamine the assumptions underpinning strategy and tactics. Instead of reassessing the changed nature of the conflict, British generals embraced the doctrine of predominant numbers, masses of men and firepower, and limitless strategic objectives as the acme of grand tactics.[113] The British generals clung to the cult of the offensive.[114]

Inside the British army, advocates for a doctrine of offensive infantry tactics simply discounted the harsh lessons of the Boer War and focused instead on the Imperial Japanese Army's successful offensive operations during the Russo-Japanese War.[115] The human cost of Japanese tactics was justified by the battlefield victories achieved in Manchuria. Britain's senior military leaders did not grasp the essential point that the goal in war is the same as in wrestling: "to throw the opponent by weakening his foothold and upsetting his balance without risking self-exhaustion."[116]

British casualties in future battles would attest to the British generals' readiness to dismiss facts they did not like. On 26 September 1915 at Loos, French and Haig sent two British infantry divisions, the 21st and 24th, in tightly formed masses against strongly manned German defensive positions protected by miles of barbed wire. The divisions attacked without smoke or gas to cover their advance and enjoyed minimal artillery support. Of the 10,000 British soldiers who attacked that day, no fewer than 385 officers and 7,862 soldiers were killed or wounded. The German defenders suffered no casualties at all.[117]

CONCLUSION

By the standards of the early twentieth century, Haldane's reforms achieved miracles. His stubborn determination to drag the British army kicking and screaming into the twentieth century was a world historical event, a turning point in the history of the British Empire and the English-speaking peoples. Without Sir Richard Haldane, Great Britain would not have had an army capable of deploying and fighting at all in 1914. His prewar military reforms were not perfect, but they were enough to prepare Britain to fight alongside the French and, eventually, with the help of Britain's American allies, to win the war.[118]

Given the relatively small size of the BEF, it is fair to ask whether the BEF's absence from Mons on 20 August 1914 would have made a significant difference to the strategic outcome along the Marne a month later. General von Kluck, the former First Army commander, addressed this question in his book, *The March on Paris and the Battle of the Marne 1914*. Von Kluck insisted that he always intended to stream into northern France and smash the open left flank of the French armies. But for the stubborn presence of the BEF in August 1914, von Kluck would have minimized his support to Second Army and driven the bulk of his force westward and north of Paris. Without the BEF, the French army would likely have found it much harder to mass French forces in the center of the line where the German Second and Third Armies concentrated their attacks.[119]

British losses in the battle of Mons and during the Great Retreat would seem modest compared with the human carnage that lay ahead. In World War I, British losses, like the losses in every participating country, were staggering. One in 16 British men between the ages of 15 and 50—nearly 800,000 men—died.[120] Many years later, Sir Winston Churchill recounted the dark days in northern France, remarking, "Battles are won by slaughter and maneuver. The greater the general, the more he contributes in maneuver, the less he demands in slaughter."[121]

It would, however, take years of experience at the front before the British armies in France could expand their control from twenty miles to one hundred twenty miles of France's four-hundred-mile front. In return, the monumental sacrifice of the French army between Christmas 1914 and the end of June 1916 gave Britain the breathing space it needed to assemble, equip, and train a truly modern army capable of attacking the Germans and contributing to victory in the war.[122]

Haldane could not answer for British national military strategy in the years after the opening phase of World War I. He was also never empowered to impose a true meritocracy on an army officer corps that still valued social connections, good manners, and smartness of drill more than character, competence, and intelligence.

Military reform, like politics, is the art of the possible. Haldane always understood this reality. Thus, he ensured that the BEF would play its vital part in the opening drama of World War I. His timely reforms guaranteed that Britain's soldiers, sergeants, lieutenants, and captains would fight courageously and effectively in August 1914. A few months after the armistice was signed, when Britain's armies stood again on British soil, Field Marshal Sir

Douglas Haig presented a book of his dispatches to Haldane. Haig inscribed the book with the following words: "*To Viscount Haldane of Cloan—the greatest Secretary of State for War England has ever had. In grateful remembrance of his successful efforts in organizing the Military Forces for a War on the Continent, notwithstanding much opposition from the Army Council and the half-hearted support of his Parliamentary friends.*"[123]

In the age of industrial warfare when the day of the small professional army was passing away, Britain's professional soldiers demonstrated exceptional courage, discipline, and resilience under conditions that would have broken most other armies.[124] The BEF remained true to Haldane's vision. The BEF accomplished "Mission Impossible."

CHAPTER 2

WAR WITHOUT END

The Battle of Shanghai, 1937

Thirteen years after Commodore Matthew Perry steamed into Tokyo Bay, a nationalist rebellion overthrew the conservative Tokugawa Shogunate, installed the Emperor Meiji in power, and implemented a program of sweeping national reform. In an act no less stunning than the revolution itself, nearly all of the former ruling families voluntarily surrendered their power to the emperor, declaring, "We therefore reverently offer up all our feudal possessions so that a uniform rule may prevail throughout the Empire. Thus, the country will be able to rank equally with the other nations of the world."[1]

By 1895, Japan achieved its goal. Japanese armies had seized Korea and defeated China in the first Sino-Japanese war. Ten years later, Japan sent shockwaves through the world when the Imperial Japanese Navy (IJN) sank or destroyed most of the Imperial Russian Fleet in the two-day battle of Tsushima (27–28 May 1905)—at the time the most significant naval action since Trafalgar. Japan's warships were newer with more modern guns and rangefinders than those of their Russian opponents. Whereas the Russians used wireless communication sets produced in Germany, the IJN used sets that had been manufactured in Japan.[2]

To the Western powers, Japan's meteoric rise to strategic prominence in northeast Asia demonstrated that the Japanese were fundamentally different from the Chinese, and, indeed, from all the peoples of the Far East. John Pershing, who served as the U.S. military attaché in Tokyo during the Russo-Japanese War, described the Japanese he saw as "a strong, virile, aggressive race, with an ambition and determination that will carry them very far in the contest of nations for power."[3]

Britain lost no time in securing an alliance with Imperial Japan to contain Russian expansion, as well as to compensate for Britain's strategic dilemma of "imperial overstretch." Under the terms of the original 1902 Anglo-Japanese Treaty, Japan agreed to secure British commercial and territorial interests in the Far East, allowing Britain's Royal Navy to concentrate in the North Sea for its future war with Germany while Britain recognized Japan's de facto conquest of Korea.[4] The treaty lapsed in 1923 after the signing of the Washington Naval Treaty, but in the run-up to World War I, the treaty placed Japan on the winning side, a position that rewarded Japan with control of Germany's Chinese and Pacific territories—lucrative gains for Japan's modest role in the war. Far more important, Japan gained Western recognition as a great power.

For a nation that rose from obscurity to great power in less than fifty years, the military triumphs over China and Russia were intoxicating. When an incident occurred on the night of 7 July 1937 involving Japanese and Chinese troops near the Lugou bridge, known internationally as the Marco Polo bridge, the temptation for Tokyo to conquer yet again was too strong to resist.

Major General Ishiwara Kanji, the dynamic Japanese army officer who masterminded the Mukden Incident (the alleged Chinese bombing of a Japanese railway) that wrested control of Manchuria away from Nationalist China in 1931, was cautious.[5] He urged restraint, telling the general staff of the Kwantung Army, "If we act now against China, the sky will fall in. Let's keep the incident from developing further and have the local command settle the issue."[6]

Concurrently, Emperor Hirohito approved the mobilization of five Japanese divisions for a campaign against the Chinese that his minister of war claimed "would be finished up within two to three months."[7] When Ishiwara heard the news, he was more pessimistic. He told his colleagues, "We may find ourselves with a full-scale war on our hands. The result would be the same sort of disaster which overtook Napoleon in Spain—a slow sinking into the deepest sort of bog."[8]

Chiang Kai-shek, the leader of Nationalist China, responded by ordering the Chinese army to attack the Japanese garrison in Shanghai, eventually sending 600,000 Nationalist Chinese troops to fight for the city of 3.3 million people, which in 1937 was the fifth largest port in the world and Asia's financial capital.[9] Chiang was well aware that Shanghai was a city where fabulously rich Chinese and European "colonials" lived like kings inside a special "international zone" next to millions of impoverished Chinese. Under the circumstances, Chiang decided to make the fight for Shanghai in Zhabei, the poor, industrial section of the city on the north side of the international zone, hoping to produce an incident that would rally the Europeans and Americans to his side in the war with Japan.[10]

For reasons that seem obtuse today, Japan's military and political leaders believed control of China, a nation torn by civil war with hundreds of millions living in poverty, would add to Japan's margin of victory in future wars.[11] Japan's national military and political leaders equated industrialization and access to markets and resources with the control of territory and peoples.

UGAKI: PRELUDE TO WAR

The appearance of Commodore Matthew Perry's "Black Ships" in Japanese waters in 1853 forced the Japanese to face a disconcerting reality: Japan's military power and the economic strength to support itself were inferior to those of the West.[12] Without a rapid transformation into a modern state, Japan itself might not survive contact with the West.

To modernize and catch up with the Western nations, Japan embraced "raw, unbridled capitalism."[13] Japan may not have had Calvinism and the Protestant culture that launched Great Britain, Germany, the Netherlands, and the United States on the economic fast track to prosperity and power, but Japan possessed the time-honored values of integrity and hard work, as well as a culturally and racially homogenous population with a deeply ingrained sense of duty and a collective obligation in all aspects of life.[14]

The same cultural values of energy and intelligence that underpinned Japanese economic modernization also catapulted the Imperial Japanese Army (IJA) into modernization. As always, revolutions in military affairs involve much more than new technology. For a national military strategy to be effective, its goals and tenets must align in harmony with the respective nation's cultural norms, geographic position, and economic potential.

In Japan, the ruling elites looked carefully at the various ways in which other great powers sought to harmonize these factors—culture, geography, and economy—within the framework of national military strategy. Thus, the Japanese embraced the American model for industrialization, the British model for ship-building and maritime power, and the German military model for land power. But it was Japan's embrace of Otto von Bismarck's Prussian-German concept of "rich country, strong military" that most profoundly influenced Japanese thinking about national security.[15]

In time, two competing strategic views emerged in Japanese thinking about security and commercial trade, a continental approach and a maritime approach.[16] The continental IJA faction argued for Japanese expansion to the "north," through Korea and into Manchuria, Mongolia, and, eventually, eastern Siberia. The maritime IJN faction urged expansion to the "south," the soft underbelly of Asia and the Pacific basin. In the first decades of the twentieth century, the IJA overpowered the IJN.[17] Eventually, the IJA drove Japan into war first with China, then tsarist Russia.[18]

In 1924, an important figure in Japanese military history, General Ugaki Kazushige, stepped into the middle of this contest for the hearts and minds of the Japanese people.[19] Ugaki served as minister of war from 1924 to 1927 and again from 1929 to 1931. He lived and studied abroad, serving twice in Germany as Japan's military attaché, from 1902 to 1904 and again from 1906 to 1907. During this service, Ugaki developed a strong affinity for the German people, their patriotic spirit, and their cultural values of integrity and hard work. On completing his service in Germany, he envisioned Japan's future strategic cooperation with Germany "as a means to keep Russia down in case our force will not be [strong] enough. I would rather prefer a Japanese-German alliance than a Japanese-Chinese one. Suppressing Russia and China from two sides, East Asia will come under our hegemony, Western Europe under Germany's."[20]

Believing control of Manchuria and, if possible, eastern Siberia was essential to Japan's long-term security and prosperity, Ugaki made a detailed examination of the massed Japanese bayonet charges and frontal assaults against Russia's fixed fortifications during the Russo-Japanese War. He was repelled by the Japanese losses and found the Japanese generals' callous disregard for human life distasteful.[21]

Ugaki also grasped the most important lesson of the confrontation with Russia: Japan's victory was more the result of Russian incompetence and the inability of Russian forces to maneuver against the Japanese than of Japanese superiority. General Kodama Gentaro, the IJA chief of staff during the Russo-Japanese War, confirmed this insight, declaring, "This greatly simplified matters for us. It also made the result of battle far greater than we had anticipated."[22] Ugaki concluded that the views of many younger IJA officers were correct.[23] In the future, the IJA would need the mobility and firepower to conduct sweeping flank attacks, enveloping or encircling the Russian enemy.[24]

When Imperial Japan was invited by President Woodrow Wilson in 1918 to join the Western allies in a joint attack on the new Bolshevik state, General Ugaki, now deputy chief of the Imperial General Staff, was assigned to plan Japan's military intervention.[25] Ugaki welcomed the opportunity and drafted the IJA's plans for the seizure and occupation of eastern Siberia. He saw intervention in Russia as an immense opportunity to reinvigorate Japan's northern strategy and expand its foothold on the Asian landmass. His far-reaching plans utilized the railways all the way to Lake Baikal and recommended their expanded use to move Japanese forces farther west if the opportunity arose.[26] However, in Russia, the IJA encountered a new Russian enemy in the form of Bolshevik cavalry forces—mobile guerrilla armies that operated over thousands of square miles, often under horrible weather conditions.

In four years of hard fighting, the Bolshevik armies scored few military triumphs, but they did wear down the IJA and push Japan's limited industrial capacity and economy to the point of exhaustion, imparting a strategic lesson Ugaki would not forget: Japan's army and its supporting scientific-industrial base were not prepared to meet the requirements of modern warfare.[27] Ugaki resolved to change this condition by infusing the Meiji-era IJA with new thinking, a new organization, and new forms of armored mobility, firepower, and aircraft. The question for Ugaki was how to finance and implement his plan.

After the IJA's four-year intervention in Siberia ended, the politics of economic stringency confronted the army with a severely constrained defense budget. A new internal debate raged regarding how, where, and against whom to fight. Once again, Ugaki's eyes fixed on Manchuria, not the Pacific, and his relations with the admirals of the IJN quickly deteriorated. He viewed Japan's enormous investment in naval power as a diversion of resources the IJA would need for the unavoidable collision that would decide Japan's strategic future: a land war with the Soviet Union.

As chief of staff, Ugaki embodied the fight for change inside the Imperial Japanese Army, which was always intertwined with its contest with the IJN for resources. Ugaki's faction consisted of the so-called revisionists, IJA officers who believed strongly that future wars would commit the army to protracted conflicts against more advanced Soviet and Western opponents, particularly the Western colonial powers in Asia. The revisionists believed that modern armaments and new organizations for combat, not numbers or morale, were the keys to victory in future warfare. Under Ugaki's leadership, the revisionist program reorganized the IJA into smaller, triangular (three-regiment) divisions and introduced new technology in the form of tanks, mobile artillery, and aircraft—all paid for with savings from an overall reduction in IJA manpower.[28]

On the other side of the debate were the IJA traditionalists, officers convinced that numerically large conscript forces could always compensate for deficiencies in weaponry and technology so long as they were imbued with strong combat spirit. The traditionalists argued that future wars would look like Japan's first and brief war with China in 1898 or the more intense Russo-Japanese War.[29] Since Japanese troops were always outnumbered by Bolshevik insurgent forces in Siberia, the traditionalists cited the IJA experience in Siberia as evidence for the importance of numbers rather than mobility and firepower. Major General Horike Kazumaro, who opposed Ugaki, expressed the traditionalist view, asserting, "We made studies, but putting it bluntly, Japan's industrial capacity at that time could not carry out all these things we've spoken of, like mechanization of the army, the development of tanks, and the use of aircraft in group formations. If we overstrained in trying to do it, it would have entailed a third and a fourth force reduction, and the army would have been broken up."[30] Though the IJA's share of the defense budget fell from 18.8 percent in 1919 to 16.2 percent in 1922, the traditionalists made sure the IJA grew smaller, but they also resisted change in its organization, equipment, or thinking about warfare.[31]

However, Ugaki's fortunes changed in 1923, when his patron and mentor Tanaka Giichi, now Japan's prime minster, appointed Ugaki as minister of defense. He was finally in a position to drag the IJA through a second revolution in Japanese military affairs.[32] The essential features of Ugaki's reform package were to:

> ➤ Reduce the army budget. Reductions included the disestablishment of four infantry divisions to offset the costs the Japanese government incurred during the four-year Siberian intervention and the Great Kanto earthquake, an approximately 7.9 magnitude quake that transformed Tokyo into a blackened wasteland of death and destruction. Discharged officers were sent to middle schools and high schools to become teachers.[33]

> ➤ Retire general officers opposing reforms. Ukagi removed the IJA's top eleven generals, prompting a Japanese journalist to record, "There was no way to treat these stone heads other than to replace them."[34] Ugaki's allies were thus put into key positions in both the army general staff and national command structure during 1925.[35]

> ➤ Change the force structure. Ugaki set forth his program to reorganize Japanese divisions from square divisions into triangular divisions. The square division was downsized by removing one regiment and skipping the brigade as an intermediate level of command between regiment and division, thereby achieving more savings in manpower without a loss of fighting power. The smaller division retained the same number of

supporting arms—artillery, engineers, and related elements—leaving the formation just as effective, but more mobile and less vulnerable to concentrated enemy fires.[36]

> Modernize the force. Ugaki secured a reduction in the IJA budget to 12.4 percent in 1927 that partially funded the purchase and eventually the development of new tanks, artillery, aircraft, and automatic weapons for the IJA. He established the bureau of supplies and equipment to supervise the IJA's modernization.[37]

In the two years after Ugaki left office in 1927, many of his reforms were predictably delayed or halted entirely.[38] Reactionaries in the senior ranks of the IJA reasserted their influence to slow or halt Ugaki's efforts to modernize the army at the expense of the numbers of men serving in the IJA.[39] Simultaneously, interservice rivalry between the army and the navy worsened, further poisoning the contest for resources and bureaucratic dominance. In later years recalling the events of his two terms as minister of war, Ugaki said, "I tried to seize the initiative, but the tendency of the army was to go in the opposite direction."[40]

It would take another nine years for Major General Ishiwara Kanji, another Germanophile in Japanese uniform, to push through Ugaki's reform program. In 1936, Ishiwara succeeded in persuading the IJA leadership to complete Ugaki's reforms by reorganizing all of the IJA's divisions into smaller triangular formations equipped with more modern weapons. The commitment of resources and manpower to Japan's invasion of China in 1937 postponed Ishiwara's implementation plan until 1940, too late for the IJA's decisive battle with the Soviet armed forces in 1939 at Nomonhan.[41] Dismayed by Tokyo's rush to war with China, Ishiwara cabled the minister of war with the following message concerning the decision to invade China proper: "Tell the Prime Minister that in the two thousand years of our history no man will have done more to destroy Japan than he has by his indecisiveness in this crisis."[42]

None of the IJA's infantry divisions that fought in the battle of Shanghai were reorganized until after 1940, long after the tactical and operational advantages of the smaller, triangular division over the large, unwieldy World War I square division were undeniable. Though Ugaki's reforms did not succeed in transforming the IJA divisions into smaller, more mobile formations, Ugaki did succeed in equipping Japanese divisions for the battle of Shanghai with twice the number of fighting men, three times the number of rifles, and double the number of crew-served weapons (machine guns and mortars) and artillery than were present in the Chinese divisions that opposed them. Despite the setbacks to modernization, thanks to Ugaki, the IJA deployed two tank brigades plus one additional tank battalion to fight in the battle.[43] As it turned out, the presence of just twenty-four tanks inside each Japanese infantry division was decisive in the battle for Shanghai.[44]

THE BATTLE BEGINS

Tokyo's deliberate escalation of the dispute with China over the Marco Polo bridge incident into full-scale war on 7 July 1937 hurled Japan's Kwantung Army into action. In mid-August, Japanese forces struck south from Manchuria to seize Beijing and Chahar. General Chiang Kai-shek suddenly confronted a difficult situation.[45] Nationalist Chinese military strength in the north was thin, and China was still weak from years of civil war between his Nationalist forces and Mao Zedong's Communists.

Confronted with a similar strategic dilemma in 1933, Chiang opted to consolidate his strength in the south and concentrate China's military power against the Chinese Communist Party, at the time a much more serious threat to Nationalist China than Japan.[46] Under the terms of the Tanggu truce that ended Japanese hostilities with China, the price paid for this temporary retreat was humiliating but small.[47] The humiliation entailed the formal recognition of Japan's conquest of Manchuria and the loss of Rehe, a portion of Inner Mongolia controlled by China.[48] Yet Manchuria and Mongolia were not historically part of China, and the regions had few Chinese inhabitants. Chiang chose to husband his resources and defend what he considered to be most important: China's core Han population. Shanghai was an entirely different matter.

Chiang could play for time in the north, but Shanghai, only forty miles from Nanjing, was the capital of Nationalist China, meaning it could not be surrendered without a fight. In mid-July, Chiang ordered General Zhang Zhizhong, a forty-two-year-old political confidant and commander of Chinese forces in Shanghai and the 9th Nationalist Chinese Army Group, to prepare his troops for an attack to drive the Japanese garrison out of Shanghai.[49]

Under the terms of the Tanggu truce that ended China's previous hostilities with Japan, a demilitarized buffer zone was established between China and the city of Shanghai (see map 3). The Chinese military presence in the city was restricted to a Peace Preservation Corps, essentially a large paramilitary police force, but Japan was allowed to maintain a military garrison in

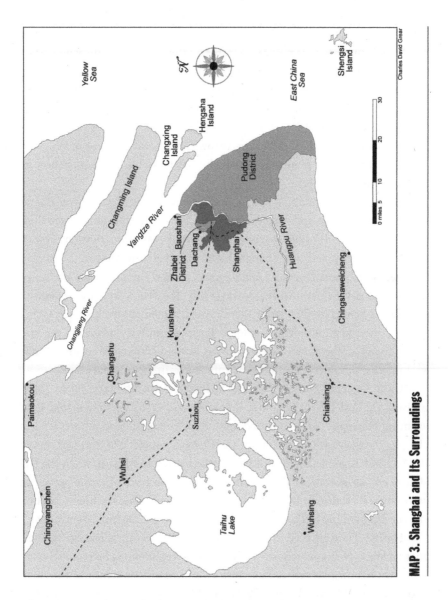

MAP 3. Shanghai and Its Surroundings

Shanghai together with the French, British, and Germans. As soon as war broke out in July, both sides began moving additional men and equipment into Shanghai: the Chinese into the ranks of Shanghai's Peace Preservation Corps and the Japanese into their fortified Shanghai garrison.

The Japanese commander tasked with the mission of seizing and securing Shanghai was sixty-year-old Matsui Iwane, a distinguished Russo-Japanese War veteran of samurai heritage who had retired from active duty just four years earlier in 1933. Matsui had served as IJA chief of intelligence under Ugaki and supported his military reforms on the German military model.

Like many officers of his generation, Matsui believed Japan's mission was to liberate Asia from Western colonial rule. Early in his military career, Matsui was strongly sympathetic to China's nationalist movement. In his younger years, he even befriended Sun Yat-sen, the leader of China's republican revolution who led the movement to overthrow China's last emperor in 1911.[50] In 1937, in a sad turn of events for Matsui, he was tasked to attack a country he had once hoped to liberate.

On reporting for duty in Tokyo, Matsui was presented with a new operational plan to invade and occupy northern China with nine to fourteen divisions while three divisions seized Shanghai and two more divisions landed in Hangzhou Bay, south of Shanghai. Once Shanghai was secured, the plan directed Matsui to advance on Nanjing and compel the surrender of China's Nationalist government. In many ways, the plan was a Japanese version of Germany's Schlieffen plan from World War I, aimed at knocking out China quickly, then turning north to refocus Japanese military power on the real threat to Japan: the Soviet Union. Moving beyond Nanjing to secure China's vast interior was never mentioned or anticipated in the original plan.[51]

Until General Matsui and the Shanghai Expeditionary Force (SEF) arrived, the 3rd IJN Fleet under the command of fifty-four-year-old Rear Admiral Hasegawa Kiyoshi would fight the Chinese on land, on sea, and in the air. Hasegawa was a veteran of the Russo-Japanese War and had served on Admiral Togo Heihachiro's flagship, the battleship *Mikasa*, when the IJN destroyed tsarist Russia's fleet in the Straits of Tsushima. He also served as Japan's naval attaché in Washington and in 1945 provided the final report on the condition of the IJN to Emperor Hirohito, persuading him to surrender.[52]

For the IJA to succeed in its fight for Shanghai, Admiral Hasegawa knew that Japanese positions ashore in the city of Shanghai must be retained at all costs. On his own initiative, Hasegawa moved quickly to reinforce the small Shanghai Special Naval Landing Force (SNLF)—literally, Japanese sailors taken off ships, issued rifles, and used as infantry on land with additional sailors. In the ten days before the IJA arrived, Hasegawa expanded the SNLF to ten thousand sailors. They would provide an important margin of victory in the battle by defending Japanese positions ashore against the attacking Chinese Nationalist army until the IJA arrived.[53]

Anticipating the decisive role that Japanese naval gunfire and airpower would play, Hasegawa also requested additional naval power. Tokyo responded by sending the 8th Cruiser Division and 1st Destroyer Squadron to reinforce the fleet. By 11 August, Admiral Hasegawa had a fleet of thirty warships in the 3rd IJN Fleet, including the 16th Destroyer and the 11th Battleship divisions plus two aircraft carriers.[54]

Three ships of the 11th Battleship Division were anchored in Shanghai harbor to provide fire support to Japanese forces in the city. The rest were located up and down the Yangtze River, where they operated without interference from the Chinese.[55] The Nationalist Chinese had a fleet of fifty-nine ships and twelve patrol boats equipped with torpedoes designed for riverine or coastal operations, but without the ability to mine the approaches to Shanghai harbor and the Yangtze River, the vessels were of little use in this battle.[56]

Knowing that all of the IJN's forces could not operate from Shanghai harbor, Hasegawa directed the *Kamoi*, 1st Carrier Division, 1st Combined Air Unit, 22nd Air Unit, and the 12th Sea Plane Division to set up bases of operations in the vicinity of the Shengsi Islands some thirty kilometers off the coast of Shanghai.[57] These units added a total of thirty-eight Type 96 attack/reconnaissance planes and twenty Type 95 fighters, all vastly superior in range and striking power to China's antiquated and numerically inferior air force.[58]

On paper, the Chinese National Revolutionary Army fielded a force of 1.75 million soldiers. As is often the case in war, the numbers were impressive but misleading. At most, perhaps 300,000 Chinese soldiers were trained and organized in any meaningful way.

Chiang Kai-shek regarded the troops that his German advisers trained as his best. Like the Japanese army officers, Chiang Kai-shek held the German military in very high esteem. His closest military advisers were Germans. One of the most famous, Colonel General Hans von Seeckt, travelled to China and provided him with a white paper that was instrumental in persuading Chiang to stand up an elite force of 80,000 men under German advisers.[59] In August 1937, these troops were better trained and equipped than the rest of the Nationalist Chinese forces, but they were still in an early stage of development and not ready to take on the IJA in pitched battle.

General Zhang, China's 9th Army Group commander, was a realist. He knew his troops were outgunned and outranged in every key category of military capability. Zhang's most promising margin of victory depended on how effectively he could exploit the Nationalist Chinese Army's numerical superiority to drive Shanghai's Japanese garrison into the sea before the IJA could land in force. By 9 August, Zhang had assembled 4 infantry divisions, a separate infantry brigade, 2 artillery regiments with 400 to 500 guns, 2 heavy mortar battalions, 2 anti-tank gun batteries, and 1 light tank battalion with 30 to 40 light tanks—a force of roughly 50,000 for the mission.[60]

Zhang's scheme of maneuver was not complex. Like many generals in Chinese history, he made virtue of necessity. He decided to exploit China's one true advantage over the Japanese: numbers of soldiers. Zhang reasoned that if he could achieve surprise, he could concentrate overwhelming numbers of Chinese troops against the Japanese defenders, eventually driving the retreating Japanese into the Huangpu River. His plan called for an assault by 20,000 troops or two divisions. One division would strike at the IJA headquarters near Zhabei, the poor industrial section of Shanghai. The other division would attack the IJA headquarters located inside a textile mill. Once these objectives were taken, Zhang planned to deploy additional Chinese forces along the coast to defeat Japanese attempts to land reinforcements.

Unfortunately for Zhang, his initial attack did not go as planned. During the morning of 13 August, Chinese troops in the Shanghai Peace Preservation Corps opened fire on members of the Japanese garrison, alerting the Japanese to impending action. Realizing that the element of surprise was lost, Chiang directed Zhang to begin his deliberate assault on the Japanese targets as soon as possible. For Zhang, that meant the next day. Zhang knew that a successful Chinese attack depended heavily on surprise, but he followed orders.

When the two Chinese divisions attacked their objectives on 14 August, they made a shocking discovery. Not only had the Japanese forces been alerted, but also the two Japanese headquarters were protected by concrete defensive barriers that were impervious to even the largest Chinese artillery (150-millimeter howitzers). Additionally, Japanese armored cars and machine guns were placed along the streets and corridors where Chinese attacks were expected to pass, and Japanese naval gunfire pulverized Chinese troops in the areas surrounding the Japanese strongpoints.

Undeterred by the failure of the first attacks, the Chinese generals sent their men into action, shoulder to shoulder, with fixed bayonets. Predictably, losses were catastrophic. Chinese flesh and bone performed poorly against Japanese steel, concrete, and machine guns. Even more disappointing, the Chinese tanks of British, French, and Italian manufacture lacked the armored protection to withstand fire from Japanese heavy weapons and provided practically no offensive capability at all. Fire from Japanese heavy machine guns penetrated the light armor and killed or wounded the Chinese tank crews.[61]

Frustrated and desperate to destroy the Japanese strongholds in the city, Zhang decided to throw in two of Nationalist China's German-trained divisions, the 87th and the 88th, in an operation he named Iron Fist. On 17 August, these elite infantry divisions attacked the Japanese strongholds using the German infiltration tactics they had practiced under the supervision of German officers on contract to train Chiang's army.

Despite the demoralizing wall of fire that greeted them, the heroic Chinese soldiers fought their way to the forward edge of the Japanese defenses. It made no difference. The attacking Chinese troops simply lacked the firepower and explosives to penetrate the defensive works, and their artillery and machine gun support was insufficient.[62] Once more, the Japanese sailors of the SNLF held their ground thanks to the concrete defensive works and the fleet's accurate, devastating naval gunfire.

In the interim, Nationalist Chinese air and naval forces struck the Japanese ships in Shanghai harbor. On 14 August, forty Chinese aircraft flew a total of two hundred sorties, attacking Japanese ships as well as troops in the city. Once again, the attacks were ineffective.[63] Chinese river patrol craft launched a successful torpedo attack against the battleship *Izumo*, scoring two hits, but did not do serious damage to it.[64] Bombs meant for the Japanese fleet fell instead on a British warship and on Shanghai's international zone, accidentally injuring or killing three thousand civilians inside an area now brimming with more than a million people seeking refuge from the fighting.[65] Japanese forces ashore sustained no losses at all.

In the first forty-eight hours of the fight for Shanghai, Japanese airpower fought the weather, not the Chinese. When the weather cleared on 16 August, the 3rd Air Fleet launched air strikes from Taipei, Cheju-do Island, Shengsi Islands, and its two carriers, *Hosho* and *Ryujo*, hit Chinese troop concentrations and airfields from Shanghai to Nanjing.[66] After decrypting the Nationalist Chinese military's encoded messages on 19 August, the Japanese established air superiority over Shanghai. By the time Matsui's SEF of 80,000 men arrived on 23 August, Admiral Hasegawa's actions had retained Japan's foothold ashore, securing Japan's margin of victory. The scales were tipping in favor of the IJA.

THE IJA ARRIVES

General Matsui's first contingent comprised two divisions, the 3rd and 11th Infantry Divisions.[67] To augment the capabilities of these two divisions, Matsui was given additional machine gun, tank, and mortar battalions, a heavy field artillery regiment, and a siege artillery battalion, adding about 100 tanks and 300 to 400 artillery systems of different calibers to the SEF for a total of 80,000 troops. Separate radio platoons were attached to major regiments and divisions, giving the SEF a significant communication advantage over the Chinese forces, which were equipped with comparatively few radios.[68] The lack of communication capabilities became a chronic weakness. Chinese defensive operations could not keep up with the frequent attacks launched by the Japanese let alone effectively monitor the actions of their own forces.

A few days later, an IJA fighter squadron from the Provisional Air Group operating in north China was added to reinforce Japanese airpower ashore.[69] By 10 September, China's small air force was largely out of action, and Japanese forces enjoyed air supremacy for the rest of the campaign.[70]

Matsui's task, however, was by no means easy. Geography still favored the Chinese defender. The maze of waterways and buildings inside Shanghai, together with the swamps, rivers, and lakes on the city's outskirts, severely restricted the movement of ground forces on both sides. If skillfully used, these waterways would favor the Chinese defender. On the north side of Shanghai is the great Yangtze River, five to ten miles wide and sixty-five to eighty feet deep. In the center of the peninsula is Suzhou Creek, an eastward flowing stream that makes a sharp northward turn into the Huangpu (formerly called the Whampoa) River, eventually converging with the Yangtze. The source of the Suzhou Creek is an area of swamps, and farther west is Taihu Lake, a body of water larger than the modern city of Shanghai itself (869 square miles). To the south of Shanghai is Hangzhou Bay, an elongated thirty-six-mile-wide inlet that gradually narrows as it reaches the Qiantang River and the city of Hangzhou.

Aside from his age, Matsui was hardly the typical army four-star general. He was remarkably fit with an exceptionally sharp mind and no shortage of personal physical courage. More important, Matsui would do early in the campaign what seemed impossible given the serious interservice rivalry that afflicted relations between the IJA and the IJN. He would make peace with the Japanese admirals.

In a discussion on 21 August aboard Admiral Hasegawa's flagship, Matsui listened carefully to the recommendations of his own staff, as well as to those of the Japanese naval officers already engaged in the battle for Shanghai. Rear Admiral Nagumo Chuichi urged Matsui to conduct two landings, which would force the Chinese defenders to fight in two directions simultaneously. (Nagumo would later command the IJN's 1st Air Fleet at Pearl Harbor and Midway.)[71]

Ultimately, Matsui overruled the IJA staff officers who urged him to make a single landing in one location in favor of Nagumo's plan for two. Matsui decided to conduct the landings in two echelons at two different locations roughly ten miles apart (see map 4). The northernmost landing would place the 11th Infantry Division in the vicinity of Chuanshakou, while the 3rd Infantry Division landed farther south near Wusong. The Japanese conducted amphibious landings along a forty-kilometer front, from Liuhe northeast of the Shanghai metropolitan area to the Shanghai docks on the Yangtze.

Matsui instructed his commanders to execute a double envelopment using the 3rd Infantry Division to capture the city of Wusong while the 11th Infantry Division pushed inward to the southwest and capture Luodian. The capture of that city—a transportation center connecting Baoshan, downtown Shanghai, and several other towns with highways—would facilitate the encirclement Matsui wanted by cutting off Chinese forces inside an area of about approximately fifty square miles.[72] The encirclement was part of Matsui's larger strategic goal of forcing the Chinese 15th Army Group to withdraw eight miles from the coast. If successful, the withdrawal would expose the left flank of the Chinese 9th Army Group, which was still fighting in metropolitan Shanghai, to Japanese assault and, potentially, encirclement.

To support General Matsui's plan, Admiral Hasegawa directed the entire 3rd Air Fleet to thoroughly reconnoiter the area and then provide the attacking Japanese divisions with close air support.[73] When the IJA formations began landing in waves on the Chinese coast, the entire might of the Japanese fleet would assemble to systematically pulverize Chinese troops and defense works.[74]

In view of Chinese weaknesses in airpower, artillery, and tanks, the Chinese had little choice but to compensate with numbers. By the time the Japanese landings started, Chiang had moved the Nationalist Chinese 15th Army Group, a force of 150,000–200,000 men under the command of General Luo Zhuoying, into hastily prepared defensive positions along the coast. Luo's mission was to stop the Japanese landings. To do so, he had 17 infantry divisions, a separate infantry brigade, and a separate artillery regiment with 600 to 800 artillery systems.[75] Chinese infantry divisions were generally 10,000 strong, or half the size of the 22,000-man Japanese square divisions.[76]

The landings began on 23 August with the Japanese SEF coming ashore near the coastal towns of Liuhe, Wusong, and Chuanshakou. Resistance near or on the beaches was sporadic, but IJA 3rd and 11th Infantry Divisions

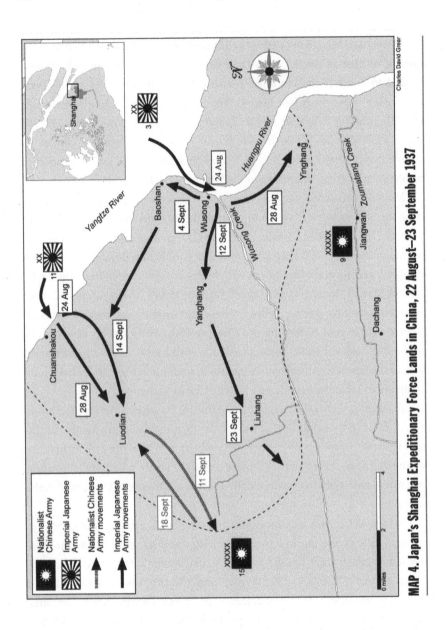

MAP 4. Japan's Shanghai Expeditionary Force Lands in China, 22 August–23 September 1937

encountered tough opposition from Chinese forces as they advanced inland to capture towns and villages. Neighborhoods and buildings that the IJA seized during the day with the aid of Japanese naval gunfire were lost to ruthless Chinese counterattacks at night. Even with the systematic bombardment of Chinese defensive positions and assembly areas, the fighting was harder than Matsui had anticipated, and he went ashore to find out why.

Upon arriving at the front, Matsui discovered that his general staff had directed the two attacking divisions to leave behind their tanks and artillery. Japanese general staff officers assumed the soft sand and ground on the coast plus the network of canals and streams surrounding Shanghai would not support the effective employment of tanks and artillery. Japanese infantry attacks bogged down due to the absence of Japanese firepower and mobility.[77]

Matsui was deeply angered by his staff's omission, and because of the lack of mobile armored firepower, five days would pass before the 11th Infantry Division would capture Luodian and the 3rd Infantry Division would capture Wusong.[78] However, far more important for the larger Japanese campaign was the fact that without the tanks and artillery, the SEF opportunity to envelop the Chinese 15th Army Group was irretrievably lost.

The town of Baoshan finally fell on 4 September. For its Chinese defenders, the battle was a fight to the death. The few Chinese units that survived that battle escaped to establish new defensive positions in and around Luodian, barely sixteen miles from the center of Shanghai. Taking Luodian would now require a deliberate assault, something Matsui had hoped to avoid.

To defend Luodian, Chiang concentrated 300,000 troops, including the survivors of Baoshan, to stop 100,000 Japanese soldiers supported by tanks, artillery, aircraft, and naval gunfire. The Chinese were too poorly equipped and trained to halt the IJA for long, but as the battle progressed, the Chinese found innovative ways to slow or derail the Japanese advance.

Under cover of darkness, Chinese soldiers mined the roads leading into their defensive positions around Luodian and launched raids to isolate and cut off Japanese outposts. To reduce their losses from the massive Japanese artillery and air strikes, the Chinese kept the forward lines lightly manned, a tactic the Germans had employed against the British and French armies in the last two years of World War I. Then, when the Japanese infantry closed in, the Chinese would appear to spring up from nowhere and attack them at close range. These tactics worked well for the Chinese, who used them repeatedly.

When one defensive line was wiped out and taken by the Japanese, the Chinese would fall back to another, over and over, until few Chinese soldiers were left alive. These diehard tactics had a profound effect. On 18 September, the Japanese attack was halted, and a thousand Japanese soldiers were killed or wounded. It is no accident that in Chinese history, the battle for Luodian is referred to as the "grinding mill of flesh and blood."[79]

For the Japanese to regain momentum, Matsui concluded that more drastic measures were needed. He recalled Japanese air forces from bombing runs on Chinese airfields and supply columns and ordered them to focus on Chinese forces holding up the Japanese attacks. On 10 September, Matsui launched a massive air assault with aircraft from the IJN 3rd Fleet and 2nd Combined Air Unit to support the IJA's infantry divisions.[80] With the relentless and massive application of airpower, the SEF was finally able to dislodge the determined Chinese from their last defensive positions in Luodian before the end of September.

By this point, the IJA had dramatically improved its coordinated use of aircraft, artillery, tanks, and infantry in daylight attacks. The result was not quite a blitzkrieg, but it was close enough in the fighting with the infantry-centric Chinese. For the Chinese, the experience was sheer terror.

Imperial Japanese Army attacks were planned and executed with precision; they began at first light with massive air attacks supported by observers in aircraft who identified and targeted Chinese positions for the artillery and naval gunfire. When smoke appeared on the battlefield, IJA infantry began advancing with tanks in the lead while fighters flew forward to search for and attack Chinese reinforcements racing to the sector under attack. This was a pattern that the IJA would repeat with great effectiveness.

Nevertheless, Japanese losses at this point in the fight for Shanghai were much higher than Tokyo anticipated; 8,000 casualties, or nearly 30 percent of Japanese losses during the entire battle for the city.[81] Even with the reinforcement of 40,000 troops from the IJA's 13th and 9th Divisions, the battle for Shanghai was beginning to resemble a bloody stalemate on the World War I model.[82] The lack of mobile armored firepower inside the Japanese forces meant that Matsui's troops could not move and concentrate quickly enough to envelop and trap the Nationalist Chinese forces as he had originally intended.[83]

Determined to regain the initiative from the Japanese no matter the cost, Chiang now committed all of his military commanders to the battle for Shanghai, directing them to fight literally to the last Chinese soldier. On 21 September, he reorganized his forces into area defense formations (see map 5). Chiang assigned specific areas to Chinese armies and army groups with defined boundaries that established command responsibility for what contemporary American military leaders call "defend to retain" missions. The river defense forces, Nanjing's capital garrison forces, and the Nationalist Chinese 23rd Army Group (as a separate command) were directed to establish an area defense south of Hangzhou Bay, far from Nanjing.[84] Seventy Nationalist Chinese infantry divisions would eventually be involved in the operation, but

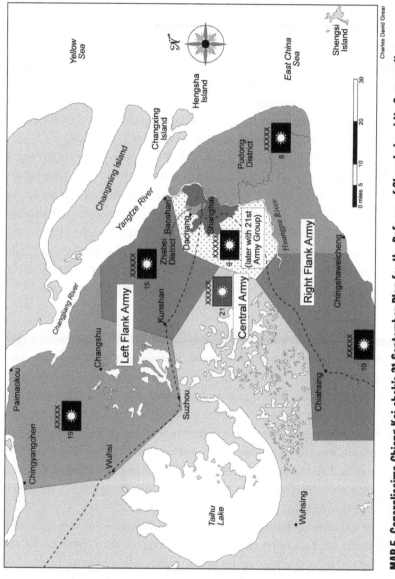

MAP 5. Generalissimo Chiang Kai-shek's 21 September Plan for the Defense of Shanghai and Its Surroundings

only the forces designated "Right Wing Forces," "Central Forces," and "Left Wing Forces" would be directly engaged in the battle of Shanghai.

Chiang's arrangement was problematic. His reorganization inserted an extra layer of command and control that slowed decisionmaking, restricted the flow of information, and reportedly caused some unnecessary confusion.[85] Moreover, instead of utilizing all nine Chinese army groups to attack and overwhelm the IJA, he initially committed only two (and later, a third) army groups to directly engage the IJA at any one time.

Chiang later said the new defensive scheme was necessary to accommodate the growing number of Chinese troops committed to defend Shanghai and its surroundings. While this may have been true, there was another reason. The IJA's war of ruthless extermination against its enemy cultivated extreme hatred in the Chinese, evoking a particularly visceral response from the Chinese soldier. Chiang wanted to put this hatred of the invader to good use.

Nationalist Chinese soldiers now killed Japanese prisoners of war as readily as the Japanese killed Chinese prisoners of war. Major General Wei Li-huang, the commander of the 67th Division, Chinese 15th Army Group, noted, "It's impossible to have a prisoner delivered to headquarters although we pay from 50 to 100 yuan upon delivery, and there are severe punishments for not doing so. The soldiers say that the prisoners die along the way."[86] Chiang could defend Shanghai and its surroundings to the last Chinese soldier because the "war of armies" was becoming a war between two peoples.[87]

THE IJA RENEWS THE OFFENSIVE

On 30 September, the IJA and IJN signed Memorandum 519, which set down the agreed responsibilities of army and navy air forces. This memorandum was crucial for attacking Japanese ground forces in gaining access to air support from both the services. Under the terms of the agreement, the 2nd Combined Air Unit, a mixed formation in northern China consisting primarily of IJN aircraft, was tasked to support the 3rd and 9th Infantry Divisions.[88] The 1st Combined Air Unit halted raids against Nanjing and instead agreed to coordinate with the IJA forces in Shanghai on a daily basis until 27 October or whenever the Shanghai phase of the operation ended.[89]

The same day the memorandum was signed, Matsui set in motion an attack southward from Liuhang through Wusong Creek, toward Zoumaotang Creek (see map 6). He hoped the attackers would quickly seize two stone bridges west of Dachang being defended by the Nationalist Chinese 33rd and 18th Divisions.

The Japanese employed the 101st, 3rd, and 9th Infantry Divisions, with the 11th Infantry Division covering the right flank from possible spoiling attacks by the Chinese 15th Army Group. The IJA 13th Infantry Division was held in reserve.[90] Chinese accounts also mention the presence of Taiwanese and Manchu units intermingled with IJA reinforcements, totaling 100,000 troops including more than 300 artillery systems, 300 tanks, and 200 aircraft.[91]

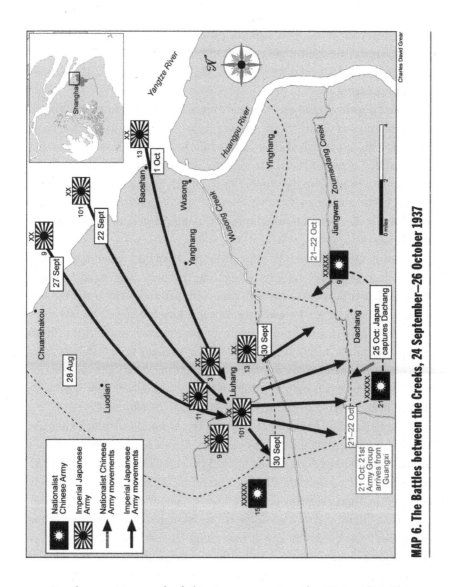

MAP 6. The Battles between the Creeks, 24 September–26 October 1937

On the receiving end of this juggernaut was the Nationalist Chinese 9th Army Group, commanded by General Zhang Zhizhong, which was now tasked with protecting the north side of Shanghai. At this point in the battle, General Zhang's troops were all that stood between the attacking Japanese and the city of Shanghai.

The 9th Army Group had 4 infantry divisions and a separate brigade, a force of 60,000 men. However, unlike other Chinese army groups, the 9th Army Group had substantially more artillery, around 400 guns, and even a separate battalion of 50 light tanks, a unique formation in the Nationalist Chinese Army.[92] General Zhang also continued to command the German-trained 87th and 88th Infantry Divisions, the best formations in the Nationalist Chinese army.

Japanese prime minister Konoe Fumimaro was unaware of Chiang's intentions and was totally reliant on the advice of Matsui and other IJA commanders, with whom he had an uncomfortable relationship. To the extent that he was able, Konoe restricted the IJA's political influence. When he agreed to integrate and escalate the combat in the north China and central China theaters by launching an October offensive, he did so reluctantly. He was skeptical that the operation would compel Chiang's capitulation and bring the conflict to a close.[93]

By early October, the IJA's strength in the Shanghai region approached 250,000 men. After several days of fighting that was often hand to hand, the IJA 9th Division broke through on 5 October and secured the far side of Wusong Creek. Here, however, the Japanese attack broke down. The Chinese defenders were waiting in carefully prepared trench works that utilized barbed wire, mines, machine guns, and artillery. From 7 to 13 October, heavy rains intervened to provide a respite from the fighting, which allowed time for both sides to replenish supplies. Then the Japanese offensive continued with the goal of eliminating all Chinese resistance north of Wusong Creek.[94]

Chiang Kai-shek had another card to play: Nationalist China's Guangxi Army of roughly 70,000 to 80,000 soldiers. Given the success of Zhang's defense, Chiang judged the timing to be right for a Chinese counteroffensive that might fully consolidate Chinese control of Dachang. With the timely arrival of the Guangxi Army on 17 October, Chiang was certain that Nationalist China's Central Army would be strong enough to regain control of the Yunzaobin River bank, the key to frustrating Japanese efforts to maneuver Chinese forces out of Shanghai. With the combined strength of the 9th and 15th Army Groups, the Nationalist Chinese would enjoy an advantage in personnel numbers over the IJA and a slight advantage in the number of artillery systems but would still labor under major handicaps in the number and quality of tanks. The Chinese also had no real defense against Japanese air strikes.

While Chiang planned his counteroffensive, the Nationalist Chinese 8th Army Group remained on the defense at Pudong, east of Shanghai city and north of Hangzhou Bay, while the 10th Army Group stayed in its defensive positions south of Hangzhou Bay. For reasons that have never been satisfactorily explained, Chiang did not employ these formations to reinforce the 9th

Army Group's flank in the north. Their mission was to simply defend their assigned areas. As a result, nine divisions and four separate brigades that could have joined the fight and diverted IJA forces from defending against the Chinese counterattack did nothing. Whether these might have tipped the balance in favor of the Chinese offensive is unknown, but the fact that they were not massed to support it is peculiar.

The counteroffensive was not well coordinated, and as a result the Chinese attackers were decimated by superior Japanese firepower. As in previous operations, the lack of experience, poor communications, woefully inadequate firepower, and incompetence in the senior Chinese ranks constrained Chinese freedom of action. Chiang's counteroffensive petered out.

On 25 October, the Japanese proceeded with their planned assault on Dachang. This offensive is worthy of attention because it was probably one of Matsui's finest operations. The Japanese attack was supported by 700 artillery systems of various calibers and 400 aircraft including 150 bombers. It was also spearheaded by just 20 tanks.[95] In a rare event in Japanese military history, the tanks were concentrated as envisioned by the Germans and, as Ugaki always urged, not broken into small groups to operate as fire support platforms for light infantry.[96]

The Chinese 33rd and 18th Divisions sustained 90 percent casualties and the bridges across the river were captured, but the 26 days of fighting also cost the Japanese 25,000 casualties.[97] When Dachang fell, the 9th Army Group's flank collapsed, and the door to Shanghai was flung wide open. The operation General Matsui had hoped to complete in a week had instead lasted for almost a month.

Chiang Kai-shek was despondent, writing, "I had hoped that after the troops from Guangxi entered the fighting, we could hold out. The military situation is shaky. It is very discouraging."[98] Chiang's fight for Shanghai was always a desperate gamble with an underequipped and inadequately trained force. Now, he began to realize he would have to salvage what he could for a war that would last for years.

THE FINAL ACT

Reeling from heavy losses, Chinese forces were totally unprepared when Japanese troops forced their way across the Suzhou River on 30 October, putting Chiang Kai-shek's remaining troops in grave danger. The combination of the loss of Dachang on 26 October and the Japanese breakthrough on 30 October meant Nationalist Chinese troops in Shanghai would have to withdraw or face certain destruction through methodical Japanese encirclement. If the Chinese army was going to survive to fight again, Chiang Kai-shek's troops would have to abandon Zhabei and Jiangwan along with other heavily defended Chinese positions. On 30 October, the last remnants of the heroic 9th Army Group, soldiers who had held the line against the IJA through seventy-five days of unimaginable hardship, finally retreated. It was the end of the 9th Army.

Chinese forces now outran the advancing Japanese. There was little the Japanese could do to catch the retreating Chinese forces. The IJA lacked the tracked armor to outpace them. When the Japanese 10th Army, composed of units from northern China, landed in Chingshaweicheng on 5 November, they encountered no real opposition (see map 7). However, the retreating Chinese were able to establish effective blocking positions with the 19th Army Group in the area north of Taihu Lake and the 10th Army Group south of the lake. These forces successfully covered the majority of retreating Chinese troops.

Within ten days, the IJA 6th Division would advance some thirty miles west and capture Chiahsing in an attempt to cut off retreating Chinese forces, while the 9th Division occupied the city of Suzhou and linked up with the rest of the SEF on 19 November.[99] Another landing by the IJA 16th Division north of Paimaokou designed to cut off retreating Chinese forces came too late to be effective. The operation failed, and the Chinese escaped yet again.[100]

The battle for Shanghai was over. General Matsui Iwane relinquished his command of the SEF and assumed command of a new, larger force, Japan's Central China Expeditionary Army, which included both the SEF and the 10th Army.[101] The great offensive to smash remaining Chinese resistance was about to begin.

As the war moved inland and away from Shanghai, the Japanese occupation authority in Shanghai restored order, repairing and reopening many of Shanghai's factories and administrative buildings. But 70 percent of Shanghai's productive capacity lay in ruins. Thousands of residential buildings, factories, and workshops were damaged or completely demolished. Tens of thousands of homeless Chinese swarmed the city's streets, and hundreds of thousands more slept in stockrooms, warehouses, temples, and parks. Before the end of 1937, 101,000 corpses, mostly civilian, were recovered from the city's ruins.[102]

Shanghai's banking community fared somewhat better. Though Japanese occupation cut off Shanghai banks from economic interaction with the rest of

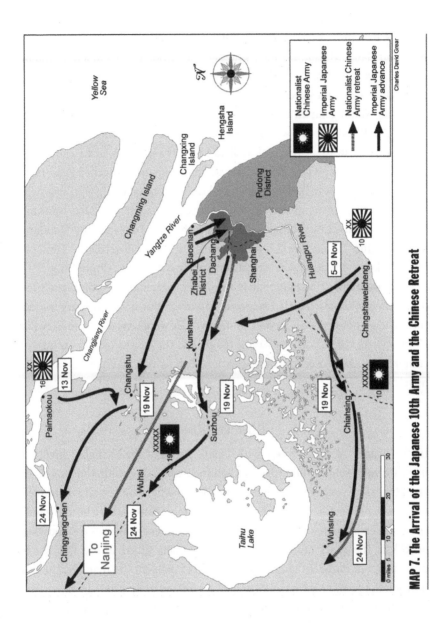

MAP 7. The Arrival of the Japanese 10th Army and the Chinese Retreat

China, the banks still functioned without too much regulatory interference from the occupying authorities. After December 1941, this situation ended, and the Japanese imposed strict controls on all facets of life in Shanghai from monetary policy to food.[103]

While Shanghai settled in for a long Japanese occupation, the fight for control of Nanjing transformed an already bitter conflict into a prolonged series of atrocities on a scale not seen since the days of Genghis Khan. Almost nine years later, Matsui, the man who once befriended Sun Yat-sen, would be tried and executed by the Allied Tokyo War Tribunal for war crimes committed against the Chinese people by his troops in Nanjing.[104]

After Nanjing, Japan's war with China evolved into the bog that Ishiwara had originally predicted—war without end. Chinese military strategy methodically adhered to the formula described in a 1936 letter to Nishi Haruhiko, who would be Japan's foreign minister when the Japanese attacked Pearl Harbor: "If war breaks out between Japan and China, the Nationalist Government has made secret plans to resist to the bitter end. If their Shanghai-Nanking [Nanjing] defense line is broken, they will withdraw to a Nanchang-Kiukiang [Jiujiang] line. If that line cannot be defended, they will retreat to Hankow [Hankou]. If the Wuhan defense collapses, they will shift to Chungking."[105]

With the fall of Nanjing, Japan's military campaign to subjugate China dragged on without result. In response, Japan's political and military leaders turned to airpower for an answer. Chinese cities were leveled and millions of Chinese were killed, but the Chinese fought on. The Japanese never seemed to comprehend the power of Chinese nationalism, which was as fierce as their own.[106]

CONCLUSION

In the history of China's war with Japan, the fight for Shanghai involved more Chinese soldiers and matériel and incurred higher human losses than any other single engagement. Before it ended, the fight for the city embroiled nearly a million soldiers in combat. For the Chinese Nationalist forces, the outcome was catastrophic. An estimated 270,000 Chinese soldiers were wounded or killed. The exact number of Chinese civilians killed in the fighting is unknown, but numbers range from 250,000 to 450,000.[107] Chiang Kai-shek's decision to commit his best units to fight for Shanghai devastated China's best military manpower. In 3 months of intense combat, Chiang Kai-shek sacrificed thousands of his army's most highly trained junior officers, compelling his forces to fight for years without the competent tactical leadership they desperately needed.

Japanese casualty figures were much lower, estimated to be around 40,000.[108] The disparity in Chinese and Japanese losses highlights the impact of Ugaki's modest modernization efforts and the high quality of Japanese troops and their leadership, but the struggle for control of Shanghai was harder and bloodier than it should have been.

Whereas Sir Richard Haldane succeeded in changing the British army just enough to play its vital part in the opening battles of World War I, the IJA failed to change enough to achieve a true margin of victory. Rather than downsize the IJA and use the savings to invest in the war-winning technologies of modern warfare—tanks, artillery, and aircraft—the Japanese generals chose to rely on masses of manpower.

The Japanese generals' preference for numbers in uniform over capability produced the bloodbath at Shanghai and the "grinding mill of flesh and blood" at Luodian. Their determination to retain the large, ponderous World War I square division structures—ideal for the attritional character of trench warfare but unsuited to rapid and decisive offensive operations—was a costly mistake. In the months it took to seize Shanghai, the generals compensated for the lack of offensive capability in their large infantry formations by committing their entire arsenal of tanks and aircraft to move forward and drive the Chinese defenders out of Shanghai.

Tokyo celebrated the fall of Shanghai as a great victory, but the Japanese victory concealed the truth that the IJA was still critically short of completing its transformation into a military force suitable to modern warfare as practiced by the Germans and Soviets. The essential lesson that decisive operations required large, mobile armored forces supported by thousands of advanced fighters and bombers went unlearned. Japanese generals such as Matsui were ferocious and courageous, commanding from the front whenever and wherever conditions demanded decisive leadership. The Japanese generals made use of the tanks and artillery they had, but the IJA still remained organized for World War I until World War II ended.

Despite the gradual introduction of newer and better tanks before war's end in 1945, the IJA never fielded more than the equivalent of three armored divisions in combat, a force woefully inadequate for operations in the Chinese and southeast Asian theaters of war.[109] Japanese tanks and self-propelled guns never attained the quality and capability of comparable equipment in the U.S., German, or Soviet arsenals. Serious weaknesses in mobile armored firepower and logistics allowed the inexperienced and ill-equipped Chinese armies to escape, regroup, and resume their attacks on Japanese occupation forces time and again.

One reason the Japanese generals failed to learn from their operations in Shanghai was the weakness of their opponents in the early stages of World

War II.[110] In Malaya, where the British opponent could not melt away into an expansive interior, the Japanese conducted a masterful campaign involving the coordinated use of tanks, artillery, engineers, infantry, aircraft, and ships, defeating a British army in February 1942 that was twice as large as the attacking force. Against the British troops defending Singapore, the quality of IJA training and aggressive leadership compensated for the IJA's numerical inferiority on the ground.[111] The conquest of the U.S.-held Philippines in May 1942, though more challenging than the campaign to take Singapore, simply reinforced Tokyo's illusion of Japanese military superiority.

Japan's modest military advantage did not last long. Two years after the fall of Shanghai, Japan's Kwantung Army was decisively defeated by Soviet armed forces on the plains of Nomonhan.[112] Japanese airpower fared better than the ground forces; superb Japanese pilots fought their Soviet opponents in the air to a draw, but airpower could not compensate for the IJA's acute weaknesses in mobility, armor, firepower, and organization.[113] Soviet army small arms, tanks, artillery, and organization were demonstrably superior to anything the IJA could field. Japan sued for peace, releasing Soviet forces in Siberia to move west in time to defend Moscow in the winter battles of 1941–42.

As American air and naval power closed the ring around Japan in early 1945 and Japanese cities were incinerated from the air, 1 million of the Imperial Japanese Army's 5.9 million soldiers were still in China, and another 780,000 were in Manchuria.[114] Chiang Kai-shek's decision to trade lives for space exacted a high price from the IJA. The defenders of Shanghai prevented the Japanese from striking directly into central China, slowing the Japanese advance long enough for the Nationalist government to begin moving a portion of its defense industries deeper into China, toward China's new wartime capital, Chongqing (Chung King).

Japan's war with China not only delayed and disrupted the IJA's modernization, it also fatally crippled Japan's northern strategy to defeat the Soviet Union, while putting Japan on a collision course with Britain and the United States. In August 1945, the calamity that Ugaki, Ishiwara, and their supporters had feared the most struck the IJA in Manchuria, when Japanese forces were annihilated in less than two weeks by Soviet armored and mechanized units consisting of 5,556 tanks together with several thousand self-propelled guns and supporting armored fighting vehicles.[115]

The hard lesson that mass and athleticism do not equate with real military capability was not lost on the postwar Japan Self Defense Forces (JSDF). Less than twenty-five years after World War II ended, the much smaller JSDF, only 4 percent of the size of the IJA at its height, already possessed thirty times more firepower than its predecessor. Emperor Hirohito's comment that "our military leaders put too much emphasis on [fighting] spirit and forgot the significance of science" still resonates in Japan.[116] Technology, not manpower, combined with superior organization and leadership, is now widely recognized as Japan's future margin of victory.

Ugaki Kazushige won his fight for change inside the IJA after all, albeit at the cost of a lost war. Today, the Japan Ground Self-Defense Force (JGSDF) fields significant armored forces and more tanks and armored fighting vehicles than the British or French armies. Japanese soldiers are highly educated, trained, and disciplined.[117] At this writing, the JGSDF is upgrading its armored force to the new Type 10 tanks while retiring the older Type 74 tanks. It is also likely that production of the Type 89 Infantry Fighting Vehicle will resume in the near future. The JGSDF is following a familiar pattern: shed old equipment first, then modernize with initial low rate production runs until the new equipment performs to expectation. In the West, this process is called rapid prototyping, and it is something much discussed but seldom seen in practice.

China's emergence as a great power in the twenty-first century must also be viewed through the lens of its war with Japan, especially the battle of Shanghai. China's inability to defend its near seas, great rivers, and coastal cities, and its vulnerability to attack from Formosa (Taiwan), Japan's unsinkable aircraft carrier during the battle for Shanghai, and the seizure of all of China's coastal cities traumatized the Chinese people. These experiences not only shape current Chinese military modernization efforts, they also figure prominently in Chinese thinking about the potential conflict with Japan and the United States, Asia's two great maritime powers.

China's recent demarcation of an air identification zone that includes the Senkaku and Diaoyu Islands must also be seen as part of a larger Chinese anti-access/area denial (A2AD) strategy with its roots in a tragic, costly war against Japanese invasion that began with the battle of Shanghai.[118] Americans would do well to keep this history in mind before leaping to conclusions about China's alleged belligerence toward the United States and its commercial interests in Asia.[119]

CHAPTER 3

REVERSAL OF FORTUNE

The Destruction of Army Group Center, 1944

uring the night of 14–15 September 1941, seventy years after Prussia's titanic victory over the French at Sedan, the armored spearheads of two German armies met at Lokhvitsa, 120 miles east of Kiev, forming an iron ring around 1.6 million Soviet troops. In what turned into the greatest battle of annihilation in recorded human history, the German Wehrmacht destroyed four entire Soviet armies and most of two others, inflicting one million casualties and capturing 665,000 Soviet soldiers.[1]

Less than three years later, on 22 June 1944, the third anniversary of the German invasion of the Soviet Union, 2.5 million Soviet troops launched an offensive, striking Germany's Army Group Center along a 360-mile front extending in a great semicircle from Mozyr on the Pripyat River to Polotsk on the Dwina River. For the first time since the Nazi-Soviet war began, the attacking Soviet forces enjoyed unchallenged control of the airspace over the battle area.

Without interference from the German Luftwaffe, Soviet armored spearheads advanced over 125 miles in less than 12 days. By the time the Soviets recaptured Minsk on 3 July, 25 divisions and 250,000 troops had vanished (killed, wounded, or missing) from the German order of battle, and Army Group Center ceased to exist.[2] Soviet premier Joseph Stalin celebrated his greatest victory over the Wehrmacht on 17 July 1944 by marching a column of 57,000 German prisoners of war led by their captured generals through the streets of Moscow.[3]

Meanwhile, like the French generals in May 1940, the German High Command (Oberkommando der Wehrmacht, or OKW) was reduced to drawing halt lines on maps—lines that advancing Soviet forces had already passed. Unable to suspend his disbelief in the unfolding catastrophe, German chancellor Adolf Hitler continued to count on the exhaustion of Soviet troops and supplies to put an end to the Soviet offensive, but American lend-lease programs provided the Soviets with thousands of trucks, jeeps, and wheeled transports to carry the supplies and replacements that kept the Red Army moving forward.

British prime minister Winston Churchill understood what had happened, exclaiming in horror to his private secretary, "Good God, can't you see that the Russians are spreading across Europe like a tide; they have invaded Poland and there is nothing to prevent them marching into Turkey and Greece!"[4] Transformed Soviet military power had not only destroyed Germany's last strength in the east, but the collapse of German military power also meant the Red Army would reach Berlin long before the Anglo-American forces could do so. Once Stalin's armies conquered central and eastern Europe, they would not leave, extending communism's conflict with the West to the heart of Europe.

For Churchill and Franklin D. Roosevelt, the question during World War II was always how to end the war as quickly as possible at the lowest cost in lives. In 1944, the Anglo-American alliance was still troubled by the chronic fear of bold, offensive operations that might expose British and U.S. forces to heavy casualties.[5] A sudden spike in casualties could cause popular support for the war inside the Western democracies to collapse.[6]

In the Soviet Union, conditions were different. Stalin's totalitarian state exerted absolute control over its enslaved population, its armed forces, and its generals. Soviet casualties were never Stalin's concern. Long before Nazi concentration camps existed, Soviet security forces maintained camp systems that consumed an estimated 17 million lives.[7] The issue for Stalin, then, was fundamentally different: how to organize and direct the Soviet state's masses of humanity and warfighting equipment against the Nazi invader to ensure that before the war ended, Soviet armies would control as much of Europe and the Eurasian land mass as possible.[8]

How the triumphant Wehrmacht of 1941 was crushed in 1944 is a story of two different military transformations. The first was a German transformation that focused on marginal, tactical changes to an existing World War I army; the second was a Soviet transformation focused on integrating and concentrating combat power on the operational level for strategic effect. Of the two, the Soviet transformation produced a decisive margin of victory. By 1944, the Soviet military leadership had fundamentally transformed warfare through the integration of ground maneuver forces with the dramatic increase in the size and power of Soviet strike (artillery and airpower) forces—a revolution in warfare that created a dramatic imbalance in military power between Soviet and Nazi forces.

PRELUDE TO WAR: THE GERMAN TRANSFORMATION

Why the German army invaded Russia in June 1941 with more horses than tanks is a curious tale. After all, by the end of the nineteenth century, Germany was a world leader in fusing science and technology, a comparative advantage that should have delivered decisive results in war.[9] Understanding why this did not turn out to be the case involves understanding that a German military designed from its inception for short, decisive campaigns in central and western Europe was incapable of waging war over hundreds of thousands of square miles in a bitter, unforgiving climate.[10] In this sense, the destruction of Army Group Center in 1944 was the culminating event in a process that began before the first German soldier set foot inside the Soviet Union.

In the aftermath of World War I, the answers to the first-order questions—*where, whom,* and *how* does the German army fight?—were fairly straightforward. The mission for the army was to develop the military means to ensure that in a future regional conflict or crisis, Germany could reach a quick operational decision through rapid decisive maneuver before its presumed opponents—France, Poland, and Czechoslovakia—could be reinforced with troops and resources from Great Britain.

What the German military leadership wanted were the tactical means to avoid a destructive war of attrition, a form of warfare that nullified the sheer fighting quality of German forces and sapped the economic and moral strength of the German people. The idea of waging total war to make Germany a world power was absent from German strategic thinking. Germany's strategic aims were limited to regaining lost territory and reestablishing itself as Europe's leading military, political, and economic power. In the German military mind, restoring tactical mobility to warfare promised to reinvigorate a traditional Prussian-German way of war, not to create a fundamentally new kind of warfare.

Colonel General Hans von Seeckt, appointed army chief of staff in 1919, was a co-architect of German national strategy. When he assumed his duties, the painful experience of running out of able-bodied men in the last year of World War I was fresh in his mind. The commander of Germany's new 100,000-man army and the leader of its clandestine general staff (an organization forbidden under the terms of the 1919 Versailles Treaty) harbored no illusions regarding Germany's fatal disadvantage in resources compared with Great Britain, France, and the United States.

Within months of the armistice's signing, von Seeckt directed three hundred German officers to examine the army's wartime strategic, operational, and tactical failures and successes. Von Seeckt was not interested in the kind of self-congratulatory after action reviews that pass for lessons learned in the contemporary American military establishment. Von Seeckt insisted on fact-based, gut-wrenching analysis. He got results. The resulting report provided detailed analyses of the successful tactical innovations that von Seeckt requested.[11] The most important innovations entailed the phased integration of artillery strikes equivalent to the firepower of several hundred B-52 bombers with small infantry assault groups or storm troops.[12] The assault groups infiltrated enemy defense lines, probing for weak points and bypassing strong points. Of special interest were General Erich Ludendorff's spring 1918 offensives—masterful operations that had employed the tactics of integrated fire and maneuver, driving a wedge between the French and British armies and advancing to within thirty-seven miles of Paris.[13]

Numerous studies and discussions sought to answer several critical questions. Why had the integration of devastating artillery fire with infiltration tactics worked but Ludendorff's offensives had failed? Why did Ludendorff not reinforce battlefield success where it occurred instead of clinging to a mechanistic plan his Prussian predecessors would have abandoned after the first shot? Ultimately, the same question was raised repeatedly: how could attacking German forces sustain the momentum of the initial assault and exploit success to achieve a breakthrough in depth from which the opponent could not recover? Answering these questions led the postwar German army in the 1920s to adopt the leadership style, tactics, organization, and equipment that would eventually provide the basis for what Western observers would call blitzkrieg, or lightning war.

The idea of exploiting new training, leadership, and technology to achieve superior fighting power at the decisive point, or *Schwerpunkt*, took hold. Officer accessions were reoriented to recruit and develop a new generation of leaders who could command under more fluid conditions of warfare and changing technology. The postwar German military leadership set out to attack the problem of command and control in future war from a new angle.

Since the technologies of telephone and radio could not confer omniscience on senior commanders remote from the action, battlefield commanders were needed who could work with broad tasking orders and use their own initiative to seize opportunities. Recognizing that a system of battlefield opportunism could only work if it rested on a cultural foundation that rewarded initiative and innovation at every level, the German military leadership stressed quality over quantity in manpower and the importance of soldier education, physical fitness, and training to cultivate initiative in battle.

The value of aircraft, particularly to attacking ground forces, was widely acknowledged, but the concept of mobile warfare spearheaded by tanks and armored infantry was still treated with skepticism. The traditional focus on short, decisive campaigns obviated the logistical problem of sustaining operations over vast distances and for long periods, an oversight that would eventually plague the German army in Russia.[14] A significant number of senior generals strongly opposed programs designed to equip the German infantry with increased mobility and firepower. Instead, they clung tenaciously to the large, slow infantry divisions that marched into battle during World War I.[15]

While von Seeckt fought these battles inside the army, he also pressed the German government for a policy of rapprochement with the Soviet Union, an act that led to the Treaty of Rapallo.[16] Signed on 16 April 1922, the treaty normalized relations between Moscow and Berlin. It did not include secret provisions for military cooperation with Germany, but at the instigation of von Seeckt, such cooperation commenced almost immediately.

Rapprochement with the new Bolshevik state not only strengthened German security, it also achieved von Seeckt's goal of reconciling Germany's need for new military technology with the development of new concepts of warfare in a period of severely constrained defense spending.[17] By trading German technology and military assistance for space inside Russia to develop and test new German military equipment, including tanks and aircraft, von Seeckt's secret arrangements with the Soviet Union skillfully circumvented the provisions of the Versailles Treaty.[18]

The German army and air force that emerged from von Seeckt's reforms were not everything he wanted. The army still reflected the preferences of Germany's military elites and their underlying Prussian military culture: a small, elite professional military force around which larger German reserve forces would assemble in time of war.[19]

Military modernization was still partial, not total. Horse cavalry and horse-drawn artillery and logistical support remained an unavoidable necessity for a nation heavily in debt with an industrial base struggling under the restrictions of the Versailles Treaty and, eventually, a world-wide economic depression. Neither von Seeckt nor his officers considered wholesale modernization to be possible or, frankly, necessary. After all, neither he nor they perceived any strategic advantage to be gained from an invasion of the Soviet Union. Rightly or wrongly, most Germans saw the Russians as allies that had fought with them to rid Europe of Napoleon. In the wars of unification, Otto von Bismarck secured Russia's support to found the second German Empire. Only the German Social Democrats were historically anti-Russian for ideological reasons.[20]

As a result, the German army Hitler inherited in 1933 was a traditional Prussian-German military institution focused on decisive battles of encirclement and annihilation in central and western Europe, an army enabled by the technologies of mobility, aviation, and increased firepower, but not a revolutionary force.[21] Hitler's decision to rapidly expand the German army into a mass conscript force did not fundamentally alter this outcome. Despite Hitler's interest in tanks, until 1939 there was no definitive proof in his mind that mobile armored firepower operating in close coordination with airpower justified the expense of building more than a few armored (Panzer) divisions. The events of 1939–1940 changed Hitler's opinion.

After the fall of France in 1940, not even the German general staff continued to question the decisive use of armored, motorized, and air forces to turn a tactical advantage into a strategic one by dislocating the enemy's force and paralyzing its command structure.[22] At the same time, neither Hitler nor his Western opponents realized that Germany's stunning victories in the West concealed serious deficiencies in the Wehrmacht's structure and equipment.

In 1940, the quality of German armor was actually inferior to that of the tanks and armored vehicles in the British and French armies. Superior doctrine, tactical leadership, and soldiering—combined with the skilled, operational concentration of armor and its revolutionary integration with supporting tactical airpower—compensated for the shortcoming.[23] The Luftwaffe was also far ahead of Soviet, American, and British air forces in terms of a coherent doctrine for conducting joint operations with the army.[24] Until the Allies and the Soviets caught up in 1944, German air-ground integration created a strategic impact.

Waging war in the West with a partially transformed army worked, but it was still a near-run occurrence. Weaknesses in British and French organization and command structures worked to German advantage; had the British and French forces operated differently and Hitler's Western offensive had failed, Germany would have been plunged into a long war at a point when it had almost no significant equipment stocks or reserves.[25] In fact, without the influx of Soviet raw materials and fuel made possible by Hitler's 1939 nonaggression pact with Stalin, Hitler's 1940 offensive in the West might not have happened at all.[26]

A year after the fall of France, Germany's armed forces were still not designed to launch attacks over 1,000 miles—the distance from Berlin to Moscow—let alone eventually defend a front of 1,200 miles, roughly the distance from Boston to Miami. The Luftwaffe had only 838 bombers in Russia, half the number that was available for the 1940 campaigns, because German air assets were still dealing with the threat from Britain.[27]

In 1941, the severe shortage of aircraft of all types because of ongoing operations against Britain left advancing German armor without the reconnaissance and strike aircraft it needed, while the shortage also severely restricted the Luftwaffe's ability to interdict Soviet rail lines transporting manufacturing equipment to the Urals.[28] But these were not the only problems that plagued the German war effort.

From the moment he took power, Hitler was ideologically committed to the creation of a new national leadership cadre headed by men who, like him, had working-class origins.[29] Hitler loathed the old elites who dominated German society. He cleansed the German officer corps of anyone who questioned or challenged his regime and rewarded those who were loyal Nazis or obedient technocrats, but he was still compelled to rely on Germany's elite classes to run the armed forces and society more than he liked. Hitler quietly discarded the Prussian principle requiring German general staff officers to provide written expressions of opposition to orders that were judged wrong and replaced it with National Socialism's demand for unconditional obedience to all orders.[30] However, it was really Hitler's promotions and gifts of cash to Germany's military elites that guaranteed their loyalty to the Nazi state. Hitler's generosity turned Germany's new crop of field marshals and colonel generals into rich men.[31]

Hitler also employed a type of affirmative action program so he could install his working-class comrades and party loyalists in power throughout German society.[32] The effect was a managed or command economy shaped by military priorities but run by a coalition of government bureaucrats, party hacks, and greedy industrialists.[33] During the first two years of war, this defective combination produced widespread duplication of effort, waste, and poor distribution.[34]

Hitler rose to power on the promise of a better life for the average German, and he aimed to keep that promise.[35] In the spring of 1942, 90 percent of Germany's defense industries were still working on a single shift basis. Moreover, Hitler's desire to spare the German people the hardship of war meant that far too much of German industry and labor were engaged in producing consumer goods.[36] The multiplicity of competing government bureaucracies and the military's demand for highly engineered, technically complex weapons systems compounded these deficiencies in defense needs by obstructing cheaper, faster methods of mass production.[37] Lieutenant General Hermann Balck, an officer who commanded in Russia, Italy, and France, described the disastrous impact of this problem on his division:

> Our worst problems in weapons development and production came from the interference of all those lackeys around Hitler and from the influence of the industry. The industry, of course, was only interested in what their position at the end of the war would be. As a result, it proved impossible to achieve standardization or a rational choice of vehicles, both armored and unarmored. The situation when I took over command of my division [the 11th Panzer Division] in Russia was so bad with respect to diversity of vehicles that I felt I had to write a very strong letter to Hitler from the front. This letter dealt with the necessity to take over the industry, to get real control over it and to standardize vehicles and engines in some reasonable way. As it turned out, Hitler was never able to gain control over the industry.[38]

In the spring of 1942, German minister of armaments Albert Speer and Luftwaffe general Edward Milch cooperated to persuade Hitler of the need to revolutionize German war production by using existing resources more efficiently. Hitler approved their recommendations, and the impact was immediate and significant. Within months, the German aircraft industry was producing 40 percent more aircraft than it had in 1941 with only 5 percent more labor and substantially less aluminum.[39]

By 1943, Germany's annual military aircraft production rose from 14,700 to 25,200, and in 1944, it rose again to 37,000—more aircraft than were being produced in the Soviet Union. Tank production also rose from 2,200 armored vehicles of all types in 1941 to 11,000 medium tanks and assault guns, 1,600 tank destroyers, and 5,200 heavy tanks—in all, 17,800 medium tanks and assault guns in 1944, an impressive figure, but one that fell short of the Soviet Union's output (see figure 1).[40]

In 1941, this level of output would have conferred a decisive advantage on the German Wehrmacht in Russia, even to the point of securing German victory in the east before January 1942, but the equipment came too late for the worn-down German forces of 1944.[41] Germany's allies—Italy, Finland,

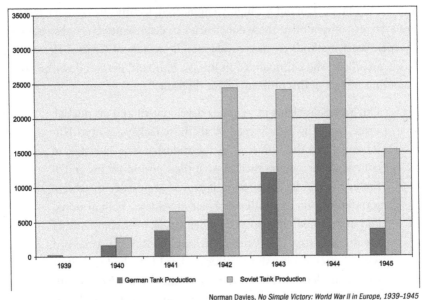

Norman Davies, *No Simple Victory: World War II in Europe, 1939-1945*

FIGURE 1. German and Soviet Annual Tank Production, 1939–45

Hungary, and Romania—also offered the potential to deploy significant forces and production capability to support the German war effort, but their collective potential was ignored or mismanaged by the Nazi state throughout the war.[42]

Hitler and his generals ignored the great paradox that "an advancing army could march from victory to victory, smashing every enemy concentration in its way, but it had to recognize that every step forward dulled its fighting edge, robbing it of precisely those qualities that made it formidable in the first place."[43] In the late summer of 1942, Hitler's forces were already so overextended that some German soldiers actually died of starvation in the front lines.[44]

By 1944, waging war in the vastness of the Soviet Union had consumed men and matériel faster than the Nazi state could replace them. Confronted with superior forces on every side, Germany could do little more than replace the matériel that was lost in combat. In the air, the demand for fighter aircraft to defend German cities from the Anglo-American bombing campaign denuded Luftwaffe strength. In April, the Luftwaffe fighting in Russia had only 500 combat aircraft to counter 13,000 Soviet planes. By the summer of 1944, the Wehrmacht's strength in the east fell to 2,242,649 troops—the lowest total since June 1941. In the front lines opposing the Wehrmacht were 6,077,000 Soviet troops.[45]

THE SOVIET TRANSFORMATION AFTER WORLD WAR I

Once the Communist Party consolidated its power over tsarist Russia, Soviet military leaders such as Sergei Kamenev, Georgii Isserson, Aleksandr Svechin, Abram Vol'pe, Mikhail Frunze, and Mikhail Tukhachevskiy debated the meaning of Russia's military failures in World War I and the Red Army's defeat in its first invasion of the West in the Polish-Soviet war in 1921. Soviet studies of World War I revealed a preference in Russian minds for the Brusilov offensive of June through December 1916 and the Anglo-French offensive at Amiens in August 1918. Both involved the systematic preparation of the offensive theater, which included the assembly of operational reserves and the establishment of logistical support centers in depth. In the years leading up to World War II, marshalling military power to overwhelm the opponent at key points became the organizing imperative for planning and executing large-scale Soviet offensive operations. For the participants in the debates that lasted for nearly a decade, these experiences administered several critical lessons. The future keys to victory seemed to depend on operational pauses and the regrouping of forces, the concentration of strategic reserves, technical competence, and the logistical preparation of whole regions for the transport and provisioning of attacking forces.[46]

When the time came to formally define warfare in Marxist-Leninist terms, the answer was straightforward: "total war." The notion of a partial military transformation on the model of the Germans or the plans of J. F. C. Fuller was considered but rejected as an inherently bourgeois concept unsuited to the needs of Soviet communism's world revolutionary movement.[47] Instead, postwar Soviet thinking created the intellectual and industrial foundations for a massive military machine designed for offensive warfare and manned by troops trained, equipped, and ideologically hardened for sweeping maneuver over vast distances.

The resulting theory of future war employed mechanized formations composed of tanks, motorized infantry, and self-propelled guns within the framework of "deep operations," the idea of striking deep into the enemy's rear areas. Deep battle emerged as an overarching concept designed to exploit the mobility of mechanized and armored forces to outflank and encircle enemy forces. Soviet operational art embraced "all arms" combat, which meant the use of aviation formations with mechanized and airborne forces that could be delivered in the enemy's rear areas. This approach contributed to the overall Soviet strategic goal of dissolving the opposing forces' capacity for defense.[48]

In 1930, the Soviet military theory of combined arms formations that could engage in multi-echeloned offensives was formally approved by Stalin.[49] He deliberately harnessed the first five-year plan, which had begun in 1928, to the militarization of the Soviet Union's national economy.[50] From 1929 onward, Stalin ensured that "80 to 90 percent of [Soviet] national resources—raw material, technical, financial, and intellectual—[were] used to create the [Soviet] military-industrial complex," converting Soviet society into a war mobilization state.[51]

By the summer of 1935, by which time millions of people in the Ukraine had already been deported or murdered through systematic starvation or shooting, industrial expansion had increased the Soviet army to more than 940,000 troops.[52] Factories turned out more than 5,000 tanks, 100,000 trucks, and 150,000 tractors, motorizing 3 rifle divisions, the heavy artillery of the army's main reserve, and much of the Soviet army's anti-aircraft artillery.[53] Then, Stalin suddenly unleashed a campaign of terror that eventually consumed 5 million more lives inside the Soviet Union.

From exile in Mexico, Leon Trotsky, Stalin's enemy in the world communist movement, called for a popular revolt to remove Stalin from power. Because Trotsky was the architect of the Red Army, Stalin reasoned that the ranks of the armed forces had to be purged of any lingering Trotskyite elements. Of course, with the exception of Mikhail Tukhachevskiy, one of Trotsky's colleagues, and a few other senior officers, Stalin did not know most of the 35,000 Soviet military officers (including numerous generals, admirals, and colonels) whom he had executed.[54] Stalin's foremost concern was to eliminate any potential alternative to his own absolute power.

Not everyone with a promising intellect perished, but Stalin's purge killed most of the Soviet military's conceptual thinkers, placing men who had recently been lieutenants in command of regiments and colonels in command of armies.[55] New officers rose to fill the vacant ranks—men such as Georgii Zhukov, who read very few books, distrusted foreigners, believed in iron discipline, and applauded Stalin's violence against the "class enemy."[56]

By early 1941, this new generation of Soviet officers was leading troops inside a force that had increased in size to 4,207,000 men.[57] This prewar force was already larger than the German Wehrmacht that would invade the Soviet Union six months later. In addition, the Soviet armed forces possessed far more tanks and aircraft than the attacking German forces: 14,200 Soviet tanks (1,861 of which were heavily armored and up-gunned T-34s and KVs) versus 3,350 German tanks, and 9,200 Soviet aircraft to Germany's 2,000.[58]

These points notwithstanding, Stalin, like Hitler in 1939, harbored serious doubts about tanks. These doubts led him to reject the brilliant concepts and innovative ideas of the men he executed. The upshot was that in June 1941, Soviet tanks were still widely dispersed, not concentrated for decisive operations. Even more troubling, only about 80 percent of the tanks in the Soviet army's 9 mechanized corps formations were operational at any given time.[59] Despite the large numbers of aircraft, only 15 percent of Soviet pilots were trained to fly at night.[60] As a result, when Operation Barbarossa began, not one of the Soviet army's 170 divisions and 2 brigades in the Western military districts bordering Germany, Slovakia, Hungary, and Romania was up to full strength.

The disaster that ensued in the wake of Hitler's invasion in June 1941 came close to destroying Stalin and the Communist Party of the Soviet Union. Ultimately, it was not the Soviet armed forces but rather the vast distances, severe winter weather (with temperatures sometimes falling below -30° Fahrenheit), and woeful inadequacy of German equipment stocks and repair parts that saved Stalin and the Soviet Union from destruction.[61] Thanks to the Wehrmacht's inability to exploit its victories before the close of 1941, Stalin's war mobilization state survived to support a crash modernization program that organized and equipped new formations and redeployed Soviet forces from the Far East to the west. The result was impressive. In December 1941, the Soviet army mobilized 291 divisions and 94 brigades, a force of 4 million men—again, a force larger than the invading Wehrmacht.[62]

Through 1941 and 1942, a series of crushing defeats and the loss of valuable territory and millions of lives compelled Stalin and his generals to finally reinvigorate the concepts and ideas developed in the 1920s and 1930s. Survival was not easy, and lessons were not learned quickly.

As late as November 1942, a massive Soviet offensive involving nearly 700,000 troops and 2,000 tanks against Germany's numerically inferior Army Group Center in the Rzhev salient, about 130 miles west of Moscow, failed miserably, costing Soviet forces at least 350,000 casualties.[63] It would take time before new formations of self-propelled anti-tank artillery, engineers, mortars, and anti-aircraft guns, along with heavily armored T-34 and T-70 tanks, were added to tank and mechanized brigades. Stalin's resistance to fundamental reform postponed the formation of tank armies composed exclusively of tanks until late 1942, a concept first contemplated in the early 1930s by many of the men Stalin's purges swept away. But in early 1943, the appearance of 5 "tank armies," new armored shock forces, had an immediate and dramatic impact on the Wehrmacht.[64]

By the standards of the superbly trained German army, Soviet tactics were often crude, even clumsy. Soviet troops were poorly educated and culturally disinclined to independent action. Russia had long been a place of petrified servitude where tens of millions of eastern Slavic peasants lived and worked on vast estates belonging to Russia's ruling classes.[65] Forced labor was common, and the individual Russian undertook no action of consequence without the sanction and direction of the Russian state.[66]

This cultural condition compelled the Soviet military leadership to make virtue of necessity. Unconditional obedience to orders at the lowest level often cost lives, but it also enabled strategic deception, as well as the rapid assembly of large air and ground forces on the operational and strategic levels. Steady improvements to the transportation and manufacturing infrastructure, much of which was beyond the reach of Germany's limited airpower, after November 1941 facilitated the deployment of armies and groups of armies across the front with real operational and strategic effectiveness. Ruthless discipline combined with the Soviet high command's (*Stavka*'s) ability to mobilize and direct resources wherever it chose created unrivaled lethality. Simplicity and rigidity on the tactical level translated into operational agility with strategic effect.

Any deviation from the plan by a single corps, division, regiment, or even rifle battalion could disrupt the entire operation. Therefore, front and army commanders discouraged "excessive" initiative by their subordinates lest they disrupt the overall offensive. As a result, throughout the war, the rifle forces and their supporting arms assigned to its operating fronts and armies, which constituted 80 percent of the Red Army, resembled a massive steamroller flattening a path through the Wehrmacht's defenses regardless of human cost. Casualties were highest when the steamroller faltered, but they were also high when it accomplished its deadly mission.[67]

Put differently, the Soviet command and control structure that mounted operations to break through Wehrmacht defenses and strike deep into German rear areas was a highly centralized, top-down, attrition-based, industrial meat grinder that squandered human life and resources on a scale that is beyond Western comprehension.[68] To ensure the meat grinder's effectiveness, when Soviet commanders failed or disobeyed, Stalin simply executed them, something Stalin's top commanders never forgot.[69]

Yet as horrifying as the steamroller was, without the machinery of terror that could wage total war—as much against Russia's own soldiers and peoples as against the Wehrmacht—Stalin and the Communist Party would not have survived the war.[70] On its own, Russian nationalism and distaste for Hitler's theories of racial superiority that presented Slavs as inferior *Untermenschen* (sub-human) were not enough to recruit the huge numbers of soldiers required for the meat grinder, Stalin's war machine.

Stalin's decades of mass murder, deportation, and collectivization inside the Soviet Union had the effect of creating substantial resistance to his regime.[71] One angry Russian woman summed up Stalin's strategic dilemma very well: "Shoot me if you like, but I'm not digging any trenches. The only people who need trenches are the communists and Jews. . . . Your power is coming to an end and we're not going to work for you."[72]

As self-defeating as Hitler's policies and the criminal acts they inspired were, the policies were unevenly applied and sometimes ignored.[73] In September 1942, the German Sixth Army fighting in Stalingrad had over 50,000 Russian and Ukrainian auxiliaries attached to its front line divisions, representing over a quarter of the divisions' fighting strength.[74] Had Hitler turned the National Socialist crusade against Bolshevism into a war of liberation, the outcome of the war in the east would likely have been different.[75]

After the United States' entry into the war, President Franklin Roosevelt's lend-lease program provided the Soviet Union with much of the logistical support and transport it needed to move forward (see table 1). Then, on 6 June 1944, American and British forces massed 6,000 ships and 11,000 aircraft to carry nearly a million men and thousands of tanks and self-propelled guns to Normandy. Within weeks, the Allied numbers inside the Normandy beachhead grew to 850,000 troops and 154,000 vehicles and drew an increasing number of German combat formations away from the eastern front.[76]

With the Wehrmacht exhausted by its own exertions, the stage was set in 1944 for a dramatic turning point in the east. "No one," wrote Marshal Georgii Zhukov in the summer of 1944, "had any doubt that Germany had definitely lost the war. This was settled on the Soviet-German front in 1943 and the beginning of 1944. The question now was how soon and with what political and military results the war would end."[77]

TABLE 1. Lend-Lease Tonnage to the Soviet Union, 1941–45

	June – Sept 1941	Oct 1941– June 1942	July 1942– June 1943	July 1943– June 1944	July 1944– May 12, 1945	May 13– Sept 2, 1945	Sept 3– Sept 20, 1945
Railroad Equipment	0	0	0	70,466	355,739	41,380	947
Trucks and Wheeled Transport	1,575	214,164	448,488	742,337	645,270	238,117	879
Metals	4,655	424,525	749,890	1,012,401	1,122,596	249,202	11,815
Chemical & Explosives	4,726	56,007	181,366	448,149	399,346	57,788	382
Petroleum	130,354	167,995	213,448	446,706	748,740	406,166	0
Machinery	15,855	29,692	168,468	487,501	475,645	68,538	2,149
Food	3,918	305,037	997,783	1,734,801	1,157,373	258,201	7,864
Other Supplies	2,623	76,224	237,776	472,968	310,501	117,207	4,008

Source: Albert L. Weeks, *Russia's Life-Saver: Lend-Lease Aid to the U.S.S.R. in World War II*

PREPARATIONS TO DESTROY ARMY GROUP CENTER

The man tasked with designing the Soviet offensive to smash Army Group Center was General Aleksei Antonov, the forty-seven-year-old son and grandson of Imperial Russian Army officers.[78] Shortly after assuming his new post as first deputy chief of the general staff in May 1943, Antonov, with the support of marshals Aleksandr Vasilevskiy and Zhukov, tried to persuade Stalin to stand on the strategic defensive in the summer of 1943, something Stalin vigorously resisted. Antonov argued that the Wehrmacht, if allowed, would inevitably attack the extensive Soviet defenses inside the Kursk salient and waste its best armored forces in doing so.[79]

At first Stalin refused, demanding another Soviet offensive—the very action the Wehrmacht was still capable of defeating, as it demonstrated after the Stalingrad disaster in the Kharkov counteroffensive.[80] To his generals' surprise, however, Stalin finally relented and approved Antonov's plan. The resulting success at Kursk confirmed the wisdom of Antonov's plan and earned him Stalin's trust.[81] Unlike Hitler, who increasingly disregarded sound military advice, Stalin heeded the counsel of men who in his eyes had proven themselves in the crucible of war.[82]

In its final form, Antonov's design for the offensive resembled the operational constructs for deep battle and successive operations envisioned during the interwar years (see map 8). The Soviet operation was planned in three

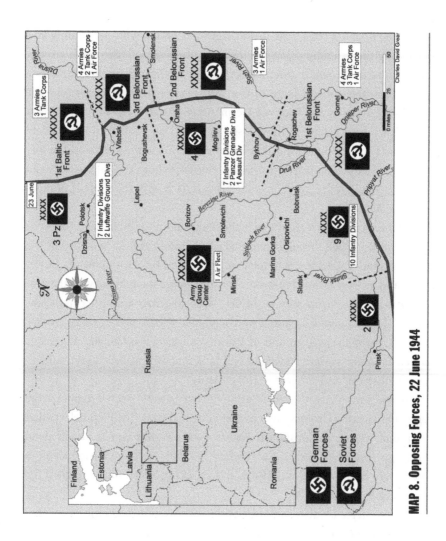

MAP 8. Opposing Forces, 22 June 1944

phases, and the attacking Soviet forces were organized in two echelons.[83] The operational objective in the first and second phases was to entrap Army Group Center and destroy what remained of it with air and ground attacks by four Soviet fronts moving west along three axes. The concept entailed the convergence of the four fronts along nearly parallel axes north, south, and west of Minsk. The resulting encirclement of German forces was to be accomplished by the simultaneous defeat of Army Group Center's flank forces, around Vitebsk and Bobruisk, as well as at Mogilev. The outcome, Antonov believed, would open the road to Minsk so that Soviet forces to its west could cut the German escape route.[84]

In the opening phase, the first echelon was tasked with penetrating and destroying the defending German forces on the flanks in the north around Vitebsk and in the south around Bobruisk. Breakthrough artillery divisions employing thousands of large caliber guns were massed together with air armies to pin down and wipe out German fighting strength in Army Group Center's forward defenses. These tasks were critical; Soviet military leaders knew from experience that if they did not annihilate the troops in the forward defensive positions strewn among Belorussia's bogs and thick woods, the Germans would retire, regroup, and counterattack with the support of rapid reinforcements.[85]

In the second phase, the Belorussian bulge in the German front was to be cut off and encircled through concentric exploitation attacks launched by the tank and mechanized forces of the first and second Belorussian fronts. Soviet commanders were ordered to strike deep and ignore their flanks with the goal of uniting Soviet forces west of Minsk, deep in Army Group Center's rear areas. All Soviet tank formations were equipped with brush and logs to carry the tanks over the soft ground of Belorussia's marshes. Combat engineers, as well as infantry, were attached to all tank and self-propelled gun units to remove obstacles and accelerate river crossings.[86]

In the third phase, the attacking Soviet fronts were ordered to pursue the remnants of Army Group Center as they retreated west. The First Belorussian Front under General Konstantin Rokossovskiy would begin its attack along the Pripyat marshes toward Kovel when the bulk of Army Group Center's forces were encircled around Minsk and attacking Soviet forces reached the vicinity of Baranovici.

The strategic objective was obviously Warsaw, not the Baltic coast. Had Soviet forces pressed northwest toward the Baltic, the resulting effect would have been much greater—similar to the impact of the German thrust in 1940 from Sedan to the French coast. However, in the summer of 1944 recapturing Warsaw involved political interests that trumped military practicality.

Marshal Zhukov and Marshal Vasilevskiy were selected by Stalin to coordinate the operations of the fronts during the offensive, a technique used repeatedly during the war. Zhukov coordinated the First Belorussian Front, the Second Belorussian Front, and later, the First Ukrainian Front. Vasilevskiy coordinated the offensives of the First Baltic Front and Third Belorussian Front. In practice, "coordination" meant that the two marshals shared aircraft of the four air armies assigned to each of their fronts.

Originally scheduled to begin on 18 June 1944, Operation Bagration was delayed until 22 June, 3 years to the day after the Wehrmacht had invaded Russia. The delay was deemed necessary to ensure sufficient Soviet forces were assembled to retake Belorussia: 2.5 million men (including 1,254,300 Soviet troops in the attacking echelons), 45,000 artillery systems (including 2,306 Katyusha rocket artillery), 6,300 tanks and assault guns, and 8,000 fighters and fighter bombers.[87] This massive Soviet force would be hurled against the German armies that were stretched thin along a 660-mile front between Vitebsk and Bobruisk.[88] The operation's name, Bagration, was chosen to honor the tsarist general who had participated in the campaign of 1812–13 to drive Napoleon out of Russia.

As the buildup for the offensive began, Antonov developed a deception plan (*maskirovka*) intended to convince the OKW that the Soviet fronts would make their main attack in the Ukraine and the Baltic littoral, not in Belorussia. *Maskirovka* entailed the collective employment of deception measures in all aspects of Soviet-Russian military operations, including actions to confuse and mislead opponents and camouflage intentions.[89] Radios were sealed to prevent their use as part of a total blackout, and false troop concentrations were organized in both sectors. All six Soviet tank armies dedicated to Operation Bagration were held in the Ukraine until they regrouped at the last moment and occupied new assembly areas farther north, ensuring two-thirds of the Wehrmacht's armored formations remained in the Ukraine when the hammer blow fell on Army Group Center.[90]

Antonov's deception appeared to work, but not because the German commanders in the front lines were fooled. Intelligence officers serving under Colonel General Georg-Hans Reinhart, commander of the Third Panzer Army, reported unmistakable signs of a Soviet buildup and impending attack in early June.[91] Colonel General Hans Jordan, commander of Ninth Army, was so alarmed by the buildup along his front that he personally informed Field Marshal Ernst Busch, the commander of Army Group Center. Busch did not listen because Hitler would not listen—a pattern that would work to Soviet strategic advantage throughout Operation Bagration and for the rest of the war.[92]

OPERATION BAGRATION BEGINS

On 19 June, German intelligence intercepted Soviet radio transmissions instructing 143,000 Soviet partisans to attack Army Group Center's rear areas. German and local (Lithuanian, Belorussian, and Ukrainian) auxiliary security forces deployed early and were able to shut down or neutralize most of the insurgent attacks, but they signaled an impending Soviet offensive no one in Army Group Center could ignore.[93]

Unfortunately for the soldiers under his command, Field Marshal Busch, Hitler's choice to command Army Group Center in 1944, subscribed to Hitler's view that the Soviet summer offensive would be launched against Field Marshal Walter Model's Army Group North in the Ukraine from the area south of Kovel.[94] Busch incorrectly perceived Belorussia as a wooded, swampy morass where rapid movement was difficult for tanks. Events would prove that Busch was totally wrong.

Busch's war record as a combat commander did not recommend him for a critical field command such as Army Group Center. Colonel General Georg von Kuechler, the commander of Army Group North, actually requested Hitler's authorization to relieve Busch of his command for gross incompetence in 1942. Hitler refused. Busch owed his field marshal's baton to his National Socialist attitudes. He was a "yes man" in the worst sense of the term, a "Marionette in [a] Marshal's uniform."[95] Busch transformed Army Group Center's headquarters into a mindless instrument for the transmission of Hitler's increasingly ludicrous orders.[96]

Busch's readiness to embrace Hitler's directives without question placed Army Group Center in a perilous position. Busch subscribed to Hitler's notion that key towns and cities could be converted to fortified places, a strongpoint defense concept that failed repeatedly during the previous winter.[97] In Army Group Center, the designated fortified places were Vitebsk, Orsha, Mogilev, and Bobruisk—sites that Busch pledged to Hitler would be defended to the last man.

Between the Third Panzer Army, Fourth Army, and Ninth Army, Army Group Center fielded the equivalent of 29 understrength divisions (with 5 more understrength divisions in reserve), or 336,573 troops together with 118 tanks and 337 assault guns in 4 understrength Panzer and Panzergrenadier divisions. The low proportion of tanks to assault guns was based on Hitler's insistence that Army Group Center would fight static defensive battles in Belorussia's forested and swampy terrain.[98]

German defensive positions were nevertheless well prepared with secondary defense lines. Millions of mines were placed in dense minefields stretching across Army Group Center's front and in depth. Behind the front were an additional 300,000 men, but these were primarily administrative, supply, training, transport, and police units, not combat troops.[99]

However, on the day the Soviet offensive began, the 3 German armies mustered only 166,673 men.[100] Since Hitler believed no imminent Soviet offensive was possible against Army Group Center, large numbers of German soldiers were allowed to go on leave. Opposing those German soldiers in the defensive line were 1,254,300 Soviet soldiers armed with 2,715 tanks and 1,355 assault guns.[101]

Alarmed by the Soviet buildup to their front, all of Busch's army commanders expressed the view in early May that the fortified places concept was self-defeating and that Army Group Center should withdraw farther west, shorten the front, and occupy defensive positions behind the Beresina River. Given the overwhelming Soviet superiority immediately in front of Army Group Center's three armies—an advantage of 23:1 in tanks, 4:1 in assault guns, 9:1 in infantry, 10:1 in artillery, and 58:1 in fighter aircraft—the withdrawal to a shorter, more defensible line in late May or early June made infinite sense.[102]

Still, Hitler refused to consider any withdrawal, resulting in the following deployments on the eve of the Soviet offensive. On the northern shoulder of Army Group Center, General Reinhart commanded the Third Panzer Army—an army without Panzer divisions or tanks, but instead having only 60 to 80 assault guns and tank destroyers, plus 60,000 horses for transport and resupply.[103] In addition to being exposed on three sides at the northern tip of the Belorussian bulge, Reinhart's force was weak in firepower and mobility, with just 7 understrength infantry and 2 Luftwaffe field divisions (air force ground combat formations) to defend 130 miles of Army Group Center's front.[104]

In its center, Fourth Army consisted of roughly 362 medium artillery systems, 205 heavy guns, 246 assault guns, 40 tanks, and 116 self-propelled 88-millimeter guns deployed primarily in an anti-tank defense role. Fourth Army's field strength was equivalent to a 1938 German army corps (50,000 men).

With almost 80,000 men, including 43,555 infantrymen, Ninth Army on the southern shoulder was stronger. Ninth Army also had 76 assault guns and 551 artillery systems of all calibers.[105] Seven thousand additional troops were placed in corps and army reserve. On the southernmost flank of the Belorussian bulge facing the Soviets' Northern Ukrainian Front, Second Army had 20,000 men, or 6 division equivalents including 2 Hungarian cavalry divisions (see map 9).

Army Group Center maintained relatively small reserves. The heaviest concentration of armor, one battalion of 29 Tiger I tanks, was committed

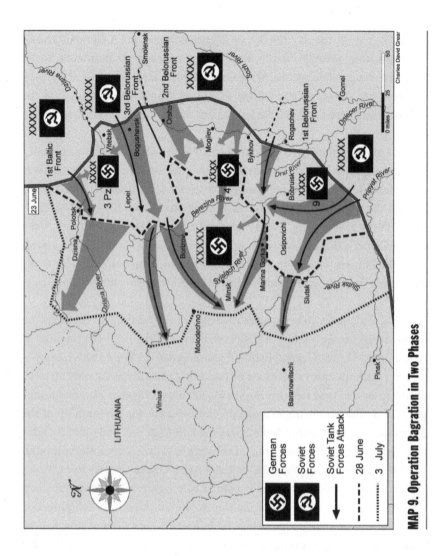

MAP 9. Operation Bagration in Two Phases

to the defense of Orsha in Fourth Army's sector. Otherwise, Army Group Center's tank strength consisted of older Mark IV Panzers fitted with long-barreled 75-millimeter guns weighing in at 20 to 22 tons. They were good tanks but were much lighter than the 36-ton Soviet T-34s. To maximize their effectiveness, the Mark IVs had to maneuver to strike the T-34s from the flank or rear. However, given the reduced availability of fuel, the ability of German tanks to maneuver was limited.

Colonel General Ritter Robert von Greim's Sixth Air Fleet headquarters was in Minsk. The airpower at his disposal to support Army Group Center consisted of 839 aircraft, of which only 40 were Me-109G/K fighters. Ground attack units included 106 Ju-87 Stuka tank busters and Fw-190 fighter bombers.[106] Because the Sixth Air Fleet lacked the fuel reserves to keep most of its aircraft flying for more than a few hours, the impact of German airpower on the battle would be minimal.

On 22 June, Soviet forces conducted probing attacks all along the front. The First Baltic Front and Third Belorussian Front launched the heaviest attacks at General Reinhardt's Third Panzer Army on either side of Vitebsk. Field Marshal Busch flew back from Hitler's residence in Berchtesgaden on the Austro-Bavarian border and began organizing reinforcements. During the night of 22–23 June, the Soviet air force's strategic bomber force followed up the probing attacks of 22 June with one thousand sorties using Il-4 and Tu-2 bombers against major German troop concentrations and artillery positions.[107]

At 5 a.m. on 23 June, 40,000 Soviet artillery systems announced the main attack. Most of the artillery strikes started with intense shelling designed to obliterate German formations in the forward defensive lines before they could retire to secondary positions. In some sectors, the initial artillery attacks were followed by rolling barrages; in other sectors where the German defenses were particularly dense, double rolling barrages were used to simultaneously attack German defenses in depth.[108] Three rocket artillery divisions added their firepower to the assault, saturating German infantry, armor, and artillery in their defensive positions. German accounts of these artillery strikes describe them as being of an intensity and destructiveness never before seen on the eastern front.[109]

As the artillery fire slackened, 14 Soviet armies attacked along a 300-mile front concentrating 27 divisions in the first echelon at 6 critical points to break through German defenses. In contrast to previous offensives, the Soviets deliberately concentrated their firepower (204 guns per kilometer) with daring and imagination. At each point of attack, on average at least 750 Soviet infantrymen attacked 80 German infantrymen—assuming any of the defending German infantry survived the initial Soviet artillery and air strikes.

Almost immediately, Third Panzer Army needed help. Its infantry trench strength was at most 11,000, far too weak to halt the 100,000 Soviet infantry and tank forces penetrating north and south of Vitebsk. Quickly discerning the outlines of the Soviet plan of attack, Reinhart urged immediate withdrawal to avoid encirclement. Busch adamantly refused, saying, "If we start withdrawing now we will all end up in the drink!"[110]

Busch eventually changed his mind. Early in the afternoon of 23 June, Busch informed OKW that Third Panzer Army's LIII Corps had to be allowed to retreat or be overrun. General Adolf Heusinger, OKW's chief of operations, agreed and urged Hitler to allow Third Panzer Army to retreat to the Dnieper River. Because this would mean abandoning Vitebsk, Hitler's designated "defended place," he denied the request.

On 24 June, Reinhardt organized a counterattack with 3 understrength divisions, roughly 15,000 men who had been sent to Third Panzer Army as reinforcements. Their mission was to break through to Vitebsk, which was now completely surrounded. They came within 6 kilometers of the city center, but their counterattack was too feeble. Even Field Marshal Busch realized it was time to abandon Vitebsk.

Colonel General Kurt Zeitzler, chief of the German army general staff, felt compelled to intervene on behalf of Busch. Zeitzler flew to Berchtesgaden to meet personally with Hitler on 24 June. After speaking with Reinhart on the phone at 3:40 p.m., Zeitzler presented the situation to Hitler, repeating Reinhart's words that "the last possible minute had arrived" and asking for permission to withdraw the remaining German forces from Vitebsk before the ring closed.[111] Hitler authorized the withdrawal of Reinhart's already encircled LIII Corps but insisted that Vitebsk must be held by the 206th Infantry Division, the understrength division reinforced with the shattered remains of flank elements.

Inside Vitebsk itself, Soviet and German troops were already fighting hand to hand for the possession of buildings serving as German strongpoints, but what the Soviets wanted most was the bridge over the western Dvina River. Marshal Vasilevskiy was well aware of the confusion in OKW, but he feared that if German forces retreated over the Dvina to establish a new defense line, the First Baltic Front's offensive on the northern flank could come to a dangerous halt. Urgent orders were issued for a river crossing.

At noon on 24 June, Marshal Vasilevskiy was relieved to learn that Soviet forces had finally crossed the Dvina during the night on improvised rafts, plank, and boats. By evening pontoons arrived, and Soviet tanks and artillery began moving behind the German defenses. As darkness covered the battlefield, Soviet tanks and infantry were closing in on Third Panzer Army headquarters.

Soviet forces had opened a breach in Third Panzer Army's sector that was roughly eighteen miles wide, allowing Soviet tanks and mechanized forces to stream by on the left and right of Vitebsk through a twenty-mile break in

Third Panzer Army's defense line. While Hitler dithered on 24 June, Third Panzer Army's divisions, essentially dismounted infantry forces with assault guns, were pulverized by Soviet tank forces supported by hundreds of heavy guns in the breakthrough divisions. Hitler's refusal to allow his commanders to exercise their own best judgment and maneuver accordingly was turning a potentially life-saving retreat into a rout.

On 25 June, Busch transmitted another of Hitler's "fight to the last man" orders to the 206th Infantry Division in Vitebsk. Oblivious to the conditions on the battlefield, Hitler actually ordered Reinhart to parachute a general staff officer into Vitebsk to personally convey to General of Infantry Friedrich Gollwitzer, the LIII Corps commander, that German forces still in Vitebsk were to fight and hold out to the last man.[112] Fortunately, the order was ignored. Eventually, 8,000 of Vitebsk's defenders broke out and rejoined Third Panzer Army in occupying defensive positions farther west, but 27,000 men perished needlessly defending Vitebsk when it was finally overrun on 27 June.[113] General Reinhardt subsequently recorded, "Constantly acting against my better judgment is more than I can do."[114] His force would live on to fight in the Baltic littoral until war's end.

On 23 June, Soviet attacks against Fourth Army initially were less successful than those against Third Panzer Army. The preliminary Soviet artillery attack by the 5th Breakthrough Artillery Corps fell on open ground, missing the German anti-tank gun positions and leaving German defenses intact. Given that the main Moscow-Minsk highway from Smolensk to Orsha was crucial to the Soviets' deep operation, this was a troubling development.

The German defenders in Fourth Army did what they had previously done. They observed the Soviet preparations and methodically plotted the Soviet artillery deployment.[115] Even when additional Soviet tanks and aircraft were hurled against the German defenders, Fourth Army picked up elements from Third Panzer Army that had been cut off and incorporated them into the fight. Miraculously, Fourth Army held on until the main roads from Orsha to Borisov were cut. Then, on 26 June, Soviet forces crossed the Dnieper north of Mogilev, putting Fourth Army at risk of encirclement.

General Kurt von Tippelskirch, temporarily commanding Fourth Army after Busch relieved General Hans Jordan, ignored another of Hitler's "stand fast" orders and saved what was left of his army pulling it away from the Dnieper. Busch was furious, screaming at von Tippelskirch over the phone, "Your behavior is in contravention with the Führer's orders."[116] Tippelskirch was unimpressed and acted in accordance with his best judgment.

Ninth Army was attacked on 24 June. Woefully understrength individual German infantry battalions defended their positions against the simultaneous attacks of two Soviet divisions.[117] General Rokossovskiy achieved almost complete surprise with a massive concentration of tanks where the Germans least expected it: in the theoretically impassable swamp lands on the southern edge of the Pripyat marshes. Within twenty-four hours, Ninth Army's forward defenses were smashed and its main forces were in danger of being encircled by a pincer movement on Bobruisk from the east and the south.

This time, Hitler responded differently. He directed the transfer of two divisions from Army Group North to support Army Group Center, and Busch authorized the commitment of Ninth Army's reserve, the 20th Panzer Division, an understrength unit with only one regiment of seventy-one Panzer IVs.[118] After a series of confusing orders from Busch and Hitler, the 20th Panzer met advancing Soviet forces near Slobodka, south of Bobruisk. The 20th Panzer destroyed sixty Soviet tanks but lost half its strength in the battle, eventually joining German forces inside Bobruisk.

Meanwhile, Orsha, another of Hitler's fortified places, fell on 27 June, trapping 40,000 German troops 14 miles east of Bobruisk. This pocket was in close proximity to the massive concentration of Soviet breakthrough artillery formations, making German breakout attempts impossible. At least 10,000 German troops were killed and 6,000 were taken prisoner; the surviving troops fled into Bobruisk, where they were once again encircled.

On 27 June Hitler granted the German troops inside Bobruisk permission for a breakout but insisted, as he had in Vitebsk and Mogilev, that a division remain in Bobruisk to defend the "fortified place" to the last man. The Ninth Army chief of staff recorded that Hitler's orders were tantamount to operational insanity.[119]

The breakout from Bobruisk began on 28 June at 11 p.m. With the 20 to 25 surviving tanks from 20th Panzer Division in the lead, about 15,000 German troops managed to break out and escape destruction when Bobruisk fell into Soviet hands on 29 June.[120] In less than 7 days of fighting, the First Belorussian Front under Rokossovskiy had captured or destroyed 366 armored vehicles and 2,664 artillery systems and killed 50,000 German troops and captured a further 20,000.[121] German forces were now being driven west into a new death trap forming in and around Minsk. On the Soviet side, events were unfolding according to plan.

SALVAGING THE RUINS OF AN ARMY

On 28 June, Hitler finally relieved Busch of his command, replacing him with Field Marshal Model, the commander Hitler had chosen from the beginning to meet the summer Soviet offensive. At this point in the battle, there was not much Model could do to rescue Army Group Center. Earlier in the year, Hitler moved the bulk of German tank strength and equipment into Army Group North Ukraine, where he expected the massive Soviet summer offensive to occur. Hitler's decision had left only a few sparse tank reserves available to Model, who could do little to forestall the fall of Minsk, already largely encircled.

The approaches to Minsk were held by perhaps 18,000 troops from various units: police, supply, and infantry formations reinforced with 125 tanks of the German 5th Panzer Division. Northwest of the city, the 5th Panzer destroyed 295 Soviet tanks. One hundred twenty-eight of the destroyed Soviet tanks were credited to the 20 Tiger tanks in 5th Panzer, but all of these successful German actions could do little more than buy time for a sensible withdrawal from Minsk, an action Hitler once again forbade. Meanwhile, the Third and First Belorussian fronts simply avoided the 5th Panzer by swinging north and south to envelop the city as originally planned. Once Minsk was encircled, Soviet airpower was skillfully concentrated to destroy tens of thousands of trapped German troops. Without food, ammunition, or motorized transport, very few German soldiers survived to fight their way west through Soviet lines.[122]

At the führer's headquarters, General Heusinger mobilized everything at his disposal to reinforce Army Group Center. While a few German formations from Army Group North moved south to assist Army Group Center, on 2 July Heusinger summoned the 6th Panzer Division from Germany, the 18th SS Panzer Grenadier Division from Hungary, the 367th Infantry Division from Army Group North Ukraine; later, the 3rd SS Panzer Division Totenkopf and even formations from as far away as Norway were ordered to the eastern front. But these additional formations were still too few in number to stop the 116 Soviet rifle divisions, 6 cavalry divisions, 42 tank brigades, and 16 motorized rifle brigades that were streaming into eastern Poland.[123]

On 3 July, the German position deteriorated further. The Germans lost Minsk, the capital of Belorussia, and by 8 July, the 5th Panzer Division was down to 18 tanks, the size of a reinforced battalion. All of the Tiger tanks were destroyed or abandoned.[124] Soviet tank forces had advanced 120 miles in

10 days, tearing a 250-mile-wide gap in Army Group Center, which was shattered and ceased to exist.[125]

Having reached the third phase of the operation, *Stavka* now assigned new objectives to the front commanders: First Baltic Front was aimed at Kaunus and Third Belorussian Front at the Molchad and Niemen River lines, and from there to Bialystok and the western Bug River. Vilnius, Lithuania's capital, was encircled and fell into Soviet hands on 13 July. Shortly after dawn on 17 July, 170,000 artillery shells fell on German forces attempting to defend a new defense line east of Lublin, Poland. Nine Soviet infantry armies crushed the German defenders, and Lublin fell on 23 July.[126] The Soviet pursuit, moving at a rate of 15 miles a day, now turned northwest toward the Vistula River and Warsaw.

Knowing eastern Poland offered little in the way of defensive terrain, Field Marshal Model ordered the 3rd SS Totenkopf division to hold a line fifty miles east of Warsaw. This new defense line meant the Soviet armed forces would inevitably end up less than four hundred miles from Berlin. The Waffen SS battle groups held long enough for the German Second Army to escape encirclement before beginning its own withdrawal west on 28 July while executing a series of punishing counterattacks against advancing Soviet tank forces.[127]

For his rapid advance into central Poland, Stalin promoted Rokossovskiy from general to marshal and ordered him on 2 August to take Warsaw with the support of two Soviet fronts moving up on his left from the Ukraine. It was not to be. On 11 August, Totenkopf finally crossed the Vistula River northeast of Warsaw and set up new defensive positions. For the next seven days, Totenkopf, together with SS Panzergrenadier Division Wiking (Viking), turned back a series of Soviet breakthrough attempts to reach and capture Warsaw.

At the end of August, German troops reported seeing Soviet troops on the east side of the Vistula building anti-tank gun fronts, a defensive tactic that placed low-profile, high-velocity, flat-trajectory guns in depth. The message was unambiguous: Operation Bagration was finally over. Stalemate ensued.[128]

Having advanced three hundred miles in five weeks, Soviet forces were overextended and exhausted. But the Soviets were now far closer to Berlin than U.S. and British forces were, although the Soviets would not renew offensive operations in western Poland until January 1945.

The destruction of Army Group Center was a stupendous military achievement, but encirclement and pursuit of the German units assigned to Army Group Center were no cakewalk for Soviet forces. Despite overwhelming superiority in every meaningful category of military power, Soviet casualties between 23 June and the end of July were much higher than was reported at the time: 440,879 soldiers, including 97,232 (roughly 30 percent of the attacking ground force) killed.[129]

CONCLUSION

Operation Bagration was the most strategically important combat operation of World War II for the simple reason that it epitomized the Soviet revolution in warfare.[130] It represented the collision of two military reforms; the Germans dramatically increased their tactical fighting power at the point of impact, while the Soviets expanded their power to dominate the whole battlespace on the operational and strategic levels. Events in the summer of 1944 showed that the Soviet transformation was the more effective of the two, as *Stavka* demonstrated its nearly full-spectrum dominance in central and eastern Europe.

Though the war would continue for another ten months, the spectacular advance of Soviet military power over the wreckage of Army Group Center into the heart of Europe ensured the destruction of the Third Reich and Stalin's conquest of central and eastern Europe. The Soviet command structure, organization for combat, and supporting doctrine for the application of military power in the form of strike—artillery, rockets, and airpower—with operationally agile maneuver forces created a margin of victory that changed the course of European and world history.

The partial transformation of the Wehrmacht that provided Germany with its margin of victory in 1939 and 1940 turned out to be insufficient for an extended conflict with Stalin's war mobilization state. Without the mobile armored firepower and the aircraft it needed to dominate the enormity of the Russian theater of war, the Wehrmacht's superior tactics could not produce the operational victories with strategic impact that Germany needed in 1941 and 1942. Russia swallowed vast numbers of dismounted German infantry, and without mobility and firepower, the World War I–styled infantry divisions were doomed to be overrun and destroyed in warfare that rewarded mobility, protection, and firepower.

As the war with the Soviet Union dragged on, Germany lost the profound edge in military capability it possessed at the outset. When the war entered its final twelve months, nearly 85 percent of the German army's supply and transport was horse-drawn, in part because there was so little fuel for wheeled vehicles and because mechanization had proceeded too slowly.[131]

The Wehrmacht was defeated in World War II because Hitler and his generals disregarded one of the most important principles of international conduct articulated about 110 years ago by Clausewitz: "No one starts a war—or rather, no one in his senses ought to do so—without first being clear in his mind what he intends to achieve by that war and how he intends to conduct it. The former is its political purpose; the latter its operational objective."[132] From July 1943 onward, the Wehrmacht in Russia lacked a definitive operational purpose and an attainable strategic objective. By January 1944, the Wehrmacht's margin of victory was effectively lost. German soldiers and the forces fighting with them from Finland, Hungary, Croatia, Romania, and Spain simply defended their assigned sectors to the best of their ability, and often to the death.

The Soviet Union won World War II in eastern Europe because the Communist Party of the Soviet Union organized its forces to achieve absolute unity of command. The appointment of senior commanders at the army and front levels with total, uncontested authority to employ and integrate all of the forces under their commands (army, navy, and air force) eliminated the interservice fights for prominence and control of resources that were common inside the German, British, and American forces. Thanks to this unique condition of unity of effort throughout the theater of war, the Soviet high command could commit troops and resources when and where they were needed quickly and efficiently on the strategic and operational levels of war.[133]

When the opportunity presented itself, a Soviet marshal could do in minutes what took General Dwight D. Eisenhower months of negotiation with U.S. and British air force commanders to do: unleash 700 long-range bombers to attack and destroy 50,000 German troops encircled by Soviet tank forces.[134] The Soviet capability to concentrate and move forces in time and space on a scale that achieved a dramatic strategic impact did not end with Operation Bagration. The subsequent Soviet campaign in Manchuria during August 1945 followed the pattern of integrated strike and maneuver operations in the Belorussian offensive, eventually providing the inspiration for Marshal Nikolai Ogarkov's Reconnaissance Strike Complex. Ogarkov extended the idea of integrating strike and maneuver forces to incorporate the growing arsenal of intelligence, surveillance, and strike assets.[135] It is no exaggeration to suggest that the successful conduct of Operation Bagration was a watershed event in Soviet military thinking and force development.[136]

In retrospect, no two armed forces ever fought harder for worse causes: the one for National Socialism, and the other for national survival as well as communism.[137] For most Germans, the suffering ended with the destruction of the Nazi state in 1945, but suffering inside the Soviet Union and in the nations Stalin conquered in the last year of World War II continued until 1989.

In 2001, the Narodnii Kommisariat Vnutreniikh Del' (NKVD, or the People's Commissariat for Internal Affairs) archives were closed when the public reacted with horror to the news that Soviet losses were certainly twice what the Communist Party admitted to during the war with Germany.[138] In 2009, Russian authorities released revised figures claiming nine million Soviet soldiers and twenty-seven million to twenty-eight million civilians were killed in the conflict, but the Russians are always "economical" with the truth. The world will probably never know the true figures.[139]

Germany rebounded dramatically. Today, Germany is once again Europe's leading political and economic power, but Stalin's legacy haunts post-Soviet Russia.[140] Were a visitor from another planet to see contemporary Moscow after seeing contemporary Berlin, he or she would conclude that Berlin, not Moscow, had won planet Earth's last great war.

CHAPTER 4

ENEMY AT THE GATE

Counterattack across the Suez, 1973

I srael's military victory over Egypt, Jordan, and Syria in the 1967 Six-Day War was so thorough and complete that General Ariel Sharon was convinced another war in the region was impossible for years, if not decades. In Sharon's words, "We [the Israelis] managed to finish it all, and after our success this time . . . the enemy is not going to be able to fight for many, many years."[1]

Sharon's statement was not hyperbole. By the second week of June 1967, Egyptian forces had lost 800 tanks, several hundred guns, and more than 10,000 vehicles, and had sustained at least 15,000 casualties.[2] In fact, the position of Israeli forces in 1967 could have been described in words similar to those Marshal Joachim Murat used regarding the Prussians in his message to Napoleon after the 1806 Jena-Auerstedt campaign: "Sire, the fighting is over because there are no combatants left."[3]

Egyptian president Gamal Abdel Nasser was distraught, and Egyptians were almost hysterical with rage against Israel. Egypt's defeat left the Sinai Peninsula and the right bank of the Suez Canal under Israeli occupation, a humiliation Nasser could not accept.[4] Having risen to power on a toxic mix of anti-capitalist, anti-imperialist, and anti-Zionist ideology, Nasser could not risk inaction against Israel without jeopardizing his leadership of Egypt, let alone his pretentions to lead the Arab world. Determined to regain the Sinai, Nasser launched a war of attrition against Israel in March 1969.[5]

The results of Nasser's war were disheartening for Egyptians; between March 1969 and August 1970, Egypt lost 109 fighter aircraft to air combat, while Israel lost 16 aircraft, most of which were shot down by anti-aircraft artillery or surface-to-air missiles. Egyptian losses on the ground were at least 10,000 dead including 6,500 civilians. Israeli losses were a few hundred.[6]

In Moscow, Egypt's inept military performance against Israeli forces raised serious questions about Egypt's ability to defend itself. This concern made a much larger and more intense program of Soviet military assistance to

Egypt absolutely essential. In Tel Aviv, views on the outcome of the war were mixed.[7] Egypt's poor military performance reinforced a popular Israeli perception: Arabs are collectively incapable of offensive operations. The problem for Israel's military leaders was more complex. The Egyptian will to fight for the Sinai was not broken, and Israel's top military leaders knew it.[8]

Gamal Abdel Nasser's death in September 1970 was mourned in Egypt and the whole Arab world. Egyptians wondered who would lead them. Eventually, a new figure rose to power—Anwar Sadat, a close confidant of Nasser who participated in the overthrow of Egypt's King Farouk in 1952. Sadat inherited a moribund economy, a bankrupt government, and a deeply disgruntled population, more than half of which was illiterate and living in abject poverty. In view of these conditions, few Western leaders would have argued for any strategy other than a purely defensive one. But Sadat was not a Western leader.

When a thousand Egyptian guns and rocket artillery systems struck Israeli positions along the Suez Canal at 2 p.m. on 6 October 1973, surprise was almost complete.[9] Five Israeli army battalion equivalents holding a one-hundred-mile front behind the Suez Canal faced five reinforced Egyptian divisions.[10] When Israeli fighters flew forward to attack Egyptian forces in the crossing sites, at least a dozen were shot down by Egypt's surface-to-air missile batteries. The Israeli air force was not prepared for close air support missions of the type and scale necessary to destroy an invading army, particularly when the invading army was heavily protected by a forest of surface-to-air missiles.[11]

Though Israeli fighters managed to strike the crossing sites, the airstrikes were not accurate or intense enough to halt the Egyptian advance. Within 24 hours, 100,000 Egyptian troops with 1,000 tanks and 13,500 vehicles moved out of Africa with speed and precision into new defensive positions on the eastern bank of the Suez Canal.[12] By 9 October, Israeli losses to Egyptian air defenses included an estimated 30 combat aircraft and 300 Israeli tanks damaged or destroyed by Egyptian ground forces.[13] These losses were unthinkable in 1967.

Within a few days, the feeling in Tel Aviv was that Israel's enemies in the Sinai were truly at the gate, but Egyptian casualties were heavy too. There are no precise numbers, but by nightfall on 9 October, Egyptian forces had sustained an estimated four thousand killed and wounded in action, along with one hundred tanks, thirty-five combat aircraft, and twenty helicopters.[14]

Decisive victories are rare in the history of warfare. But successful counter-offensives that rescue hard-pressed armies and air forces from operational and strategic errors beyond their influence are even more uncommon. However,

Israeli army and air force commanders reacted intelligently to battlefield reverses that would have stymied many other armed forces. The Israeli military leaders accepted bad news, something few people are inclined to do in war or peace. They learned quickly from their mistakes and adapted their tactics and organization to cope with the unanticipated battlefield conditions.[15]

On the night of 15–16 October, only nine and a half days after the war began, Israeli armored forces struck back, crossing the Suez Canal into Africa and turning the tables on Egypt. How and why this feat of arms was achieved, together with its profound strategic impact on Egypt and the Middle East, is the story of Israel's margin of victory, one embedded in Israeli culture, leadership, training, and technology.

EGYPT'S PATH TO WAR

In April 1972, Anwar Sadat went to Moscow to inform Soviet leader Leonid Brezhnev that Egypt had no choice but to go to war with Israel to retrieve its territory and its honor. The burden of maintaining large standing armed forces was consuming more than a quarter of Egypt's national budget; the Suez Canal remained closed, depriving Egypt of much-needed revenue; and Egypt, the nation that once supplied the Roman Empire with grain and gold, depended for its survival on subsidies from Libya, Saudi Arabia, and Kuwait.[16] To Sadat, these conditions were intolerable and could not continue.

Brezhnev was not enthralled with the prospect of a new Arab-Israeli conflict. Soviet-American détente was in full swing, and the post-1967 stalemate—no peace, no war—corresponded in many important ways to both Washington's and Moscow's strategic interests.[17] But Sadat reckoned that Brezhnev was in no position to say no, and he was right.

To preserve the Soviet Union's critical bridgehead in the Middle East, Brezhnev reluctantly capitulated to Sadat's demands.[18] Generous military aid and assistance from the Soviet Union would increase, albeit with restrictions. The Soviets would not supply long-range missiles or bombers capable of striking Israel. Soviet aid would furnish Egypt with the capability to defend itself, particularly with the massive supply of anti-aircraft weapons, but little more.[19] Until he expelled Soviet military personnel from Egypt in July 1972, Sadat always took whatever equipment, training, and assistance he could get, but he was firm in his opposition to Soviet command of Egyptian troops. He also never allowed Soviet advisers to hold key positions inside Egypt's defense establishment.[20]

Despite substantial Soviet military assistance, Sadat knew he could not regain control of the entire Sinai by force of arms alone. Seizing and then securing the whole of the Sinai was beyond Egypt's military capacity. In addition, Israel's alleged nuclear strike capability was never far from Sadat's mind. An Egyptian attempt to invade Israel itself entailed unacceptable risk and in Sadat's view was unnecessary to attain his goals.[21] Sadat was also reluctant to embrace the "long war" strategy that attrition entailed, given the factors that constrained Egyptian military performance.[22] He was confronted with the daunting challenge of Israel's demonstrated military superiority in practically every key category of national military power.[23] The first challenge was cultural, while the second involved time, distance, and the Israeli enemy.

First, Sadat was well aware that he could mobilize Egypt's mass of nearly 38 million people with appeals to nationalism, social justice, and Islam, but he also understood that Egypt's fragile society lacked staying power. Although the daily caloric intake in Egypt had risen from 2,300 calories a day in the 1950s to 2,500 calories a day in the 1970s, debilitating diseases such as tuberculosis, typhoid, and malaria were still widespread, and unemployment among the millions of Egypt's urban poor was high.[24] A failed offensive threatened to court the kind of social unrest that political opponents might use to remove him from office.[25] Sadat had no intention of providing his enemies with such an opportunity.

Egypt's pool of technically trained people was also small. In 1897, 91 percent of Egyptian men and 99 percent of Egyptian women could not read or write.[26] By 1973, the combined literacy rate for men and women in Egypt had climbed to nearly 36 percent. This was a significant improvement, but it was not nearly enough to provide the Egyptian armed forces with the human capital it needed to man and operate complex weapons systems.

General Saad el-Shazly, the Egyptian chief of staff, noted that these constraints on Egypt's military capability could not be easily overcome. Egyptian soldiers were not trained to act independently, seize the initiative, or advance new ideas.[27] If anything, Egyptian culture discouraged such behavior, meaning that Egypt's soldiers could only do what they rehearsed to do. In military terms, that meant they could execute set-piece operations but not much more.[28]

Second, conducting a deliberate river crossing under fire is one of the most challenging and dangerous military operations any modern armed force can undertake. Crossing operations demand extensive reconnaissance, detailed planning, and exhaustive rehearsals, as well as significant coordination of air defenses, combat engineers, and fording equipment with attacking ground forces. Since the far side of the Suez Canal was already firmly in the hands of the Israeli armed forces, crossing was an even more daunting task.

After occupying the Sinai side of the canal in 1967, the Israel Defense Forces (IDF) constructed intricate barriers and fortified defensive positions along the canal. Israeli defensive measures included flammable liquid storage points that could be ignited by remote control, turning sections of the canal into a pool of fire. Although not terribly effective—the weapon was installed only at two points for show (one of which was subsequently dismantled)—it had a significant psychological impact and figured prominently in Egypt's operational planning. In addition, the Israeli army maintained mobile tank reserves in depth that the Egyptians assumed could move rapidly to attack them in the crossing sites.

After reviewing the situation, many of Egypt's senior military leaders doubted their ability to coordinate and execute such an operation. Some even concluded the operation had little chance of success unless the Israelis were truly surprised by the Egyptian offensive. Egyptians are also loquacious people. Keeping a large-scale operation secret inside Egypt would be difficult, yet without the element of surprise, an offensive would simply fail.

Together with Defense Minister Ahmed Ismail, Sadat devised a simple war plan with straightforward goals.[29] The plan precluded the need for specific readjustments or complex revisions once hostilities commenced.[30]

Sadat presented his concept for the crossing and seizure of the far side of the canal to Egypt's senior military leaders and directed them to prepare detailed plans for the execution of the attack, which Sadat named Operation Badr (see map 10). Sadat, however, surprised his commanders because he would not share the exact date for the attack with them even though he had already decided to attack on 6 October. He also directed that Egypt's junior officers undergo intensive retraining programs and that thousands of university students be conscripted into the Egyptian army and air force. Sadat thought this was the best and easiest way to provide a larger pool of technically trained officers and soldiers.[31]

On Sunday, 30 September 1973, Sadat met with his top military leaders to explain what he sought to achieve with Egypt's armed forces. His strategic goal was "to challenge the Israeli theory of 'security' with military action according to the capabilities of our armed forces. . . . [I]f we can successfully challenge this notion it will lead to certain results in the near and far future."[32] Sadat's plan entailed a series of actions that diverged sharply from the expansive strategy and thinking of his predecessor, Nasser. The plan was to:

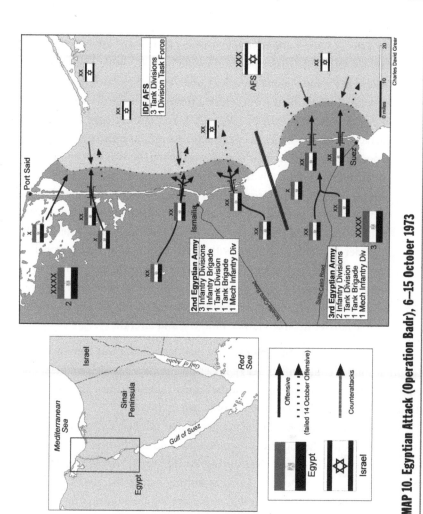

IDF AFS
3 Tank Divisions
1 Division Task Force

2nd Egyptian Army
3 Infantry Divisions
1 Infantry Brigade
1 Tank Division
1 Tank Brigade
1 Mech Infantry Div

3rd Egyptian Army
2 Infantry Divisions
1 Tank Division
1 Tank Brigade
1 Mech Infantry Div

Port Said

Ismailia

AFS

Suez

Ismailia-Cairo Road

Suez-Cairo Road

Charles David Grear

0 miles   10   20

Mediterranean Sea

Israel

Sinai Peninsula

Gulf of Aqaba

Red Sea

Gulf of Suez

Egypt

Offensive

(failed 14 October Offensive)

Counterattacks

Egypt

Israel

MAP 10. Egyptian Attack (Operation Badr), 6–15 October 1973

> capitalize on Syria's simultaneous attack to seize the Golan Heights in order to achieve Egypt's objectives while Israeli forces are fighting on two fronts.[33] Sadat was acutely sensitive to the fact that Germany's two-front dilemma led to its defeat in World War II, and he wanted the Israelis to confront similar circumstances.

> cross the Suez Canal at five sites and then establish bridgeheads with a depth of ten to fifteen kilometers along the canal in the Sinai. The troops were to advance on a broad front but avoid engaging in the mobile armored combat that Israeli forces excelled in.

➤ turn the Egyptian offensive into a strategic defense. After crossing the canal, a strong defensive position would be built inside a narrow strip of land in the Sinai along the Suez Canal. With their backs to the canal, Egyptians would fight from under a protective umbrella, perhaps one of the densest networks of SA-2, SA-3, and cutting-edge SA-6 Soviet surface-to-air missile batteries in modern military history.[34] Egyptian generals learned from their experience during the War of Attrition that Israeli pilots deliberately avoided high concentrations of SAM sites. The creation of thick forests of fixed SAM batteries to protect Egyptian forces on both sides of the canal was a result of this experience.[35] Sadat also said he wanted to integrate the aforementioned systems with shoulder-fired SA-7 missiles with several thousand rocket-propelled grenades and hundreds of AT-3 Sagger wire-guided anti-tank missile launchers. These, he said, would be augmented by hundreds of towed and recoilless anti-tank guns. Sadat's concept was to present an impenetrable barrier to Israeli tanks, infantry, and aircraft.

From Egypt's impregnable defensive positions, Sadat was convinced the Egyptian soldier could inflict heavy losses on the Israeli tanks, soldiers, and supporting equipment. This outcome, he argued, would achieve Egypt's larger strategic aim of "shattering the myth of Israeli invincibility."[36]

For tactical inspiration, Egypt's generals and colonels did not have far to look. They studied the logistical requirements and the tactics that launched Soviet forces over river after river during World War II. In the twenty-three months leading up to October 1973, assaulting across the Suez Canal and establishing a defense was integrated into every major training exercise conducted by the Egyptian armed forces.

No army in the world crossed as many rivers under fire more often and more successfully than the World War II Soviet army, but Egypt introduced an innovation that the Soviets had never considered: the use of high-pressure water cannons. These were designed to erode the foundations of the massive sand walls the Israelis constructed along the canal and blast openings in them.[37]

Instead of training to strike deep into the Sinai, the Egyptians trained to advance cautiously on a broad front, securing numerical superiority where it counted most—at the crossing sites. Chief of Staff of the Egyptian Armed Forces General Shazly later credited Soviet-inspired concepts of deception with creating the conditions for success in the opening phase of the operation. Lulling the Israelis into a false sense of confidence was essential:

For three or four years we had kept five infantry divisions stationed by the canal, each deployed in defensive formation over
a sector of 10–12 kilometers wide. They remained in those positions. We relied on the enemy to monitor this and to conclude
that the divisions were not massing for an assault. Our secret
was that each division was to storm the canal over a sector only
three to four miles wide—and those assault sectors were within
each division's existing sector. During our years of preparation,
so many trenches had been dug that the defensive lines of each
division could act not only as the concentration area before the
attack, but could also hold the reinforcements and bridging
equipment. So each division had to move only very little before
the attack.[38]

To the offensive-minded Israelis, the idea of crossing the canal and then
halting to establish a defense was incomprehensible, but the slow, cautious
advance by Egyptian troops was quite intentional. Sadat's operational design
had a purpose: to overcome what Israeli officers called the Arab soldiers' "barrier of fear."[39] In the aftermath of the 1967 war, this barrier exerted a deeply
demoralizing influence on Egyptian forces.

This was not the first time in the twentieth century that a cautious, set-
piece battle was planned with the goal of restoring confidence in an army.
When Field Marshal Sir Bernard Montgomery reflected on the British Eighth
Army's battles with Erwin Rommel's Italo-German army, he reached similar
conclusions. The demoralized character of the British troops did not escape his
notice when he took command. He immediately set out to meet the German
and Italian enemy on ground the Eighth Army selected and defended in depth.
He reasoned that by systematically preparing British soldiers to defend terrain
they knew intimately, the same soldiers who had retreated for months would
successfully halt the German attacks on 31 August and 1 September 1942.[40]

Montgomery later recounted the experience: "We had a good heavy tank
and it contained a good gun; we had a great weight of artillery . . . but the
training was not good and it was beginning to become clear to me that I would
have to be very careful, and that I must ensure the formations and units were
not given tasks which were likely to end in failure. After all, the British Eighth
Army had suffered 80,000 casualties, and the re-born Eighth Army was still
full of untrained units."[41] Montgomery's solution involved thorough training and rehearsal to the point of exhaustion. British infantry and engineers
rehearsed breeching the anti-tank minefields. Gunners rehearsed quickly

setting up anti-tank guns to halt German counterattacks before bringing forward British armor.

How much of Sadat's cautious and limited offensive was inspired by Montgomery's command of the Eighth Army is difficult to know. Sadat does not
specifically credit Montgomery's successful rebuilding of the Eighth Army's
morale and combat effectiveness with influence, but Sadat was also decidedly
pro-German and anti-British during World War II. However, Anwar Sadat was
also a graduate of the British military school established in 1936 for Egyptian
officers, and he was able to closely observe the British Eighth Army in Egypt
during its long campaign against the Germans and Italians in North Africa.[42]

What is known is that Sadat's approach worked. It overcame the Egyptian
soldiers' barrier of fear. The plan's success in battle was recorded by Brigadier General Fahim Shedeed, chief of staff of Egypt's Second Army Division.
The parallel with Montgomery's preparation of the Eight Army in the fall of
1942 seems indisputable: "It was incredible. The [Israeli] troops we had once
regarded as supermen seemed to have been overcome with fear. . . . We had
counted on achieving surprise and, by God, we achieved it. It was so complete
that the enemy became quite unnerved when he saw the waves of Egyptian
infantry crossing the canal in broad daylight. . . . And he ran. Believe me, he
ran. In many instances, he left his tanks and he ran."[43]

Sadat had reason to be pleased with the progress his forces were making
in the spring of 1973. The routine assembly and deployment of Egyptian forces
into positions along the Suez Canal together with the incremental increases
in Egyptian warfighting equipment positioned near future crossing sites did
not alarm the Israelis. Sadat and his generals felt increasingly confident that
Egypt's armed forces could achieve the limited objectives envisioned in Operation Badr. But Sadat also knew that limited war is fought in theory for political goals that do not have to result in the total subordination of one state's will
to another. Naturally, there was never any guarantee that the Israelis would
pierce the fog of war to discover that Sadat's war was truly limited in scope.
Moreover, Sadat knew that the leaders of the United States and the Soviet
Union would wait only so long before meddling in the conflict. Yet Sadat took
comfort in the idea that "if we [the Egyptians] could recapture even 4 inches
of Sinai territory (by which I meant a foothold, pure and simple) . . . the whole
situation would change."[44]

When the Israelis cooperated with Sadat's strategic ploy during the opening attack on 6 October, Sadat and his generals were understandably relieved.
By 10 October, the Egyptian Second and Third Armies with 800 tanks and

90,000 troops had repelled all counterattacks and consolidated their positions inside 2 bridgeheads, 1 held by Second Army north of the Great Bitter Lake, and a second held by Third Army south of the Little Bitter Lake. The depth of the Egyptian bridgeheads varied from 4 to 9 miles. Sadat's "Montgomeryesque" approach to planning and execution had worked brilliantly.

Sadat wanted to avoid moving beyond the range of the air defense umbrella concentrated along the canal. Exposing Egyptian ground forces to the Israeli air force was an experience no one in the senior ranks of Egypt's armed forces wanted to repeat.[45] Yet that is precisely what the Egyptians eventually did. Whether Sadat was pushed by Syrian president Hafez al-Assad to relieve pressure on Syria's armed forces or the Egyptian offensive was always part of the larger operational plan is still debated. However, Egyptians and Israelis do know that Sadat rejected a cease-fire proposal from the Soviets on 12 October and ordered his forces in the Sinai to attack the Israelis. This was a set-piece action that did not work.

At first light on 14 October, the Egyptians attacked east out of their bridgeheads with 4 reinforced brigades in the direction of the Mitla Pass, the Gedy Pass, Tasa, and Baluza. The attacks (2 in the Second Army sector and 2 in the Third Army sector) were too widely dispersed on a 120-mile front to present the Israelis with the threat of a serious breakthrough, and by midday, the Egyptians had lost between 200 and 250 of the 400 tanks in the offensive by attacking across open ground dominated by Israeli tanks and aircraft. At the same time, fewer than 25 Israeli tanks were hit, and Israeli casualties were light.[46] Egypt had shot its bolt. The strategic initiative now passed irrevocably into the hands of Israel's military leaders.[47]

ISRAEL'S PATH TO WAR

Contemporary military analysts in the United States, Europe, and Northeast Asia tend to view the Israeli army as similar in content and character to the armies of other modern scientific-industrial states. The true picture is far more complex.

During 3 decades of the British mandate in Palestine, the Jewish community was protected by several underground militia organizations with fierce reputations: the Haganah (1920), Irgun (1931), and Lehi (1941).[48] The Haganah ("the Defense"), the largest of the three, assisted British authorities to aggressively suppress the Arab rebellion by fielding 10,000 men on a more or less full-time basis along with 40,000 additional reservists. The Haganah and its

World War II offspring, the Palmach ("Shock Companies"), both fostered initiative, resourcefulness, and independent leadership in the conduct of guerrilla warfare.[49] These acquired characteristics decisively molded the character and shaped the thinking of Israel's post–World War II military leaders.[50]

After Germany's defeat in May 1945, David Ben Gurion, president of the Jewish Agency Executive, was determined to establish once and for all time the Jewish state. In Palestine, he was already leader of the Jewish community and, in the view of many Israeli Jews, "the inevitable man" who was destined to lead the new nation. Ben Gurion argued forcefully that the survival of the new Jewish state required much more than a large guerrilla force: "There will be war [when the British leave Palestine]," Ben Gurion insisted. "The Arab States will be united and will jointly fight us. There will be a battle front. It will no longer be the fight of a squad or a platoon. We have to establish a modern army. We have to think of the means of a modern army."[51]

In the summer of 1945, Ben Gurion turned to the Jewish veterans of the British army for answers. They had the expertise and leadership to transform Palestine's Jewish guerrilla fighters into a modern army capable of defending the future Israeli state. Thirty thousand Jews from Palestine served in the British army during World War II.[52] Most important, the British army created a Jewish Brigade Group in 1943, a force of five thousand men who fought as an integral part of British armies in North Africa and Italy.

These Jewish veterans supplied much of the expertise that standardized the doctrine, training, and structure of the Israeli regular reinforced brigades on the British army model.[53] The reinforced brigades of tanks, infantry, and artillery that emerged from this period would also spearhead operations in Israel's subsequent wars with its neighbors.

In the years after Israel's independence, senior military leaders continued to build and expand the Israel Defense Forces. These men were primarily "doers," combat commanders who learned their trade in a dynamic wartime environment that rewarded initiative and originality. Historian and IDF veteran officer Dr. Eitan Shamir explains:

> The outstanding young officers who emerged during these formative years had gained their knowledge through the trials of war rather than in the halls of military academies. For example, the founders of the armored corps learned their trade by trial and error and "endless debate." Some military literature was available, and officers such as Lieutenant Colonel Uri Ben-Ari,

who later commanded the famous Seventh Armored Brigade, reportedly read and experimented with German panzer tactics. Nevertheless, limited access to the experience of foreign militaries forced the IDF to devise its doctrine nearly from scratch. This turn of events allowed the IDF to tailor fighting methods to its specific needs and encouraged experimentation.[54]

Israeli military inventiveness also meant that Israeli army formations in the 1950s and 1960s operated as independent forces with objectives, targets, and timetables. Detailed plans and centralized command structures were largely unknown to them. Higher headquarters sometimes intervened to coordinate the movement of different formations, but the influence of these headquarters was limited. Higher commanders simply ensured that tactical leaders at the brigade level and below adhered to objectives, targets, and timetables. Complex coordination on the operational and strategic levels was seldom required.[55]

Tactical doctrine likewise evolved over time from whatever mix of weapons and demonstrated action (in the air or on the ground) proved successful. Without a culture that rewarded improvisation, originality, and aggressiveness, the IDF simply could not function. Equipment sets were always diverse and included tanks, guns, and aircraft from many Western nations, as well as captured Soviet equipment. Effectiveness depended on how well IDF officers cobbled together fighting units from a mix of equipment. The practice was both a constant irritant and an unavoidable necessity.

Though largely self-taught, many Israeli officers were actually exposed to a broad range of Western and Soviet military thinking and organizations. These encounters were crucial, but there is another factor in the evolution of Israeli military culture that should not be discounted. The youthful quality of Israel's early military leaders meant their minds were receptive to new ideas, concepts, and technologies.

Yigael Yadin was only thirty-two years old when he became IDF chief of staff in 1949. His military career began at age fifteen during the Arab Revolt when he joined the Haganah. His successor, Mordechai Makleff, was thirty-two when he assumed his duties. Moshe Dayan, who lost his eye with the Palmach scouting for British troops in Lebanon during World War II, became the fourth IDF chief of staff in 1953 when he was only thirty-seven. When Ezer Weizman assumed his duties as Israeli air force chief of staff, the former World War II Royal Air Force pilot was still in his thirties.[56]

All of these men were tough task masters who trained their officers in unconventional ways. To compensate for the IDF's small size, they emphasized individual responsibility, inventive tactics, and daring leadership.[57] Their preference for demonstrated talent and guts over education and social standing infused the IDF with a degree of energy and imagination seldom seen in Western military organizations, which tend to reward longevity of service rather than performance.[58] Only the youthful and dynamic leaders that rose to command inside the revolutionary armies of France in 1789 come close in comparison.[59]

Extensive combat experience against a known opponent—the Muslim Arab—translated into a strong preference for offensive action designed to surprise and unhinge the Arab enemy, a preference inextricably intertwined with the elasticity of mind that youth and imagination bring to warfare. By the fall of 1973, twenty-five years after the War of Independence, the aforementioned combination of unusual thinkers and hands-on experience elevated the IDF to the peak of its power. Israel's 1973 military establishment had several important features:

> By 1971, Israeli defense spending had risen to 24.7 percent of the gross national product, resulting in an increase in brigade strength from twenty-six in 1967 to thirty in 1973. These brigades were consolidated under the command of permanent division headquarters and staffs with an enhanced capability planning and execution on the operational as well as tactical levels.[60]

> In 1973, the IDF was commanded by a unified, national general staff that directed the operations of air, land, and sea forces. The Israeli chief of the general staff, also known as the commander in chief of the IDF, was responsible for achieving unity of command and effort across the armed forces. In Israel's two-front war, the national general staff played a vital role in the strategic allocation of military resources and capabilities across the theater. In a war in which people and assets had to shift constantly between two fronts, none of the major commanders was ever completely satisfied.

> In 1973, Israel's standing army comprised 80,000 active-duty personnel, but the army's true strength depended on 220,000 well-educated and technically skilled reservists.[61] In 1973, the need to react quickly and then project and sustain forces on 2 fronts (Syria and Egypt) was

made more challenging by the long and extended interior lines Israel acquired in 1967.

> From the 1950s onward, the Israeli general staff developed a strategic-operational doctrine designed explicitly for war with its Arab neighbors. By 1973, this doctrine stressed decisive maneuver, emphasizing flank attacks over head-on collisions and decentralized over centralized command. Based on the 1967 war, the IDF's presumed strength was the coordinated use of armor and airpower. By 1973, the Israeli army was in fundamental terms a mobile, tank-based army, ideally suited for rapid decisive operations with the support of the Israeli air force's flying artillery.

> Notwithstanding the political contests for power between various political factions inside the Israeli government, officer selection in the IDF was (and still is) merit-based. Of those selected for officer training before 1973, only 50 percent became officers. However, few soldiers remained to become long-serving noncommissioned officers. Consequently, the 1973 Israeli army depended heavily on aggressive junior officer leadership for its effectiveness in action.[62]

General Shmuel "Gorodish" Gonen, commander of the IDF Southern Command in October 1973, was very much a product of Israeli military culture and experience.[63] When the Egyptians attacked across the Suez Canal, he did not immediately comprehend the magnitude of the offensive, but his experience and training told him to attack—the tactic that had secured victory for Israel in every war with the Arabs since 1948.

Thinking the Egyptians could be bullied into a full-blown retreat, Gonen decided to commit two-thirds of one Israeli division in one attack to defeat three reinforced Egyptian divisions. Individual Israeli tank companies counterattacked entire Egyptian brigades with abandon. In short order, they were surprised to discover that the Egyptian troops did not collapse as they did in 1967.[64] It would take ten to twenty hours for Gonen, along with the rest of Israel's senior military leaders, to figure out that Israeli forces in the Sinai Peninsula were fighting a full-scale offensive, not just another cross-canal raid like the ones they experienced during the earlier War of Attrition.

The IDF's intended blitzkrieg with tanks and fighter aircraft was suddenly and swiftly neutralized.[65] To be fair, no one in the Israeli military establishment anticipated an effective Egyptian tactical defense of lethal anti-tank missiles protected by dense, impenetrable air defenses, but that is exactly what happened.[66] After 8–9 October, the Israelis fought a defensive battle with force conservation as the prime directive, something midway between defense and delay. Holding ground in itself was not judged to be as important as causing Egyptian casualties. While the Israelis completed their mobilization, recovered and repaired tanks, reorganized their units, and studied the new lessons of the opening battles, inflicting losses on the Egyptian enemy was the overriding objective.

In 1973, all of Israel's military leaders wanted to fight as they had in 1967: in a fluid battlefield environment that rewarded Israeli initiative. Initiative was the historic key to concentrating superior Israeli fighting power at the decisive point. When these battlefield conditions did not emerge, acrimonious debates ensued between General Gonen and his subordinate commanders. More to the point, Gonen flew into rage after rage to the point that his behavior created confusion and disarray inside Southern Command. The decision was made that new leadership was needed, and on 10 October, former IDF chief of staff General Chaim Bar-Lev arrived to command Southern Command.[67]

ISRAELI FORCES STRIKE BACK

From the moment the Egyptians attacked into the Sinai, crossing the canal behind the Egyptian bridgeheads was foremost in Israeli military minds. Soon after assuming command of the southern front, Bar-Lev wanted to cross the canal behind the Egyptian defenses, but his instincts told him that any Israeli counterattack that did not precipitate the collapse of the Egyptian front was probably pointless. Still, when the fighting on 14 October ended with significant Egyptian losses in tanks, Bar-Lev concluded the time to decisively counterattack across the Suez Canal had arrived. He issued a verbal order on 14 October directing the crossing operation—code name "Abirei-Lev," or Operation Valiant—to begin at 5 p.m. on 15 October.

Operation Valiant was based on prewar plans developed while Major General Ariel Sharon was the commander of Southern Command. His plan called for a two division crossing to establish a bridgehead in Africa from which an attack would be made either to the north or the south. Bar-Lev retained the plan in outline but modified it to accommodate a very narrow approach to the canal, about two and a half miles wide—an operational constraint that eventually cost time, lives, and resources. Once across, the plan was to annihilate the Egyptian bridgeheads from behind and encircle the remaining Egyptian forces in the Sinai.

General Sharon's 143rd Armored Division, with 240 tanks reinforced by a parachute brigade, 2 engineer battalions, and 3 reduced infantry battalions, was tasked with establishing the Israeli bridgehead and conducting the crossing operation. Sharon was also directed to conduct diversionary attacks on the canal's east bank to persuade the Egyptians that the Israelis intended to envelop the flanks of Egypt's northern bridgehead.

Sharon was a born leader, a dynamic commander whom soldiers unhesitatingly followed. Unfortunately for his superiors, Sharon was also an unruly subordinate with an insatiable appetite for public adulation and attention.[68] Sharon's decision to disobey orders on 8 and 9 October is a case in point.

On 7 October, IDF chief of staff General David "Dado" Elazar ordered Israeli forces to hold a line approximately ten kilometers from the canal.[69] He also specifically directed Israeli division commanders not to move closer than three kilometers toward the Suez Canal so as to reduce their exposure to the Sagger anti-tank missiles that were on the Egyptian embankment (the Egyptian earth ramparts on the west side of the canal were taller than the Israeli ones so Egyptian troops could shoot into the Sinai). Ignoring these orders, Sharon made one last attack on 9 October to regain some high ground overlooking the canal in the central sector near Matzmed. During the night of 8–9 October, Major Yoav Brom, Sharon's brilliant divisional reconnaissance battalion commander, probed undetected until he found a point at which the two Egyptian armies were not connected. On reaching the Suez Canal near Matzmed, the young major reported the absence of any Egyptian troops on either side of the canal. After a thorough reconnaissance to identify the Egyptian positions on either side of this "seam," he withdrew to Israeli lines.[70]

The strategic importance of this officer's discovery and his phenomenal achievement—penetrating to and withdrawing from the seam undetected—cannot be overstated. Thanks to Sharon's disobedience, the reconnaissance battalion commander's initiative produced what Americans call a "game changer."

Armed with this information, the Israeli military leaders decided upon a course of action. At the appropriate time, General Avraham Adan's 162nd Armored Division with 200 tanks would exploit Sharon's crossing and move south to encircle the Egyptian Third Army. Then, General Kalman Magen's 252nd Armored Division with 140 tanks would follow Adan's division into Africa.[71] General Yitzak Sasson's division of 125 tanks together with a diverse collection of infantry formations would remain on the defense in the Sinai to contain any Egyptian offensive moves.

On 15 October, Adan moved his division to an assembly area one mile west of Tasa in preparation to cross. Sharon established his headquarters in Tasa, east of the canal. Sharon's division was centrally located and was in possession of bridging and amphibious equipment from 13 October onward.

On 15 October, there were still no Egyptian troops on the east bank of the Suez Canal near Deversoir, an abandoned airfield on the African side of the canal across from Matzmed. As a result, Matzmed was selected for the crossing operation. If the Israelis could cross at Matzmed, they could reach the Plains of Aida on the other side, a broad expanse that would support the rapid penetration of Adan's tanks into Egypt.[72]

To the south were the Geneifa Hills, a hill mass that dominated the proposed zone of attack in all directions.[73] To the northwest of the crossing site were several more bridges over the Ismailia Canal. The capture of these bridges by Sharon's force would offer additional protection to the bridgehead against Egyptian counterattacks from the north.

The Geneifa Hills also contained several surface-to-air missile batteries that threatened the Israeli air force. If Egypt's air defenses were to be destroyed, the Israeli army would have to do the job. In 1967, the Israeli air force enjoyed a profound strategic advantage after an Iraqi pilot flew his new MiG-21 to an Israeli airfield. Israeli pilots were able to thoroughly study the aircraft.[74] Israeli pilots enjoyed no such advantage in their 1973 contest with Egypt's Soviet-supplied air defenses. Israeli air force officers had not physically studied the Soviet air defense technology that now presented Israeli pilots with a new and dangerous threat.

Sharon's plan for the crossing called for a massive artillery strike on the far side followed by light infantry assault. A parachute brigade would cross in rubber boats and secure the far side. Then, tanks on 18 motorized wheeled rafts called Gilowas would begin crossing into Africa. Three Gilowas linked together could carry 1 52-ton M-60 tank. Eventually, the plan called for a massive rolling floatation bridge, 10 feet wide and 590 feet in length, to be towed down Akavish, a narrow asphalt road, to the crossing site. There the bridge would be pushed into the river until it reached the far bank.

In Sharon's sector there were two parallel east-west roads, about a mile and a half apart leading to the canal and Matzmed's "yard," an area of about 2,500 square feet surrounded by earthen barriers. The yard was the perfect place to marshal forces before sending them across the canal. Akavish snaked through sand dunes where off-road movement for anything other than tracked vehicles was next to impossible. The other road running to the canal was called Tirtur, an unpaved dirt road that could still support heavy, wheeled transport because of its hard-packed gravel composition.

In time, Sharon would come to appreciate just how aggressively the area north of the roads was defended by Egypt's 16th Infantry Division and 21st Armored Division. Together the two divisions had about 120 tanks, 200 Sagger missile launchers, and roughly the same number of towed and recoilless anti-tank guns. Equally important, these Egyptian divisions controlled highly defensible terrain, a hilly area the Israelis called "Missouri" and "the Chinese Farm." [75] The maze of irrigation ditches and embankments separating the cultivated fields that stretched across the Chinese Farm area made it a strong position. [76]

Before crossing the canal, however, the Egyptian forces blocking the planned routes also had to be moved aside or at least engaged so they did not see or fire at the column of paratroopers moving to the crossing site. Sharon accomplished this task on 15 October by sending one tank brigade to conduct a diversionary, head-on attack from the east (though it was not to press home so as to avoid excessive casualties). A second tank brigade entered the empty area between the two Egyptian armies and then attacked Egypt's Second Army from behind its rear flank from south to north (see map 11). This second attack pushed Second Army's flank slightly northward. Israeli armor screened and protected the paratroopers as they drove directly to the canal area. Consequently, the assaulting paratroopers met no resistance and rapidly secured the west bank. Despite these successes, the timetable for the operation began to slip almost immediately.

In 1973, the Israeli army made very limited use of helicopters, primarily because they were vulnerable to Egyptian ground fire if they flew low and to Egyptian air defenses if they flew high. When Bar-Lev issued the order to cross the canal, Sharon's paratroopers were actually deployed in defensive positions around the Mitla Pass. Many hours would pass before the parachute brigade reached the staging area, where it was supposed to find rubber boats for the assault across the canal eighteen miles east of Tassa. Because of the risk to helicopters in the air defense environment, the paratroopers moved to the battle areas on tracked or wheeled vehicles. [77] When they finally crossed the Suez Canal at 1:30 a.m. on 16 October, more than seven hours later than planned, they did so initially with only part of the parachute brigade. [78]

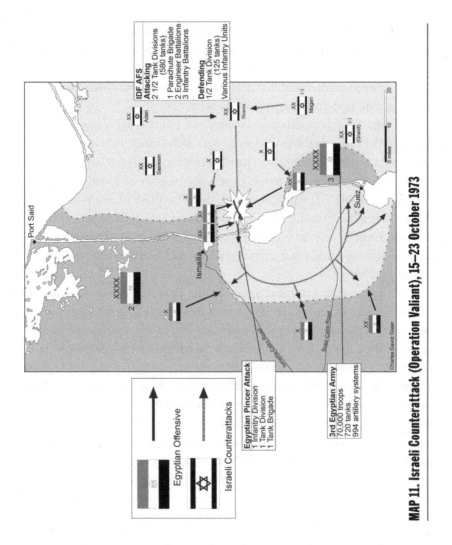

MAP 11. Israeli Counterattack (Operation Valiant), 15–23 October 1973

Over the next seven hours, the Gilowas moved twenty tanks, seven M113s, and two thousand paratroopers across the canal. To ensure their crossing remained undetected as long as possible, the paratroopers concealed themselves in the heavy undergrowth along the canal, and the tanks hid inside the abandoned hangars on the nearby Deversoir airfield.[79] At 2 a.m., Sharon crossed into Egypt and took personal command of his small force in Africa.

While Sharon established the bridgehead in Africa, his deputy division commander, Jack Even, attempted to control the Akavish Road and the traffic that moved across it. In a scene reminiscent of the German columns snaking through the Ardennes on 13 May 1940, hundreds of Israeli vehicles loaded with fuel, ammunition, and engineering equipment moved bumper to bumper in a twelve-mile-long traffic jam. Wheeled vehicles that attempted to pass around the traffic jam careened into the dunes and became mired in the soft sand.[80] Concurrently, Sharon's brigade-sized attacks on Missouri and the Chinese Farm stalled with serious losses in men and equipment, but they nonetheless diverted Egyptian attention from the crossing site and the paratroopers now operating on the canal's west bank.

In the light of the 15–16 October full moon, Egyptian tanks and infantry poured fire from the slopes of Missouri's small hills into the advancing Israeli armor, repelling the attacks and disrupting movement over the nearby roads, Akavish and Tirtur. In the space of a few hours, Sharon's diversionary attacks cost the division 70 of its 280 tanks and at least 300 killed. Losses included the complete destruction of the tank company attached to the parachute brigade still located on the east bank of the Suez Canal.

Unable to concentrate significant volumes of accurate, high-angle fire from mortars and artillery together with airstrikes, the Israelis were compelled to fight through tough terrain that provided the Egyptian infantry and tanks with ideal fields of fire. Egyptian armor and infantry again fought more ferociously than the Israeli senior leadership had expected. Lieutenant Colonel Amnon Rashef, then deputy commander of the parachute brigade assigned to Sharon's division, described the scene: "In all directions, the desert was covered with a vast fleet of burning and smoking tanks, vehicles, guns, transporters; dead infantry lay everywhere. . . . The remnants of the Israeli forces were there too, and frequently, the distance between them and the Egyptian vehicles was no more than a few yards."[81]

At the tip of the spear on the African side of the canal, things went much better. Before the sun was up, Sharon's force set out to attack anything of military value they found within a 5- to 6-mile radius. In short order, they found and destroyed several surface-to-air missile batteries without any interference from nearby Egyptian combat units. Sharon was so elated with the unopposed buildup of his force in Egypt—now a force of 50 tanks, 2,000 paratroopers, and a dozen long-range 175-millimeter guns—that he urged Bar-Lev to send Adan's division over the canal as soon as possible.

The battle had changed. It was no longer a set-piece action. Decisions had to be taken quickly at every level, but Egypt's centralized command system was proving too slow and too remote from the battlefield to react effectively. It was not until noon on 16 October, from the comfort of his office in Cairo, that General Shazly noted the first report of Israeli tanks operating west of the

Suez Canal. Shazly describes the confusing scene near the canal: "Some of our rear SAM [surface-to-air missile] units, stationed almost ten miles behind the canal, began to report attacks by enemy tanks. Nobody seemed to know where the tanks had come from. They would appear in the vicinity of a SAM battery, shell it from around 2,000 yards (these rear batteries had no long-range anti-tank weapons) and, then, disappear unhindered, to appear again who knew where. The reports spoke of 7 to 10 tanks in each party."[82]

Instead of rapidly assembling a capable force to decisively attack the newly discovered Israeli crossing site on 16 October, the Egyptian military leadership dithered. After confirming the accuracy of the reports, Shazly met late in the afternoon with General Ismail to decide how to deal with the Israeli penetration into Egypt. Despondent that so much of Egypt's fighting power was sitting idle on the Sinai side of the canal, Shazly wanted to withdraw several tank and infantry battalions with anti-tank missiles to the west bank where they could be employed in defensive positions around the Israeli penetration.

Ismail disagreed. He wanted the 21st Armored Division with Egypt's Second Army on the canal's east bank to attack southward and the 25th Independent Armored Brigade with Egypt's Third Army on the canal's east bank to attack northward on 17 October in a pincer movement. The idea was to crush the Israeli thrust to the canal on the east bank in a vice, cutting off and surrounding the Israeli forces already across the canal. Shazly countered that to reach the Israeli force in the crossing zone, the 25th Independent Armored Brigade would have to move twenty-five miles with its left flank on the canal and its right flank exposed to enemy attack. In Shazly's view, the operational risk was too great.

When the two men could not agree, Shazly pressed Sadat for a decision. Sadat surprised Shazly with his anger. Sadat was furious with Shazly's readiness to withdraw troops from the Sinai: "Why do you always propose withdrawing our troops from the east bank? You ought to be court martialed. If you persist in these proposals I will court martial you. I do not want to hear another word."[83]

Humiliated by Sadat's remarks, Shazly backed down and ordered the 21st Armored Division and the 25th Independent Armored Brigade to prepare their attacks for 17 October in accordance with Ismail's plan. This attack and those that followed it on the west bank of the canal would be poorly coordinated and would have little chance of stopping the Israeli armored units moving into Africa, let alone out of the bridgehead to the south and north.

While the Egyptian high command debated what to do next, Israeli defense minister Moshe Dayan arrived at Southern Command headquarters where he received reports on the night's heavy fighting in the crossing zone. Dayan was sufficiently concerned that he asked Bar-Lev whether the crossing operation should be called off.[84] Bar-Lev dismissed the idea of postponing the crossing and told Dayan, "There is nothing at all to discuss."[85]

More than 129 years ago Ulysses S. Grant wrote, "The distant rear of an army engaged in battle is not the best place from which to judge correctly what is going on in front."[86] Grant's opinion was shared by the stolid Bar-Lev, who believed Dayan was too focused on the problems behind the crossing zone. From where he stood, Dayan could not comprehend the success at the tip of the spear and the criticality of securing and quickly exploiting that success. Dayan also neglected to note that Egyptian losses on 16 October were very heavy, much heavier, in fact, than Israeli losses.

These points notwithstanding, Bar-Lev could not ignore the threat to the crossing zone in the Sinai. He could not logistically support two divisions on the African side of the canal until the corridor leading to the crossing site was substantially widened and secured.[87] This was the second uncompleted mission of Sharon's tank brigade fighting at Missouri and the Chinese Farm. The Tirtur Road was still not open, and the first pontoon bridge was stuck in traffic on the Akavish Road. Whenever Israeli tank units drove the Egyptians out of one area, the Israelis were attacked from a new direction by the same Egyptian infantry and forced to withdraw with heavy loss of Israeli lives and equipment. As long as the Egyptian infantry maneuvered freely through the irrigation ditches and hills, they could block the Akavish and Tirtur Roads.[88]

Stiff Egyptian resistance inside the Chinese Farm forced eighteen Israeli tanks to tow the roller bridge off the Akavish Road and across the desert where it had broken down. Hours, if not a whole day, would be needed to repair the bridge, all while Egyptian infantry and tanks could still hurl a wall of fire at Israeli forces on the two roads from their positions at Missouri and the Chinese Farm. The problem was that Sharon's division no longer had the strength to execute all of its assigned tasks.

Bar-Lev's solution was to order Adan's division to open the Akavish and Tirtur Roads and move the remaining bridging equipment to Matzmed. This represented a significant departure from the original plan. He also decided that light infantry would be needed to root out and destroy the Egyptian anti-tank units occupying the hills and irrigation ditches along the roads in a six-mile-long stretch of desert. As a result, he assigned a parachute brigade under

the command of Colonel Uzzi Ya'iri to Adan's division. In theory, this decision made sense. In practice, it did not.

Colonel Ya'iri's first battalion of four companies arrived in darkness and
prepared to attack over terrain they had never seen. Specific intelligence regarding where the Egyptian defenders were located was not available. Rehearsals
were out of the question. The pressure on Ya'iri to act quickly meant that his
officers would not have time to conduct reconnaissance patrols in the area
before they attacked. Even more troubling, fire support officers (artillerymen)
were not assigned to Ya'iri troops. He and his men would have to depend on
Adan's division artillery, an organization they did not know, for support.

Adan later wrote in his account of the ensuing battle: "Because of the full
moon and the enemy's abundance of anti-tank weapons and in view of the
combat experience we had accumulated here, I was not suggesting any tanks
or armored personnel carriers go along—but of course we would have tanks at
the ready to come to his aid should the need arise."[89]

This passage suggests that conditions were not conducive to success. It is
especially hard to understand what persuaded Adan that paratroopers with
no protection, only small arms for firepower, and no mobility save their own
legs would succeed in the face of overwhelming firepower from prepared
defensive positions where Israeli armor had not. The enemy situation was not
clear to Adan. In the minds of Adan and the paratroopers, the mission was a
sweep to locate and kill or drive off a scattering of small groups of Egyptians
sniping with anti-tank missiles at the Israeli traffic on Akavish and Tirtur and
nothing more. They were wrong.

From their prepared defensive positions, the Egyptians had no difficulty
targeting the paratroopers with fire from artillery and machine guns when
they moved toward the Egyptian lines shortly after midnight on 17 October.
In what must have been a superhuman effort, the paratroopers managed to
come within fifteen to twenty yards of the Egyptian defenders, but their attack
stalled. The paratroopers were pinned down by heavy fire in the same ditches
they were supposed to clear. In addition to tank support, what the Israeli paratroopers needed was a volume of high-angle fire from mortars, artillery, and
airpower, not lightly armed infantry with flat-trajectory direct-fire weapons.
Unfortunately, these assets were either not considered necessary or not readily
available.

Adan now told Ya'iri to focus his troops exclusively on clearing Akavish Road, but Ya'iri's lead battalion was pinned down and could not move.
Throughout the night, Adan sent tanks and armored personnel carriers to

evacuate the wounded paratroopers, and by 9:30 a.m. Adan withdrew them entirely.[90]

None of these events interrupted the steady stream of fire exchanged between Israeli and Egyptian tank forces north and south of the Akavish Road, but there was good news. The fear of infiltration by the paratroopers seems to have diverted Egyptian attention long enough for General Dovik Tamari, Adan's deputy division commander, to pack up and move the pontoon bridging equipment down the Akavish Road to Matzmed.

Just as dawn began to break at 4:45 a.m., the pontoon bridging equipment was lumbered into the Matzmed yard. With the pontoon bridges safely under construction at Matzmed, Adan attacked at 8 a.m. in a wide arc toward Missouri and the Chinese Farm with four tank battalions (about eighty tanks). Adan's battalions collided almost instantly with Egyptian elements of the 16th Infantry and 21st Armored Divisions.

In the next 5 hours, an enormous tank battle raged inside the 8-square-mile area encompassing the Tirtur and Akavish Roads and the southern edge of the Chinese Farm. When the fighting finally ended around noon, the Israelis held the Tirtur Road. The narrow corridor leading to the crossing site along the Akavish Road was open and secure. Surviving Egyptian units from the 21st Armored and 23rd Mechanized Divisions withdrew north to Missouri. Egyptian soldiers still held most of the Chinese Farm, however, and from Missouri Egyptian fire could still sweep the edge of the Tirtur Road. But the Israelis attained their key objective. Inside the area where the fighting occurred, there were 250 destroyed tanks, one-third of them Israeli.[91]

On the west bank of the canal, the Egyptians finally awoke to the Israeli presence. In the 24 hours since the first report of Israeli tanks reached Cairo, the Egyptians deployed 144 guns of varying calibers with which to strike the Israeli bridges. At dawn on 17 October, these guns now began to fire on the Israeli crossing site almost without pause, causing heavy casualties among the engineers and the infantrymen assembling the pontoon bridge. A few tanks sank with their crews on board when their Gilowas were struck halfway across the canal. Then, Egyptian infantry and tanks attacked Sharon's tanks and paratroopers. All of the attacks were repulsed but at the cost of many Israeli lives and ten more tanks in Sharon's force.[92]

Egyptian air force fighters also attacked the bridge site but with much less success than the Egyptian artillery. When Egyptian surface-to-air missile batteries shut down air defense operations to allow the Egyptian aircraft to attack, Israeli fighters swooped in and shot them out of the sky. Egyptian losses on 17 October included sixteen fighters and seven helicopters, the latter destroyed when they flew low to drop napalm on the pontoon bridge.

BREAKOUT AND ENDGAME

After more than forty-eight hours of hard fighting to secure the crossing zone into Africa, Israel's senior commanders on the southern front met at Adan's command post on a hill near Kishuf at noon on 17 October. The purpose of the meeting was to discuss future operations, including the breakout from the bridgehead. Almost immediately, Sharon insisted that he lead the attack south out of the bridgehead behind Egypt's Third Army, an idea repugnant to Adan. As far as Adan was concerned, his troops had fought hard to complete the mission originally assigned to Sharon—to secure the crossing zone. Now, instead of securing the bridgehead as originally planned, Adan was convinced that Sharon wanted to monopolize the glory that came with the exploitation attack.[93]

General Elazar, the Israeli chief of staff who was present for the meeting, intervened to settle the matter before the discussion became too heated. For the moment he insisted the plan would not change. Sharon would continue to hold the bridgehead and corridor, and Adan's division would pass through the bridgehead to exploit. When the time was right, Sharon would join Adan while Magen protected the bridgehead.[94]

In the midst of this tense discussion, a new challenge presented itself. The Egyptian pincer attack first planned by Ismail on 16 October was finally materializing. Israeli aerial reconnaissance reported that one hundred T-62 tanks were moving from south to north along the eastern shore of the Great Bitter Lake in the direction of the Matzmed crossing site. The L-shaped ambush that Shazly feared now unfolded. Since Adan's forces were still engaged in fighting around the Chinese Farm and Missouri, disengaging and exploiting the bridgehead would be no easy task.

Bar-Lev agreed to Adan's request to release his third brigade from the southern front's operational reserve, and Adan issued instructions to his units. His brigades in contact with the Egyptian enemy had to extend their fronts to allow tank battalions on the flanks to withdraw, rearm, refuel, and reposition to fight the advancing Egyptian brigade, but Adan's forces moved quickly into position to ambush the Egyptians.

The one hundred Egyptian T-62 tanks were deployed in columns on flat terrain next to the Great Bitter Lake while most of Adan's tanks were concealed behind the low hills on the Egyptians' right flank. As the Egyptians moved north, Adan sent two battalions south to encircle the Egyptians from behind, ensuring there would be no escape.

At roughly 2:30 p.m., Adan's tanks opened fire. Of the ninety-six Egyptian tanks in the attacking column, eighty-six were destroyed in less than an hour of fighting.[95] Some of the Egyptians' Soviet-made amphibious tanks in the reconnaissance unit attempted to flee into the lake, but they struck an undetected minefield and were destroyed. By 4 p.m., the Egyptian 25th Brigade was completely annihilated. Adan's division lost three tanks.[96] Shazly's worst fears were realized.

Egypt had squandered its last opportunity to halt the Israeli crossing, and events now moved faster than Sadat and his generals ever thought possible. By midmorning, the Israeli breakthrough into Egypt was well under way. More than one hundred Israeli combat engineers and infantrymen died, and hundreds more were wounded erecting the bridges over the Suez Canal, but the sacrifice was not in vain. By 4 a.m. on 18 October, two of Adan's brigades were inside the Israeli bridgehead on the west bank of the canal.

Based on their experience in 1967, artillery failed to keep up with advancing Israeli tank forces, leading Israeli commanders to depend on airstrikes to support advancing tank forces.[97] Consequently, in the opening days of the Yom Kippur War, Israeli commanders did not employ artillery and mortars efficiently or effectively.[98] These missteps were now corrected.

In the Sweetwater Canal area, Adan's breakout force from the bridgehead met tough resistance from dug-in Egyptian infantry and artillery. This time, Israeli battalion and company commanders systematically applied combined arms tactics—heavy suppressive fires from tanks and artillery—to outflank and annihilate Egyptian infantry positions. When Adan's brigades moved west and south, they advanced rapidly but methodically.

One brigade advanced through the Geneifa Hills to destroy Egyptian surface-to-air missile sites. Another brigade moved south along a parallel road on the east side of the Geneifa Hills, and a third advanced south toward Mina, bypassing Egyptian positions whenever possible. Egyptian artillery batteries that had shelled the crossing site were overrun and destroyed. Hundreds, then thousands, of Egyptian prisoners fell into Israeli hands. Adan also captured Fayid Airport, a great operational asset. The airport was instantly transformed by Israeli crews to serve as a supply base and to fly out wounded soldiers.

As Adan broke out to the west and south on the morning of 18 October, Sharon's forces attacked north in the direction of Ismailia, a city of 500,000 located halfway between Port Said and Suez City. Sharon's units had little difficulty pushing Egyptian paratroopers off the sand rampart north of the crossing site to enlarge the bridgehead.

Sharon's second brigade now crossed the canal and moved north to take Orcha, a large Egyptian logistics hub defended by an elite commando battalion. In a bloody action that included hand-to-hand fighting, Israeli infantrymen rooted the Egyptians out of their defensive positions with grenades, supporting tank fire, and sometimes bayonets. The Egyptians did not give up easily, but Orcha was secured by nightfall.

The next day, Sharon continued the drive toward Ismailia with Israeli air support. Without the protection afforded by air defenses, the Egyptians had little choice but to fight a delaying action back to the outskirts of Ismailia. Here, on 21 October, fierce Egyptian resistance inflicted heavy losses on the Israelis. Sharon was forced to halt his advance. Ismailia was just too large an objective for Sharon's small force.[99]

For the first time in the campaign, the Egyptian MiG fighters moved out of their hangars to launch massive attacks against advancing Israeli tank forces. This last-ditch effort had little effect and broke down completely when the MiG-21s could not hold their own in air-to-air combat with the Israelis.[100] Egypt's military leadership had recognized too late the importance of the crossing site. Magen's division had already crossed the Suez Canal and was moving south, covering Adan's western flank. Israeli tanks were within easy striking distance of Cairo, while Egyptian forces had little with which to stop the Israeli advance toward Suez City on the southern end of the canal.

Until now, Sadat had turned down Soviet offers to negotiate a cease-fire arrangement, but he no longer had any choice in the matter. With the conflict turning decisively against Egypt on 19 October, Sadat reconsidered the earlier Soviet proposal and contacted Prime Minister Alexei Kosygin to discuss a cease-fire arrangement. A short time later, on the same day, 19 October, U.S. secretary of state Henry Kissinger was on his way to Moscow with, as President Richard Nixon phrased it, "full powers" to negotiate a resolution of the crisis.[101]

A U.S.- and Soviet-sponsored cease-fire outlined in United Nations Resolution 338 was supposed to take effect on 22 October at 6:30 p.m., but United Nations (UN) peacekeepers were not yet on hand to supervise it. In view of the peacekeepers' absence, Dayan decided that Israeli forces should continue the attack south and cut the Suez-Cairo road. Still, he cautioned Adan not to seize Suez City (essentially a ghost town after the War of Attrition) unless Adan thought it possible to do so without significant casualties. Adan described the way in which he interpreted his orders: "In order to conquer Suez City—'provided there is no Stalingrad situation'—we thought we would employ the armor technique of bursting in while firing all around in order to produce a shock effect. We believed that a massive aerial bombardment, over a few hours, along with a sustained artillery barrage, would prepare the ground for the armored breakthrough. The cumulative effect of this would, we thought, lead to the surrender of the city."[102]

At 5 a.m., as artillery fire fell on Egyptian positions around and inside Suez City, Adan received an order from Southern Command to cut short the artillery preparation and dispense with the planned airstrike. Southern Command was reportedly concerned that time might run out before the UN observers arrived to enforce the cease-fire. Adan saw no reason not to attack. He saw no evidence that his attack into Suez City would resemble "Stalingrad" and ordered his two brigades to begin their attacks. While one brigade moved on the western side of the city to secure the refineries, another moved down the main boulevard of Cairo into Suez followed by a battalion of paratroopers in armored personnel carriers.

To Adan's astonishment, within a few minutes of entering the city, twenty-four Israeli tank commanders were killed or wounded, and the paratroopers advancing with the tanks came under intense Egyptian fire from the surrounding buildings. The paratroopers who jumped from their armored personnel carriers to take cover in adjacent buildings were now cut off inside the town. Several hours would pass before the concentrated application of Israeli artillery fire and tank support enabled the trapped forces to disengage and withdraw from the city.[103] Tank crews and paratroopers were not trained to cooperate, thorough reconnaissance was not conducted, no rehearsal was held, and the quality of resistance (including the use of rocket-propelled grenades and anti-tank missiles) was grossly underestimated. The outcome was a disaster.

Israeli casualties in the fight for Suez City were approximately 80 killed and 120 wounded. Since Adan had already surrounded the city, thereby cutting off the Egyptian forces still on the Sinai side of the Suez Canal, Israelis who lost sons, brothers, and husbands in the fighting were furious. They could not understand why the attack had ever been launched.[104]

In Moscow's view, the Israelis' undisguised contempt for the UN resolution was totally unacceptable, while Leonid Brezhnev suspected Kissinger was playing for time to improve Israel's strategic position. Brezhnev's suspicions were justified. Kissinger had informed the Israelis that if they required additional time for military dispositions, the United States would understand. Later, when the Israelis launched their offensive against Egypt's Third Army, Kissinger wrote facetiously that "[he] had a sinking feeling that [he] might have emboldened them."[105]

Disturbed by Israeli behavior, Brezhnev informed the White House that if Washington would not work with Moscow to enforce the cease-fire, the Soviets would act alone. He was not bluffing. Brezhnev turned to the Soviet armed forces' most politically reliable force, the seven airborne divisions. These were put on alert while the airlift was assembled to move them. Before the crisis ended, officers in the National Military Command Center were somewhat surprised to discover that the command post for deploying Soviet airborne forces was established in the Caucasus. Seven ships carrying 40,000 Soviet naval infantry also began moving to the Mediterranean.[106]

What happened next was unprecedented in the history of the United States. The Washington Special Action Group, which included Henry Kissinger, General Alexander Haig, Chairman of the Joint Chiefs of Staff Admiral Thomas Moorer, and Secretary of Defense James Schlesinger, issued an alert raising the readiness level of U.S. conventional and strategic forces from Defense Condition (DEFCON) IV to DEFCON III, the highest peacetime stage of military readiness.[107] In addition to the military alert, the group drafted a message for delivery to the Soviet embassy informing Brezhnev that his "suggestion of unilateral action was regarded as a matter of the gravest concern."[108]

The Soviet response to DEFCON III was surprisingly restrained. Brezhnev seems to have concluded that it made no sense to start a war with the United States over Egypt.[109] Simultaneously, Kissinger pressured Tel Aviv to halt offensive operations and sent a message in President Nixon's name to Sadat. In the message, Kissinger asked Sadat to drop his request for Soviet assistance or risk U.S. military intervention. Sadat quickly complied with the request, and the threat of Soviet intervention permanently receded.

The first talks to formalize the cease-fire arrangements between Israeli major general Aharon Yariv, former chief of Israeli intelligence, and Egyptian major general Abdel Ghani el-Gamasy started at 1:30 a.m. on 28 October and lasted for 3 hours.[110] At this point in the war, the Egyptians still held the narrow strip on the Sinai side of the canal. The strip contained an as-yet-undefeated Egyptian force of approximately 70,000 men, 720 tanks, and 994 artillery systems.

To everyone's surprise (including Sadat's), Egyptian forces surrounded in the Sinai maintained their combat integrity, and Second Army's position remained secure on both banks of the Suez Canal.[111] In the frequent absence of firm leadership from above, Egypt's soldiers accomplished Sadat's strategic aim of holding on to the Sinai and inflicting serious losses on Israeli forces. However, it must be said that the timing of superpower intervention rescued 30,000–40,000 troops of Egypt's Third Army from almost certain destruction.[112]

The war that began with a tragic miscalculation on Israel's part ended in victory for Israeli arms. The presence of Sharon's division just outside of Ismailia and Adan's and Magen's divisions controlling Egypt down to the Port of Adabiah left Israel in a position of strategic advantage the Egyptians could not deny.

CONCLUSION

The timely intervention of the United States and the Soviet Union prevented the IDF from encircling and destroying Egyptian forces along the Suez. Israel halted its operations, and in the weeks that followed, the two armies disengaged from their respective positions. What the Israeli government wanted was, in fact, achieved: a secure border with Egypt and the certainty that no further military offensives would be launched from Egyptian soil against Israel. At the same time, Egypt succeeded in regaining its lost territory in Suez and in retrieving its honor on the battlefield. In an event unique in the annals of modern warfare, Egypt and Israel both achieved limited but attainable political-military aims.

As the war in the Sinai drew to a close, a new war erupted inside Israel. For the first time in the country's short history, Israeli generals who were accustomed to being treated as demigods were subject to serious criticism.[113] The IDF's brilliant recovery and counterattack across the Suez received scant attention from an angry and despondent public.

The questions directed at the IDF leaders were endless. Israelis wanted to know why the sudden departure of the Soviet military advisory group from Cairo airport late on the evening of 4 October did not attract more attention.[114] Israeli citizens wanted to know why nothing was done when, two days before the war started, Israeli airborne reconnaissance revealed that Egyptian artillery normally found in rear areas had moved forward together with motorized ferries in the infantry divisions along the Suez Canal.[115] Moshe Dayan later noted, "The prevailing feeling of security, based on the assumption that the Arabs were incapable of mounting an overall war against us distorted our view of the situation."[116] Dayan's statement was true, but it did not satisfy the Israeli public.

Israel's losses in the Yom Kippur War were also much higher than Israelis expected; 2,502 Israelis were killed, 7,251 were wounded, and 297 were taken prisoner. Egyptian losses were on the order of 11,000 killed, 25,000 wounded, and 8,350 prisoners of war, or approximately 7.25 Egyptian casualties for every Israeli casualty. About 60 percent of all Israeli casualties were on the Egyptian front. For a nation of 3 million, these losses were extremely high. If the United States had experienced equivalent losses, 200,000 American soldiers would have been killed.[117]

Arthur Wellesley, the Duke of Wellington, described the battle of Waterloo "as the nearest run thing you ever saw in your life."[118] The same may be said of the Yom Kippur War. From 13 October onward, the arrival of ammunition and spare parts from the United States allowed Israeli ground units to exhaust most of their ammunition without fear of running out of rounds. Without the timely delivery of seventy-five new U.S. fighter aircraft, it is doubtful that the Israeli air force could have sustained wartime operations over Israel, Syria, and Egypt.[119] In point of fact, Israeli forces prevailed in 1973 because Israeli officers did not *send* their men into battle; they *led* them into battle. Senior commanders routinely went to the points on the ground where the action was critical and ensured the Israeli fighting forces received the resources they needed to be successful.[120] In the Egyptian military such behavior was the exception, not the rule.

While Israeli commissions met to assign blame for the war's early missteps, Israelis did not fully appreciate the IDF's substantial margin of victory in terms of organization, technology, and human capital that had reversed the disasters during the first ten days of the Sinai campaign and eventually secured battlefield victory. Israel's unified military command structure with supporting general staff ensured that the two-front war did not overtax Israel's military resources. The Israeli high command's strategic decision to hold first in the Sinai while Syria's offensive was halted and then destroyed took advantage of Egypt's planned halt. When circumstances demanded it, the IDF's highly trained and educated officers and men made it possible to rapidly reorganize and reequip with new aircraft and tanks before resuming the offensive against Egypt. These actions constituted a margin of victory that Egyptians could not match.

Meanwhile, the Israeli armed forces underwent a dramatic expansion and technological makeover.[121] Tank and artillery systems were modernized and increased in number, while infantry became fully mechanized, replacing the IDF's antiquated and inadequately protected World War II–era halftracks with M113 series vehicles.

The number of armor brigades increased from 11 in 1973 to 33 in 1982 due to a commensurate increase in tanks from 1,225 in 1973 to 3,800 in 1982. Tanks were also outfitted with 60-millimeter mortars, an innovation designed to immediately suppress anti-tank guided missiles with smoke and high explosive rounds. In the air, Israeli aircraft were outfitted with the newest electronic countermeasures, and modern command and control systems were introduced. At sea, Israel invested heavily in submarines and fast attack boats armed with missiles and torpedoes.[122]

Today, the IDF is on a different path to reform, one that focuses primarily on immediate threats rather than on possible future threats in five, ten, or fifteen years. Although stopping short of terminating universal service, Israel's parliament, the Knesset, approved a dramatic military restructuring plan in 2013 that shifted investment in the IDF away from armored formations in favor of Israeli airpower, intelligence collection, and cyber warfare.[123] With its funding increased, the air force set out to build the capacity to support a tenfold increase in the number of targets it can detect and destroy.[124]

This approach is once again under review by a new chief of staff. The reason is that the emerging force mix is unlikely to stop a barrage of rockets and missiles with airstrikes alone.[125] Target sets also do not automatically equate to strategy or influence. Recent IDF operations in Gaza would seem to reinforce this conclusion.[126]

Converting the Israeli army into a light force of riflemen (dismounted or on wheels) that depends on airstrikes for survival and effectiveness is perilous. From southern Lebanon, Hizballah can fire rockets (and, from protected positions, missiles) for six months without pausing. Surface-to-surface ballistic missiles and barrage rockets may be countered at great cost with current and future missile defense systems, but these systems cannot provide seamless or perfect protection. The penetration of a few projectiles will always create severe damage and casualties in densely packed civilian population centers.

These carefully concealed sites are also notoriously hard to target. Only the decisive use of mobile armored forces in offensive maneuver operations, combined with the striking power of the Israeli air force and high-angle mortar, artillery, and rocket fire, will first pin down and then fix these mobile targets for armor and infantry to finish them off. Effective maneuver forces do not emerge overnight. Likewise, the Israeli army that fought and defeated Egypt and Syria emerged over the course of many decades. Israelis should keep these points in mind as they ponder future changes in the IDF's organization and capabilities. Israel's experience in a series of wars has repeatedly taught the critical lesson that "one size does not fit all"—diversity of capability is vital to success.

For Israel and the West, the good news is that Sunni and Shi'ite Islamist forces are engaged in a bloody struggle for dominance across the Middle East, a struggle that is likely to last for years if not decades. Yet regardless of which alliance of states and peoples emerges to dominate the Middle East, Israelis know there can be no enduring regional stability until its Muslim Arab neighbors recognize the State of Israel within its current borders and halt their efforts to diplomatically undermine and militarily threaten Israel.

Russia's sudden move into Syria in August and September of 2015 changed the potential outcome of the Middle East's ongoing conflict and added new complexity to Israeli security. If the Shi'ites prevail with Russia's help, Iran and its allies in Damascus and Baghdad will maintain a "Shi'ite Crescent" tightly tied to Russia, increasing the likelihood of more sophisticated weapons reaching Hizballah. If the Sunni Arabs and Turks prevail, the outcome puts the Kaliphate or a Sunni Islamist Front allied with Turkey and Saudi Arabia (and, more distantly, Pakistan) on Israel's Golan frontier. In this case, the implications for instability in Jordan and Egypt with consequences for Israel are profound.[127]

It is much too early to tell which alliance of states and peoples will be dominant in the Middle East. But unless Turkey follows Egypt into a secularist reaction against Islamism, Sunni Islamists may yet outlast Russian influence and prevail in the region over Shi'ite Iran, making an advanced conventional war more likely.[128] Turkey is the one Muslim nation in the region with the cohesion, culture, economic strength, and military power to lead the region's Sunni Arab states in an armed confrontation with Israel.[129]

As has occurred in Russia, Iran, and China, Turkish president Recep Tayyip Erdogan is reducing the legislative branch to a forum for debate and a vehicle for assessing public opinion. Real decisionmaking power increasingly rests with him. As a committed Sunni Islamist, Erdogan has no interest in destroying the Kaliphate since its principal aim is the destruction of the Shi'ite presence in the Middle East. He is far more determined to crush Kurdish opposition because he sees the Kurds as the principal threat to Turkish security and as a potential ally of Iran and its Shi'ite partners in Iraq and Syria. How Erdogan's policies will play out in the shadow of Russian military power in Syria and on Turkey's Caucasian border is impossible to predict.[130]

From its inception, Israel has fought and defeated a host of nonstate actors, from Nasser's *Fedayeen* terrorists to the Palestine Liberation Organization, but the advent of new regional alliances, Shi'ite or Sunni, resurrects the specter of advanced conventional warfare. Turkey's growing power and contempt for the West and Israel should be kept in mind.[131] It would be unwise for Israel's contemporary leaders to dismiss such a development by betting heavily on perfect intelligence and flawless airstrikes, which would ignore the Israeli army's need for accurate, devastating firepower from tracked armored platforms. Quincy Wright noted the impact of unanticipated adjustments in international relations some years ago: "A single unexpected change in international relations, such as that of the Soviet-German pact in 1939, had an influence on many relations in a way which this method [quantitative analysis and conventional wisdom] could not foresee."[132]

From the vantage point of Egyptians, Anwar Sadat's clever diplomacy underpinned by the performance of his courageous soldiers set the stage for a negotiated peace between Egypt and Israel that eventually returned control of the Suez Canal and the Sinai to Egypt. Sadat's achievement redeemed Egypt's honor and created the idea in Egyptians' minds that their war was in fact a victory for Egypt. The resulting agreements ended years of destructive conflict between Egypt and Israel and continue to provide the basis for mutually beneficial security cooperation in the Sinai.

Egypt is once again mired in crisis with cultural and economic problems that are even more profound than they were in Sadat's time. Corruption in Egypt's national and provincial governments, not to mention the police and security organs, is pervasive. Disputes over "turf" and shares of income from bribery, extortion, and smuggling are commonplace, and these features of Egyptian life are unlikely to change. These are some of the reasons why the removal of Hosni Mubarak from power was not going to create instant prosperity or accelerate Egyptian political development in the direction of a secular, pluralistic, social democracy.

For the moment, the Egyptian army has succeeded in arresting Egypt's slide into chaos by halting the Islamists' use of democratic action to supplant Egypt's moderate, secular order with a political system that subjugates the population to Islamist principles. How long this condition will last is impossible to know.

How the Egyptian military leadership and the government it backs will cope with a population projected to grow over the next ten years at the speed of one million people a year is also a mystery. What can be said with certainty is that unless Egyptian and Arab society in general change in fundamental ways, whatever the courage or proficiency of individual Arab officers and soldiers, the armed forces of the Arab world are unlikely to acquire the capabilities required for success in war with Israel or the West.[133]

CHAPTER 5

LOST VICTORY

Desert Storm and the Battle of 73 Easting, 1991

On 2 August 1990, Iraq's armed forces invaded the small, oil-rich state of Kuwait. Just as the Israelis had been taken by surprise on 6 October 1973, Iraq's invasion and occupation of Kuwait caught the White House flat-footed. Intelligence reports concerning the Iraqi troop buildup in southern Iraq had reached the White House, but the size and suddenness of the Iraqi offensive were totally unexpected.[1] Without any significant forces in the region, not even a regional forward command post, Gen. H. Norman Schwarzkopf, USA, Central Command (CENTCOM) commander-in-chief, had few immediate options.[2]

Fortunately for the United States, Saddam Hussein did not exploit his victory in Kuwait and continue his attack to seize Saudi Arabia's oil fields. His profound strategic error put time on the side of the United States, and when the buildup of American and coalition military power began in Saudi Arabia, Saddam's failure to launch preemptive strikes with the substantial theater ballistic missiles and aircraft at his command was fatal.

American military power resides primarily in the continental United States, from which it must launch thousands of miles to reach opponents. In 1990, America's unchallenged maritime supremacy permitted the United States to marshal its capabilities and those of its allies to create a massive local superiority in forces and matériel. By November 1991, the buildup of forces in Saudi Arabia and the Persian Gulf encouraged Schwarzkopf to tell his generals before the attack to "pin [the Iraqi Republican Guard] with their backs against the sea, then, go in and wipe them out. . . . Once they're gone *be prepared to continue the attack to Baghdad* [emphasis in original]."[3]

From the moment the U.S. Air Force obliterated Iraq's air defenses and established unchallenged U.S. and coalition air supremacy over the Kuwait theater of operations, the outcome of the 1991 Persian Gulf War was decided. From 20 January onward, a U.S.-led ground offensive around the open desert flank of Iraq's static defenses in Kuwait was unstoppable. Any Iraqi attempt to maneuver or concentrate ground forces risked immediate and shattering air attack, but the United States ignored this critical strategic advantage.

Instead, each service—Army, Air Force, Navy, and Marine Corps—was allowed to fight its own war, attacking the way it preferred to fight.[4] In contrast to what Japanese, German, Russian, and Israeli commanders would have done—violently exploit unchallenged air supremacy—Schwarzkopf and his commanders mimicked the World War I British offensive on the Somme in November 1916, a lengthy, concentrated artillery bombardment of the enemy's defenses followed by a slow, deliberate attack by Army, Marine, British, and coalition forces on line.

American and coalition casualties were negligible, but when the shooting stopped, 700 tanks and 1,430 armored fighting vehicles of Iraq's force in Kuwait and southern Iraq along with most of the 80,000 troops in the Republican Guard Corps had already escaped destruction.[5] America's undeclared war with Iraq dragged on.

Nevertheless, the 1991 Gulf War provided a fleeting glimpse of twenty-first-century warfare; Schwarzkopf directed global military power to the points in time and space he regarded as critical to the campaign's success, confronting Iraq with a new form of multi-dimensional, strategic envelopment unprecedented in twentieth-century warfare. After Desert Storm, there was real potential to move beyond single-service, industrial-age warfare, to build highly mobile, joint, integrated, aerospace, and sensor-dominated forces with extraordinarily accurate and devastating striking power—forces capable of achieving precise effects rapidly and simultaneously. Many of these effects came together in the Battle of 73 Easting on 26 February 1991, a lost victory that showcased the dramatic advances in the American way of war at the end of the twentieth century.

PREWAR DEVELOPMENTS IN IRAQ

Saddam Hussein's rationale for invading and occupying Kuwait involved more than control of Kuwait's oil and the wealth it would give him. He also seems to have coveted the leading role in the Arab world, a job up for grabs after Egypt's peace agreement with Israel. Saddam had no intention of ceding leadership of the Arab world to his only rival for the position, Syrian president Hafez Assad.[6] At the same time, Saddam assumed Washington would not interfere with his seizure of Kuwait, and he discounted the impact of American military superiority if it did get involved.[7]

Saddam Hussein was not an educated man. Like Stalin in Russia, he spent much of his life clawing his way out of a dysfunctional childhood, then climbing to the top of the Baathist Party apparatus using the tools available to him: murder and intimidation.[8] Yet unlike Stalin, Saddam made no attempt to learn about the world beyond Iraq. Before meeting French prime minister Jacques Chirac in Baghdad in December 1974, Saddam never seriously considered traveling outside of the Middle East. However, after the delivery in 1976 of a French nuclear reactor (which was later destroyed by the Israelis in June 1981), he decided to visit Paris, his only trip to the West.[9] Not much is known about the trip, but Saddam does not seem to have learned much about the West or its ties to the Anglo-American oil protectorates in the Persian Gulf.

In 1980, with Iran still in the grip of Ayatollah Ruhollah Khomeini's revolutionary confusion and disorder, Saddam concluded he could overwhelm Iran's weakened armed forces. In the last week of September 1980, he launched a surprise offensive against Iran, using most of his 200,000 troops, 2,000 tanks, and 450 aircraft in an attack to seize Iran's oil fields in Khuzestan. For Saddam, war with a weak Iran was an opportunity to reenact the battle of al-Qadisiyya, the victory in 636 AD of a numerically inferior Muslim Arab army over a decayed Sassanid Persian army that produced the Muslim conquest of Iraq and, eventually, all of Persia.

Initially, Saddam's forces made some progress, but his army moved slowly and captured little territory. Like the Egyptian army of 1973, his lavishly equipped Arab army was incapable of rapid, decisive offensive operations. Its relatively modern Soviet tanks were indisputably better than Iran's older Challenger tanks of British manufacture, but the underlying cultural foundation for initiative, creativity, and independent action simply did not exist inside Iraq's army.[10]

Contrary to Saddam's expectation, less than two years after Iraq's invasion began, Iranian forces not only fought Iraq's army to a standstill, they also launched massive offensive operations, expelling the Iraqi army from Iranian soil.[11] For a time, the Iranian revolution seemed like it might reach into Iraq to install a new Shi'ite Islamist regime in Baghdad and expand its power into the Arabian Peninsula.

From Washington's perspective, Iran's ferocious counterattacks into Iraq looked disturbingly similar to the Bolshevik attack on Poland in 1920, an offensive that Vladimir Lenin and Leon Trotsky hoped would open the path to Berlin for the Red Army. Without realizing it, Khomeini's resolve to punish Iraq for its unprovoked attack on Iranian territory and to reintegrate

Shi'ite Iraq into greater Persia transformed a small, interstate war between two historic rivals into a regional military contest of strategic dimensions. Secretary of State George Shultz concluded that America faced a new threat, one potentially more dangerous and troublesome than the Soviet presence in Afghanistan: the exportation at gunpoint of Iran's anti-Western Islamic fundamentalism to the rest of the Middle East.[12]

When Iranian forces seemed poised to penetrate Iraq's defensive lines in 1984, President Ronald Reagan signed a national security directive authorizing intelligence sharing with Iraq. This included satellite photography and communications intercepts, advantages analysts subsequently described as having rescued the Iraqi army from near-annihilation in several key battles with the Iranians.[13] Based on the assumption that Iraq's dependence on external trade, particularly the importation of food from the United States, could be used to control Saddam Hussein's behavior, the Reagan administration opted to ignore the illegal transfer of U.S. weapons from third-party countries to Iraq. The arms transfers provided a significant boost to the Iraqi army's defensive capability. The arms and armaments included tube-launched, optically tracked, wire-guided (TOW) anti-tank missiles, helicopters, small arms, mortars, and munitions, primarily from neighboring countries such as Egypt, Jordan, Kuwait, and Saudi Arabia. The United States also turned a blind eye to the supply of materials and technology from German manufacturers that was eventually used in the production and employment of chemical weapons against Iran.[14]

In retrospect, the Reagan administration overestimated Tehran's military potential. Iran's armed forces, including both the remnants of the shah's regular army and the revolutionary masses that made up the Iranian militias, were never capable of delivering the killing blow that Khomeini's strategy demanded. Composed primarily of dismounted infantrymen with a few tanks in support, Iran's offensives relied heavily on human wave attacks that had little chance of success against Iraqi defenses based on tanks integrated with mines, barbed wire, and artillery fire.

Iraq's ground troops inflicted huge casualties on Iran's assaults, but both sides suffered heavy losses. By 1988, as many as 1 million had died, but the war ended in stalemate.[15] Neither side profited from the experience; Iran's oil-rich Khuzestan province and economically prosperous Basra in Iraq were destroyed, ruining both economies. Confronted with Iraq's grim economic condition, Saddam looked westward in search of the fiscal means for postwar reconstruction. Eventually his eye fell on Kuwait, a wealthy emirate with little or no defensive capability.

With the restoration of peace, Saddam began to examine the use of air and naval forces in the future as a way to reduce the cost of fighting on land. He became enamored with mobile theater ballistic missiles, weapons that had played a major role in what the Iraqis called "the Battle of the Cities," but he also clung to his irrationally inflated view of the Iraqi soldier's fighting power.[16] To Saddam, the number of casualties sustained by the Iraqi army in its battles with Iranian forces was a measure of Iraqi courage, strength, and effectiveness in battle.[17]

Saddam never understood that it was Iran's lack of mobile armored firepower and its reliance on masses of infantrymen, not the courage or skill of Iraq's soldiers, that had prevented Iran from exploiting its penetrations into Iraqi defenses.[18] The fact that Iraq's Arab soldiers could defend their positions within the rigid framework of rehearsed defensive tactics obscured the reality that Iraqi soldiers and officers lacked initiative and flexibility.[19] Iraq's soldiers were not comparable to the Turkish soldiers of World War I, men determined to return home as victorious *Gazis* (Muslim warriors) or to die as *Sehits* (martyrs) and go directly to Paradise.[20]

Telling Saddam the truth was always risky. The few Iraqi army officers who studied German and Israeli military operations discovered it was best to say nothing to their superiors, and they adopted this mindset toward Saddam. A display of too much professional understanding might offend Saddam and lead to summary execution.[21] Like Adolf Hitler, who obsessed over the numbers of divisions he had (however hollow they became in the last year of World War II), Saddam delighted in boasting about the Iraqi army's fifty-six divisions or nearly 1 million men. Like the Nationalist Chinese Army in 1937, the true condition and capabilities of the Iraqi armed forces were not nearly as impressive as the numbers suggested.

On the ground, Iraqi army units were loosely organized on the original British army model adopted between 1922 and 1945, but brigades and divisions were unevenly equipped and only superficially trained. Iraq's tank holdings, for instance, still included Chinese and Soviet tanks from the 1960s. Very few Iraqi tank units were equipped with night vision, modern range finders, or advanced stabilization technology, and training was poor. According to Israeli sources, very few Iraqi tank crews could hit targets beyond a thousand yards, and could only do that if the targets were stationary.[22] To make matters worse, Iraq's soldiers had to be conscripted into the army against their will. The staggering losses experienced during Iraq's war with Iran decidedly dampened Iraqi enthusiasm for another war.[23]

After the Iran-Iraq War, the Republican Guard formations, a 12-division force of nearly 100,000 men, became Saddam's Praetorian Guard. Saddam personally selected the best and most politically reliable army officers to command Republican Guard formations.[24] In contrast to the Iraqi army's older equipment, the Republican Guard divisions were provided 1970s vintage Soviet T-72s, BMPs (*boyevaya mashina pekhoty*, or infantry fighting vehicle), and ZSU 23–4 air defense guns. Before he invaded Kuwait, Saddam added six paramilitary divisions to the Republican Guard Corps. During the invasion and occupation of Kuwait, these units remained inside Iraq to preserve order and ensure Saddam's Stalinesque grip on Iraq's population. He harbored no illusions about his regime's dependence on coercion for survival.

Iraqi air defenses looked formidable, but they were not integrated to the degree that would present an impenetrable barrier to American air forces. By Western commercial air standards, Iraqi air force pilots did not fly enough hours in monthly training to be declared safe. When the United States and its coalition partners attacked Iraq from the air on 17 January 1991, Saddam was surprised by the damage, but he still expected his army and especially the Republican Guard to triumph over American military power. His illusion died hard.

After forty days of air strikes and less than twenty-four hours of ground attack, Saddam's army crumbled much like the Egyptian and Syrian armies of 1967 did, with Iraqi soldiers defending southern Kuwait surrendering in droves.[25] Only the Republican Guard Corps deployed in southern Iraq, far from Kuwait's border with Saudi Arabia, remained intact and capable of presenting resistance.

During the evening of 25 February 1991, Saddam decided to preserve as much of the Republican Guard Corps as he could. He ordered Republican Guard commander General Ayad Futayih al-Rawi to abandon Kuwait and move as much of his force over the Euphrates as the confusion and chaos in Kuwait would allow.[26] To cover the withdrawal of his force and slow the advance of attacking U.S. ground forces, al-Rawi created a rear guard comprising Iraq's Republican Guard Tawakalna Division and supporting Iraqi army units.

PREWAR U.S. MILITARY DEVELOPMENTS

President George H. W. Bush had long felt that it was in the vital national security interest to secure a permanent military presence in the Persian Gulf, ostensibly to protect the then-vital flow of oil to the United States and its allies in Europe and Asia.[27] President Bush's speech to the American people on 16 January 1991 reflected this view, but his words also suggested that his decision to fight Iraq was about more than merely ejecting Saddam Hussein from Kuwait: "When we are successful, and we will be, we have a real chance at this new world order, an order in which a credible United Nations can use its peacekeeping role to fulfil the promise and vision of the UN's founders."[28]

For President Bush, Operation Desert Storm was more than a war to remove a menacing Arab dictator. It was a neo-Wilsonian moment, a fresh opportunity for the world's only superpower to reshape the world in liberal democratic terms.[29] President Bush's national security adviser, Lt. Gen. Brent Scowcroft, USAF (Ret.), was more sober-minded: "If Saddam withdraws with most of his forces intact, we haven't really won."[30]

Schwarzkopf agreed in principle with the president and his White House advisers, but in the fall of 1990 he remained unconvinced that he could dislodge the Iraqi army from Kuwait with only the XVIII Airborne Corps and the Marines. U.S. intelligence reported that Iraq would defend Kuwait with 540,000 troops, more than 4,200 tanks, 2,800 armored personnel carriers, and approximately 3,100 artillery systems. Iraq's forces also possessed more than 700 combat aircraft and a multilayered air defense system, a navy of missile-firing patrol boats, and Chinese manufactured Silkworm surface-to-surface missiles for coastal defense.[31]

To Schwarzkopf, the numbers were troubling. His comment that "nobody wanted another Vietnam" resonated strongly with his generals in CENTCOM and Washington.[32] None had seen significant action since the Vietnam War, and none had ever maneuvered large mobile, armored forces in a fluid battlefield environment. It was clear that few, if any, relished the opportunity now.[33]

One reason for the generals' apprehension was their collective ignorance of the Middle East. Not only was the geography of the Middle East totally unlike that of Southeast Asia, but also the Arab opponent was different from the North Vietnamese opponent. Another reason was the tendency to misjudge just how much the character and the composition of the Army had changed since the end of the Vietnam War.[34]

It was true that Army ground forces were still organized in 1991 as they were in 1942, inside Gen. Lesley McNair's triangular divisions, but in the years after Vietnam the Army had radically reformed its institutional training with advanced collective training facilities. Impressed by the increased lethality of armored fighting systems demonstrated in the 1973 Yom Kippur

War, Gen. William E. Depuy and Gen. Paul F. Gorman adjusted the emphasis in Army training from winning battles to specifically winning the first battle of the next war.

For the first time, the Army specified missions, tasks, conditions, and standards that were to be met by individual units in routine training exercises. As a result, a very high state of training was institutionalized across the force through the Joint Readiness Training Center at Fort Chaffee, Arkansas, the National Training Center at Fort Irwin, California, and the Combat Maneuver Training Center at Hohenfels, Germany.[35]

In the aftermath of Vietnam, the Army also altered its parameters of modernization, equipping its World War II organization for combat with the most lethal and capable warfighting equipment in Army history. The modernization wave that began in the immediate post-Vietnam era reached a high point in 1983 with the arrival of the heavily armored M1A1 Abrams Main Battle Tank (MBT) with 120-millimeter (mm) smooth bore cannon, a precision weapon system with a laser range finder that fired a depleted uranium warhead at one mile per second out to ranges of three thousand meters.

In addition to the M1A1 MBT, the Army also fielded the Bradley fighting vehicle (BFV) with 25-mm cannon and TOW anti-tank missile, the AH64 Apache attack helicopter, and the Army Tactical Missile System, the longest-range surface-to-surface missile in the Army inventory, along with its companion, the Multiple Launch Rocket System. The Army also had recently introduced the Joint Surveillance Target Attack Radar System (JSTARS), a new technology that promised to greatly improve the senior commanders' view of the battlefield.[36]

Thanks to the hard work begun in the 1970s, the Army in 1991 was a muscular, well-oiled machine designed to fight and defeat Soviet ground forces in Central Europe within the framework of the AirLand Battle doctrine, a concerted effort to coordinate aggressive maneuver on the ground with deep attack by the Air Force.[37] The Army's soldiers, sergeants, lieutenants, and captains were aggressive, intelligent, highly trained professionals, especially in the combat formations that would spearhead the attacks into Iraq.[38] Unlike the senior officers who commanded them, they were also eager to fight.

Schwarzkopf's attitude toward the war with Iraq changed substantially after Bush unhesitatingly granted his request for deployment of VII Corps, a force of 110,000 troops with thousands of the newest tanks, armored fighting vehicles, artillery systems, and attack helicopters, from Germany to the Persian Gulf.[39] When he presented his plan of attack to an assembly of division

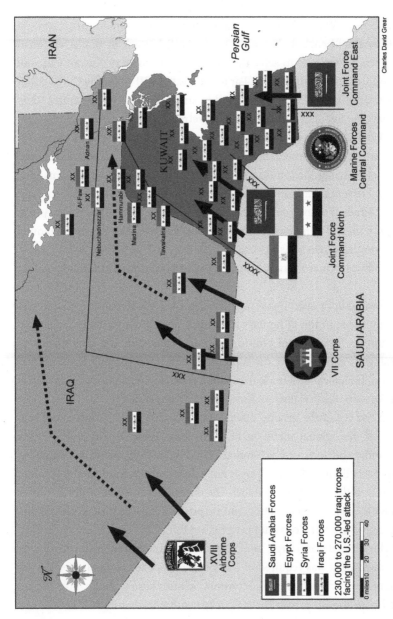

MAP 12. Gen. Norman Schwarzkopf's Battle Plan

Charles David Grear

and corps commanders on 14 November, Schwarzkopf was noticeably more confident and animated than he was in the early fall of 1990.

Schwarzkopf talked enthusiastically about his new plan to go around the flank of Iraqi defenses in southern Kuwait rather than through them (see map 12). Along the Saudi-Kuwaiti border near the Gulf coast, 110,000 Marines under Lt. Gen. Walter Boomer and a Saudi task force were to thrust straight into Kuwait and encircle Kuwait City. A parallel attack by pan-Arab forces in western Kuwait was to seize the road junction north of Kuwait City and block Iraqi routes of withdrawal. Far to the west, XVIII Airborne Corps under Lt. Gen. Gary Luck, USA, was ordered to strike deep to the Euphrates River and block the Republican Guard's line of retreat.[40]

Yet the centerpiece of Schwarzkopf's plan was his "Hail Mary" play: VII Corps' attack around the flank of Iraqi forces in Kuwait. Schwarzkopf made a point of stressing the importance of VII Corps' mission to its commander, Lt. Gen. Frederick M. Franks: "We need to destroy—not attack, not damage, not surround—I want you to destroy the Republican Guard. When you're done with them, I don't want them to be an effective fighting force anymore. I don't want them to exist as a military organization."[41] In Schwarzkopf's mind, the Republican Guard was Saddam Hussein's power base, his true "center of gravity."

Schwarzkopf's operational intent to eliminate the Republican Guard was explicitly stated in the 17 January 1991 operations order to the U.S. and coalition forces: "Attack Iraqi political-military leadership and command and control; gain and maintain air superiority; sever Iraqi supply lines, destroy chemical, biological and nuclear capability; *destroy Republican Guard forces in the Kuwaiti Theater*; liberate Kuwait" (emphasis added).[42]

On the eve of the ground offensive in February 1991, Schwarzkopf reiterated his operational intent to Lt. Gen. John Yeosock, Third U.S. Army commander and, technically, General Franks' boss: "I do not want a slow ponderous pachyderm mentality. This is not a deliberate attack. I want VII Corps to slam into the Republican Guard. The enemy is not worth a shit. Go after them with audacity, shock action and surprise.... Let me make it clear, John. You cannot have VII Corps stopping for anything."[43]

Schwarzkopf was a large, loud man who screamed at subordinates, but he understood what was required of VII Corps: a race to the Euphrates leaving a trail of destruction behind it. However, Schwarzkopf's combustible temper made his relationship with the VII Corps commander difficult. Franks was a diminutive figure with snow-white hair, slow in speech and extremely cautious in his approach to everything.[44] Like Schwarzkopf and most others of his generation, Franks surrounded himself with officers who reinforced his beliefs. In Franks' opinion, the three U.S. Army armored divisions and one British armored division Schwarzkopf gave him for the mission of destroying the Republican Guard were not enough.[45] Though he did not specifically say so, Franks' experience in Vietnam suggested he was acutely sensitive to the Third Army's grim forecast that VII Corps would take 20,000 casualties in the first 5 days of fighting the Iraqi army.[46]

In view of his cautious nature, Franks focused on wheeling his 3 enormous 18,000- to 22,000-man divisions on line and then concentrating them into what he called his "clenched fist" for a decisive blow upon reaching the Republican Guard Corps. Traffic control and density of force dominated this thinking. The option of organizing VII Corps for speed and of exploiting U.S. air supremacy, leaving unneeded equipment (especially much of the corps' heavy artillery and superfluous baggage) behind, was absent from his mind. Franks never seems to have considered putting brigades of armor in column behind the VII Corps cavalry advance guard and driving rapidly north toward the Euphrates River.[47]

The possibility that Iraqi troops might lack the stomach for a real fight, or the historical fact that no Arab army had defeated a European force in the previous 500 years, did not enter into Franks' calculus.[48] As late as 21 February, 2 days before the ground offensive began, he wanted 500,000 hand grenades. Schwarzkopf's deputy Gen. Cal Waller was shocked: "Why do you need 35,000 TOW rounds? And hand grenades? This is a mobile armored corps. Where are you going to close with the enemy so that every man in the corps needs five hand grenades? Who in the hell are you going to throw them at?"[49]

THE VIEW FROM THE AIR

Airmen viewed the prospect of war with Iraq through a different lens. Air Force chief of staff Gen. Merrill McPeak knew the Cold War had transformed his service into the world's most technologically sophisticated and potent mix of bombers, fighters, and fighter-bombers, a force Iraq had no chance of defeating. On 17 January 1991, he had one thousand operational F-15C, F-15E, F-16, F-4G, F-111, A-10, and B-52 aircraft based in and around Saudi Arabia.[50] In his view, the combination of high-altitude attack and the employment of precision guided munitions meant that the Air Force could strike with impunity to destroy more targets with fewer munitions, a capability that would magnify the striking power of American airpower on an undreamt-of scale.

McPeak sensed that Iraq's armed forces were weak. He was convinced that Bush's decision on 8 November 1990 to double the size of American ground forces was based on the Army generals' misguided fear of Iraqi military power, and he said so to Chairman of the Joint Chiefs of Staff

General Colin Powell. Powell was not sympathetic; like Schwarzkopf and Franks, Powell did not understand what he could not physically count. In Powell's mind, the Vietnam War had been lost because of "too few boots on the ground."[51] In Powell's mind, as well as in the minds of his Army peers, overwhelming force meant overwhelming numbers.

McPeak dropped the matter, but he and his officers in CENTCOM continued to view the war with Iraq as a fresh opportunity for airpower to validate two cherished principles with their roots in World War II. The first was that airpower is most effective when applied in a comprehensive, unitary way by the joint force air component commander, who in 1991 was Lt. Gen. Charles "Chuck" Horner, USAF.[52] The second was that precision strikes from the air would paralyze and terrorize the Iraqi state, conditions that would lead to the collapse of resistance without the use of ground forces.[53]

To direct centralized air operations, Horner needed a communication system that patched together Air Force, Navy, Marine Corps, and coalition air force pilots with senior commanders in Saudi Arabia and the White House. Without such a network, Horner could not transmit the air tasking order, which provided detailed targeting directions while coordinating weather forecasts, intelligence assessments, airborne surveillance operations (Airborne Warning and Control Systems and JSTAR assets), and bomb damage assessments.[54] In August 1990, the necessary command and control (C2) structure did not exist.

Meanwhile, Horner had to contend with Army and Marine Corps ground commanders who distrusted his centralized control of airpower. Horner, a distinguished "Wild Weasel" pilot in the Vietnam War, was unflappable and persisted in his argument for centralized authority.[55] Ultimately, Schwarzkopf backed Horner's demand for the centralized control of airpower. Horner received the C2 network he needed, along with a massive influx of the equipment with supporting electronics and expertise required to plan and execute the air campaign. Thanks to these developments, including the abundance of aircraft, airfields, and tankers as well as the Iraqi military's inability to interfere with U.S. and coalition operations on the ground in Saudi Arabia or with the U.S. Navy's six carrier battle groups at sea, Horner was able to run the air war as he wished and still accommodate all service points of view on the priorities of the air campaign.[56]

Past attempts to bring enemy nation-states to their knees with airpower alone had failed, but in 1991, the Air Force's faith in precision, stealth, and superior targeting inspired by Col. John Warden's concept of strategic air warfare promised a better outcome. Warden's thinking rested on the assumption that "at the strategic and operational levels, inducing the enemy to make the desired concessions requires identification and attack of those parts of the enemy state and military structure which are most essential to his ability and desire to wage war."[57]

Horner modified Colonel Warden's original blueprint for the air campaign, but Warden's insistence on linking target selection for air strikes to the desired political-military end state survived to shape the conduct of the air campaign.[58] In broad outline, the plan was an amalgamation of Schwarzkopf's operational intent, Warden's strategic inspiration, and Horner's vision of a four-phased plan.[59] Phase I was a strategic air campaign against Iraq, with Iraqi air defenses, leadership, power, and oil the target sets. Phase II was an air campaign against Iraqi air forces in Kuwait. Phase III consisted of attrition of Iraq's ground force to neutralize the Republican Guard and isolate the Kuwait battlefield. Finally, phase IV would be a ground attack to eject Iraqi forces from Kuwait.

As is often the case with any military operation, only the first 2 to 3 days of the air campaign were planned in any detail.[60] Contact with the enemy changes things. In the days that followed, target selection was determined by the damage done to the high-priority targets in the first 48 to 72 hours. Yet after 3 days of air operations and the loss of several coalition aircraft, Horner felt compelled to restrict all future bombing missions to medium altitude, or 10,000 to 15,000 feet above the reach of Iraq's anti-aircraft artillery and infrared surface-to-air missiles. The restriction increased aircraft survivability and reduced losses but allegedly at the expense of bombing accuracy.[61]

These points aside, once Horner launched the air campaign, McPeak's perception of Iraqi weakness was validated. Iraq's air defenses were shattered in the first two days, and Iraq lost fourteen aircraft to coalition fighters in air-to-air combat during the first week of the air war. The Iraqi air force presented no real challenge to U.S. and coalition air forces.

In one 24-hour period, more targets inside Iraq were struck by U.S. and coalition air forces than by the Eighth Air Force in Europe during 1942 and 1943.[62] In 40 days of continuous operations, U.S. and coalition aircraft flew over 100,000 sorties, dropping 88,500 tons of bombs and inflicting serious damage on Iraqi military and civilian infrastructure as well as ground forces.[63] U.S. and coalition air supremacy was absolute.

Air strikes were conducted across the breadth and depth of Iraq simultaneously and in parallel, not executed in the sequential manner of previous campaigns. It was also the first time in the twentieth century that a unified, joint approach in the conduct of air operations was applied. It did not matter which service or country "owned" the aircraft; the air campaign plan was assembled on the basis of capability required to hit the target and achieve a particular effect.

Between 28 and 31 January, airpower also played a decisive role in the ground fight for Khafji, a small town inside Saudi Arabia near the border with Kuwait. Coalition air forces delivered 262 individual air strikes in 2 days, effectively annihilating Iraqi ground forces that tried to attack into Saudi Arabia. On 30 January, F/A-18s dropped 100 MK-83 1,000-pound bombs on Iraqi forces assembling for the attack, the largest bomb tonnage carried in a single naval mission. Only one U.S. aircraft was lost to an Iraqi shoulder-fired air defense missile, a Special Operations AC-130H along with its crew of 14.[64]

In spite of these noteworthy achievements and modest losses, the forty-day air campaign did not attain Warden's desired end state. Iraqi command and control was neither broken nor permanently paralyzed. McPeak's fervent hope that airpower would at last defeat an army in the field without the use of attacking ground forces did not materialize.[65] Despite the use of every type of strike and reconnaissance aircraft, the hunt for mobile missile launchers achieved little, if any, success.[66]

During Desert Storm, the Iraqis fired 88 Al Hussein theater ballistic missiles (more commonly known as SCUDs), including 1 in the direction of the Saudi Arabian port of Al Jubayl. This particular missile struck early in the morning of 16 February 1991, approximately 150 meters from the port and less than 400 yards from the USS *Tarawa*, which had arrived only 13 hours earlier with 2,000 Marines. The SCUD's warhead failed to detonate, but the attack confirmed that despite the punishing air campaign, Iraq's command structure was still acting effectively on intelligence received from agents in Saudi Arabia.[67]

The amount of damage the air campaign actually inflicted on Iraqi ground forces before the U.S. and coalition ground war began is still a contentious issue. Iraqi army divisions, especially those in the front lines in southern Kuwait, were understrength by roughly 120,000 troops when they first established defensive positions along the border with Saudi Arabia. After Kuwait's occupation began in August 1990, Iraqi policy allowed frequent leaves, meaning that a large number of soldiers, absent when the air campaign began, never rejoined their units. Applying these decrements to the original Defense

Intelligence Agency estimate produces a revised estimate of no more than 250,000 to 300,000 Iraqi troops in the theater on 17 January 1991, or at least 240,000 fewer troops than originally claimed by U.S. intelligence sources.[68]

Nevertheless, the air campaign unquestionably achieved Schwarzkopf's desired end state.[69] As far as Schwarzkopf was concerned, airpower was really a new, more lethal form of long-range artillery that could be used to wear down the opposing force in preparation for his ground assault.[70] After all, Schwarzkopf was a veteran of the Vietnam War. Experience taught him to believe in attrition. With the assistance of his Air Force commander, he pored over the numbers of tanks, guns, and armored fighting vehicles that coalition pilots reported they had destroyed or damaged each day.[71]

Neither Schwarzkopf nor Horner conceived of airpower as a massive, mobile strike arsenal on the Soviet model, an arsenal designed to stun and dislocate Iraqi forces. Neither general considered exploiting air supremacy for near-simultaneous attack with U.S. Army maneuver forces on the German model in the first seventy-two hours.[72] Against a more capable Asian, European, Russian, or even Turkish adversary, the generals' predisposition to wait for the air campaign to slowly grind down the opposing ground force could have been fatal to the U.S.-led campaign. As things turned out, Iraq's armed forces were too weak for it to matter.

THE BATTLE OF 73 EASTING

The collision of 840,000 troops and roughly 8,000 tanks of the United States and coalition forces with Iraq's army that officially began on 24 February was not the contest the generals expected. Of the 220,000 120-mm tank cannon rounds moved to the theater by the U.S. Navy, only 3,600 rounds were actually fired.[73] B-52 aircraft delivered 40 percent of the conventional weapons dropped by coalition aircraft in Desert Storm, and B-52s pounded Iraqi defenses in front of the 85,000-member Marine Expeditionary Force (MEF) when it punched through them along Kuwait's southern border in less than an hour. Lieutenant General Boomer, the MEF commander, told Schwarzkopf that it looked like the entire Iraqi army was about to break and run.[74] Schwarzkopf listened to Boomer and accelerated the timetable for the ground offensive.[75]

Under conditions of U.S. air supremacy, the 2nd Armored Cavalry Regiment (ACR)—a force of about 4,200 soldiers with a mix of 126 M1A1 tanks, 115 Bradley fighting vehicles, 24 155-mm self-propelled artillery guns, along with 50 reconnaissance and attack helicopters—should have easily covered the 120 miles of flat, open desert between the Saudi border and the Republican Guard Corps in about 8 to 10 hours.[76] That did not happen.

Map 13 shows a series of phase lines denoting objectives inside a rectangular box stretching from the Saudi Arabian border to the Republican Guards' known assembly area. The control measures may have made sense in Western Europe during the two world wars when American armies of citizen soldiers attacked on foot from trench to trench or town to town, but in the flat, featureless Iraqi desert, devoid of significant obstacles to movement, the control measures were meaningless. They simply slowed movement. The VII Corps commander's obsession with controlling movement in the name of "synchronization" and the fear of meeting the Iraqi enemy on an empty gas tank where the Iraqi "hordes" would somehow manage to slip by hundreds of American fighter jets and surprise the 2nd ACR and the corps behind it made rapid movement impossible.[77]

As the spearhead of VII Corps, 2nd ACR had sporadic contact with Iraqi army units on 24 and 25 February, but they were one-sided affairs; fights ended in seconds with bursts of 25-mm rounds, mortar fire, and the surrender of hundreds of Iraqi soldiers.[78] Yet reports of Iraqi weakness had no detectable influence on the behavior of Franks and his commanders. Each night, Franks halted the entire VII Corps to regain command and control. During World War II, the German army took full advantage of its opponents' halts to prepare defenses and organize counterattacks.[79] Fortunately for VII Corps, their enemy was Arab, not German.

The depressing influence of these halts troubled the 1,100 soldiers of Cougar Squadron (2nd Squadron, 2nd ACR). Sergeant Russell Holloway, the twenty-four-year-old gunner on the headquarters BFV that functioned as the squadron's forward command post, expressed a sentiment that was widely shared by Cougar Squadron's soldiers on the evening of 25 February: "I burned with fear that I would return to Germany without fighting. It would be hard for me to over emphasize what an unbearable shame that would have been for me at the time."[80] Sergeant Holloway need not have worried.

Disturbed by VII Corps' position after two days of operation, Powell called Schwarzkopf during the afternoon of 25 February to ask why VII Corps was not moving. After listening to Schwarzkopf's description of events, he told Schwarzkopf, "Can't you get VII Corps moving faster? Call General Yeosock. Tell him the Chairman is on the ceiling about this entire matter of VII Corps. I want to know why they're not moving and why they can't attack an enemy

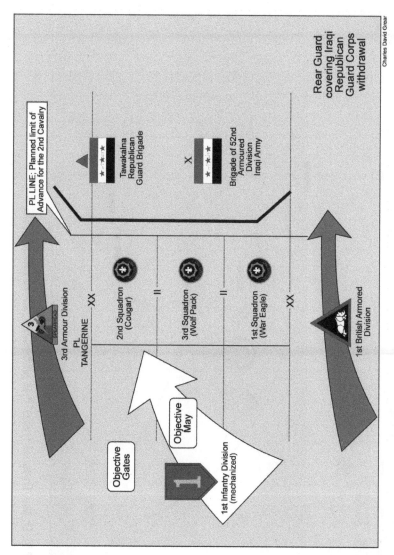

MAP 13. The Battle Plan for 2nd Armored Cavalry Regiment, 26 February 1991

that has been bombed for more than thirty days. They've [VII Corps] been maneuvering for more than two days and still don't even have contact with the enemy. . . . We should be fighting the enemy by now."[81]

Franks got the message. During the night of 25–26 February, he issued new orders and a supporting plan that moved the 2nd ACR's three squadrons on a line spanning eighteen miles of flat open desert directly in front of the rear guard detachment of the Republican Guard (see map 14). On 26 February, the order from regimental headquarters read: "2nd ACR attacks East to fix

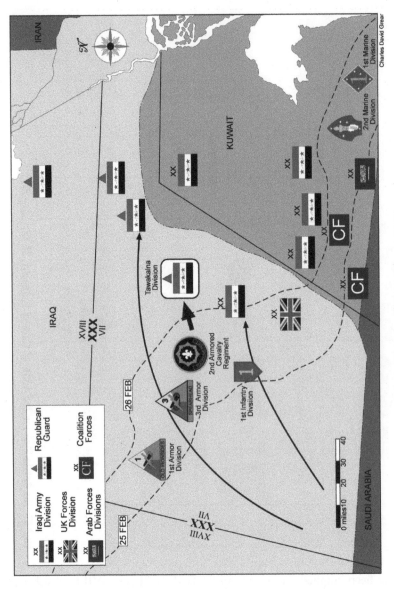

MAP 14. Lt. Gen. Frederick Franks' Plan for VII Corps, 25–26 February 1991

Tawakalna Mechanized Division; on order, 1 ID [1st Infantry Division] passes through 2nd ACR to continue the attack East . . . acknowledge, over!"[82]

The regimental commander gave each squadron a zone of attack six miles wide and six to ten miles deep. The squadrons on Cougar's right, 3rd and 1st Squadrons, deployed three troops forward in their respective zones. Cougar Squadron opted to attack in a box formation with two troops forward followed in line by another troop and Cougar's tank reserve of fourteen tanks. Each cavalry troop consisted of nine tanks, thirteen BFVs, and two 4.2-inch mortars. This gave each troop a three-mile front—a necessity given that the M1A1 MBT fired a projectile that would fly eighteen miles before stopping unless it struck a target.

Mid-morning, Cougar Squadron moved into the box formation, and Eagle Troop was designated its main attack on the right flank of the squadron. As the supporting attack, Ghost Troop occupied the left flank. Fox Troop followed Ghost Troop in support, and Hawk Company, the squadron tank reserve, followed behind Eagle Troop. The howitzer battery moved in the middle of the box, directly behind the lead troops.

On 26 February, the weather was terrible. Gale force winds and blowing sand mixed with stinging rain added a new dimension to the skies overhead, already blackened by smoke from Kuwait's burning oil fields.[83] The weather was ideal for an attack on an enemy that lacked thermal sights.

Despite the intensifying storm that by early morning cut visibility to thirty yards or less, Cougar Squadron's forty-two M1A1 MBTs, forty-one BFVs, eight 155-mm self-propelled howitzers, and six 4.2-inch mortars swung into action. Together with the rest of the regiment, Cougar Squadron now began a series of slow, deliberate moves to a succession of lines that the regimental headquarters had designated "limits of advance." These limits were unconnected to any terrain features—they were simply north-south grid lines on the map.

What the cavalrymen did not know was that Franks and Col. L. D. Holder, the 2nd ACR commander, were utilizing the ground moving target indicator radar provided by the recently fielded JSTARS to micromanage 2nd ACR's movement. Franks and Holder believed they could move the squadrons from grid line to grid line with the object of placing the leading edge of the regiment just outside the range of Iraqi tank and missile fire. Unhappily, the concept of remote-control command far from the actual point of impact on the battlefield constrained the squadrons to advance blindly toward the defending enemy. In a sandstorm, radar could not provide a pristine picture of the enemy, let alone the battlespace.

In the featureless desert smothered in blowing sand and dust, global positioning systems (GPS) were the only means the squadrons had of determining where they actually were. Only the lead scouts in BFVs had GPS. With each successive halt, the squadrons had to report their front line positions, a tedious, time-consuming exercise.

Time dragged as the squadrons moved forward. Between 10 a.m. and noon, the squadron received orders to move first to the north-south grid line designated 52 Easting, then to the 55 Easting, then to the 57 Easting—a process over which the advancing troops had no influence whatsoever. For roughly four hours Cougar Squadron's lead troops drove forward through blowing sand. As they advanced, they destroyed Iraqi mechanized infantry operating in what was clearly a security zone in front of the main Republican Guard defense. Scouts and tanks identified Iraqi targets through their thermal sights, alerted their mortar crews, and, when confident the glowing images were actually Iraqi fighting vehicles or positions, destroyed what they found.

It was not long before Iraqi artillery fire began falling in among the American tanks and BFVs moving at twenty to twenty-five miles per hour. At first the artillery rounds exploded overhead; then, more and more rounds struck the desert floor with a dull thud. Only one trooper—a tank driver—was injured by artillery. Cougar Squadron's troops simply drove around or through the artillery fire. With the rapid loss of their forward outposts, the Iraqi artillery could not shift fire or adjust the bursting height for their rounds.

Cougar Squadron soldiers did not hesitate to pull the trigger. No one halted. In training, the officers treated the squadron's Abrams tanks, Bradley fighting vehicles, and 155-mm self-propelled guns of the squadron howitzer battery like a large guided missile. Once launched into battle, Cougar Squadron was trained not to stop.[84] Offensive battle drills were second nature. In the twelve months leading up to the fight, Cougar Squadron had achieved what Depuy and Gorman set out to achieve with their reforms: it put the right people into the right leadership positions, natural born leaders who were not always the best garrison soldiers.

On reaching the 68 Easting, regimental headquarters again halted the 2nd ACR's cavalry squadrons. In Cougar Squadron's zone of attack, perhaps four hundred yards to the right of Eagle Troop, Iraqi troops opened fire from a small cluster of adobe buildings. As if on a gunnery range in Germany, Eagle Troop scouts coolly hit the kill switch on their 25-mm chain guns and fired controlled bursts of 25-mm high-explosive incendiary tracer shells into the buildings.

One scout section launched two TOW missiles while another spotted and cut down defending Iraqi troops on the side of a building near a parked BTR 60-S, a Soviet manufactured eight-wheeled armored car that resembles the Stryker armored truck. In an engagement that signaled how much the situation was changing, a barely visible T-72 tank about eight hundred meters to the right of Eagle Troop scouts fired a round that exploded short, directly in front of an Eagle Troop Bradley.

For the first time on 26 February, Cougar Squadron was exchanging fire with an enemy tank. Eagle Troop's nine tanks now moved to the front and let loose with two volleys of high-explosive rounds that blasted through building walls. Any Iraqi soldiers in the buildings were not likely to have survived. The firing stopped.[85]

At 4:18 p.m., regimental headquarters issued a new north-south grid line as the limit of advance, the 70 Easting. As Cougar Squadron advanced, the sand storm briefly slackened, improving visibility to perhaps eight hundred yards. However, the blowing sand and low ceiling meant that no aircraft, fixed-wing or rotor-driven, were flying overhead.[86]

The two cavalry squadrons on Cougar's right promptly halted at the 70 Easting. Cougar Squadron did not halt.[87] On the right flank, Eagle Troop had been designated the main attack hours earlier but, like the rest of the squadron, had encountered a few isolated outposts. This situation was about to change suddenly and dramatically.

With permission to advance to the 70 Easting, Eagle Troop pushed over the slight rise to its front and immediately recognized a line of T-72 tanks positioned in revetments. Eagle Troop's commander in the lead tank instantly engaged the enemy, firing a high-explosive anti-tank shell at the nearest T-72. Three seconds later, a sabot round screamed into the second T-72 tank, blasting its turret into the air. In what would become a familiar pattern for the next four hours, secondary explosions ripped apart the tanks as though they were made of plywood. The attack to the 73 Easting had begun (see map 15).[88]

Seconds later, the concussion of more explosive cannon fire split the air as four more Eagle Troop tanks rolled forward next to the troop commander. Now moving at twenty to twenty-five miles per hour, the attacking tanks engaged four more T-72s at nine hundred yards. On impact, the sabot rounds flipped the Iraqi tank turrets, sometimes twenty to thirty feet into the air, while burning debris pinwheeled in all directions. Any T-72s that did not explode belched plumes of smoke and fire from beneath them. In no more than three minutes, fifteen Iraqi T-72 tanks burst into flames barely three hundred yards in front of the advancing tanks.

Iraqi tank crews were obviously surprised. Gunners reported that their Iraqi opponents engaged and destroyed while still attempting to traverse their main guns onto the advancing American tanks and BFVs. A few Iraqi tanks got off a round before dying, but not many. The crash of metal against

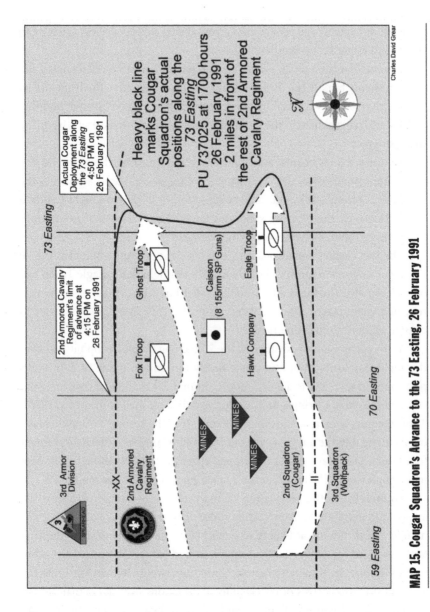

MAP 15. Cougar Squadron's Advance to the 73 Easting, 26 February 1991

metal inside and outside of the American tank turrets could not be heard as round after deafening round after round crashed into the Iraqi tanks and BMPs. Secondary explosions from fuel and ammunition that cooked off added to the thunderous noise. The sight of Iraqi tanks splintering into pieces and bunkers erupting in flames thrilled American tank commanders and gunners. If any of Cougar Squadron's soldiers ever doubted their ability to dominate the Republican Guard opponent, these doubts now vanished with the total collapse of the Iraqi enemy's defense.

The backbone of the Iraqi Republican Guard defense was now effectively broken. However, Eagle Troop's rapid advance and the resulting loss of the T-72 tanks did not reduce the volume of Iraqi small arms fire. In fact, as the tanks and Bradleys closed with the Iraqi defensive positions, the volume of small arms fire increased, but the effects were still modest. Exhilarated by the success of the tanks in smashing through the Iraqi defenses, Eagle Troop scouts rushed in from the flanks or from behind the advancing tanks to cut the surviving infantry down at point-blank range.

Iraqi troops who survived the initial assault ran into the waist-deep trenches or the deep bunkers next to the burning tanks. Wherever the Eagle Scouts spotted Iraqi infantry, they opened fire with their 25-mm automatic cannon, inflicting horrible damage on the defending Iraqi soldiers. Iraqi troops who emerged from hiding in the bunkers died in a hail of grenades thrown by BFV commanders as they drove through and around the Iraqi defensive positions.

Having penetrated the forward defensive strongpoints, Eagle Troop's tank gunners used their thermal sights to see through the fires and smoke. Two thousand meters to their front, Iraqi troops were scrambling to mount seventeen more T-72 tanks parked in a coil. Presumably this was the tank reserve designed to deal with any breach of the defense by American forces. Eagle Troop tanks did not wait. Led by the troop commander, they accelerated in the direction of the Iraqi tank reserve, which was demolished seconds later as the Iraqi crews were still mounting their tanks.

The offensive tactics of emphasizing extreme violence delivered on the move at speeds of twenty to twenty-five miles per hour, which Cougar Squadron practiced from November 1990 to the beginning of February 1991, paid handsome dividends. In the first fifteen minutes of the battle, firing roughly sixty-three 120-mm main gun rounds, Eagle Troop's tank crews destroyed all thirty-nine of the defending Republican Guard tanks in their zone of the attack.[89]

On the left flank, Ghost Troop struggled through poor visibility, scattered minefields, and Iraqi Republican Guard forward outposts to stay on line with Eagle Troop. Before Ghost Troop caught up with Eagle Troop, its scouts discovered and destroyed Iraqi outposts at intervals of about two hundred yards, which told the Ghost Troop commander that the Republican Guard's main defensive line could not be far ahead. On nearing the 73 Easting, the troop commander pulled the troop together for what he rightly anticipated would be a close, sharp fight with the main Iraqi defense. While the platoons reported their positions to the Ghost Troop executive officer, Ghost Troop's lead tank platoon leader asked his troop commander for permission to move his four tanks forward through a large cloud of smoke, presumably from burning vehicles in Eagle Troop's zone of attack that was blowing across his front. The Ghost Troop commander did not hesitate: "Make your move!"[90]

The four Ghost tanks emerged from the mix of sand and smoke at a little after 4:30 in the afternoon. On penetrating the smoke, the platoon leader saw tanks and BMPs to his front and yelled through the radio, "Enemy tanks direct front, direct frontal fire!"

Firing their main guns as they moved forward, the drivers, gunners, loaders, and tank commanders were filled with that strange emotional mixture of apprehension and elation that is inseparable from offensive action. In the space of a few seconds, Ghost Troop's four lead tanks engaged and destroyed the mix of T-72 tanks and BMPs, driving directly into the Iraqi company strongpoint. At first, they ripped a big hole in the middle, turning through and around the bunkers that stood near each of the T-72 tank and BMP fighting positions.

Then, the unexpected—an ever-present companion in close combat—occurred. The advance of Ghost tanks dissolved into chaos. An estimated fifty Iraqi infantrymen in dark green uniforms streamed out of the bunkers amidst the burning wreckage and opened fire on the Ghost tanks with rocket-propelled grenades and AK-47s from a range of less than twenty yards. Try as they might, the American tank commanders could not depress their 50-caliber machine guns low enough to kill the attacking Iraqi infantry. In a feat of courage that surprised the Americans, an Iraqi soldier climbed into one of the few BMPs that were not on fire and managed to get into the gunner's seat. He must have identified the American platoon leader's tank; he fired the 73-mm cannon, sending a round directly over the platoon leader's head.

The Iraqi infantry were getting too close. The American platoon leader ordered his tanks to follow his lead and pull back to a position from which the four tanks could engage the masses of Iraqi infantry running and firing at them from all directions. Seconds later, the drivers threw the tanks in reverse and rolled backward, in some cases over Iraqi soldiers who were too seriously wounded to move out of the way.[91]

To cover the withdrawal, the tank gunners fired their 7.62-mm machine guns, bringing down a number of charging Iraqi troops. When the American tanks were on line, about one hundred meters west of the Iraqi company strongpoint, they halted and opened fire. Red-hot tracers from 50-caliber machine guns gushed into the Iraqi infantry. At the time, tank commanders could not comprehend why the Iraqi soldiers left the defensive position to charge the tanks. Perhaps the Iraqi soldiers actually thought they had driven off the tanks.

No one will ever know what the Iraqi soldiers thought. In the space of a few minutes, the fighting was over, and the desert was covered with dead. Ghost Troop tank commanders felt a profound sense of relief that the fight was over, but they continued searching the desert in all directions for more Iraqi troops. It was quiet. The only thing the tank commanders reported they could hear was the sound of their own blood humming in their ears.

As visibility was now improving, Ghost Troop's scouts closed up on the flanks of the tanks and began launching TOW missiles into groups of Iraqi tanks and BMPs assembling in the distance.[92] The fighting was not over, but the two cavalry troops had penetrated the Iraqi rear guard defense. There was now nothing between Cougar Squadron and the Euphrates River but a shattered, retreating army. With no more targets to its immediate front, Cougar Squadron halted its advance and reported its position to the regimental headquarters. Cougar Squadron's leadership now began piecing together what had happened. Closing with and destroying a defending force armed with tanks, armored fighting vehicles, artillery, and anti-tank missiles made it impossible to report in detail what happened until the enemy was sufficiently broken to allow for a pause to inform the regimental headquarters of the battle and its outcome. It was 5 o'clock in the afternoon.

At 6 p.m., the regiment ordered Cougar Squadron to halt, break contact with the enemy, and retire to the 70 Easting limit of advance, but Cougar Squadron did not withdraw. Eventually, the regiment granted permission for it to remain in a defensive line roughly 2 miles in front of the regiment. Though prohibited from advancing further east, Cougar Squadron continued to engage the Iraqi enemy to its front. Republican Guards counterattacked several times over the next 3 hours, especially where Ghost anchored the VII Corps' left flank. Cougar Squadron's 8 155-mm guns fired 1,100 rounds to repel Iraqi counterattacks and engage Iraqi forces beyond the range of 120-mm tank guns and TOW missiles, but the Iraqi rear guard was destroyed. Everywhere, mounds of metallic refuse and human remains marked the path of Cougar Squadron's attack. In the words of its soldiers, the desert had been transformed into a "heavy metal graveyard."[93] At the cost of 1 Bradley,

1 soldier killed in action, and 6 soldiers wounded, the attack to the 73 Easting left the 1,100 men of Cougar Squadron in complete control of the desert as far as the eye could see.

Hours later, when the Iraqi brigade commander and a few hundred survivors became Cougar Squadron's prisoners of war, the brigade commander reported that the bulk of his 2,500-man Iraqi Republican Guard brigade, a force of 140 armored vehicles including 70 tanks, 44 trucks, and 32 bunkers, was gone. He also stated that he had lost only 2 tanks to air strikes in the 40 days of air attack, but he lost the remainder of his tanks in the opening minutes of Cougar Squadron's assault.[94]

The Battle of 73 Easting was a battle of annihilation, a testimony to the superior combination of training, technology, and leadership that General Depuy and General Gorman began building in the mid-1970s.[95] Thanks to the sandstorm, the unexpected direction from which the attack came, and the speed and violence of Cougar Squadron's assault, even an opposing Soviet force would not likely have survived it.[96] Within a few short hours, less than half of Cougar Squadron's combat force, no more than five hundred soldiers equipped with nineteen M1A1 Abrams tanks, twenty-seven Bradley fighting vehicles, four 4.2-inch mortars, scores of M113s, and twelve M109 155-mm self-propelled howitzers engaged the Iraqi enemy, reducing more than seventy tanks, seventy armored fighting vehicles, forty-four trucks, and thirty-two bunkers of the Republican Guard to smoldering debris.

Cougar Squadron demonstrated yet again the immense power of mobile armored firepower in the attack when disciplined, professional soldiers are courageously led into action from the front. German general Hermann Balck, an experienced veteran of many battles on every front in World War II, noted the importance of courageous and dynamic leadership from the front during offensives in a 1979 interview: "It's quite remarkable that most people believe that the attack costs more casualties. Don't even think about it; the attack is the least costly operation. . . . In the attack, there are only 3 or 4 men in the division who carry the attack; all the others just follow behind. In the defense, every man must hold his position alone. . . . That's why he's easily uprooted. Nothing incurs higher casualties than an unsuccessful defense."[97]

Though Saddam Hussein did not ask for a cease-fire, just twenty-four hours after Cougar Squadron fired its last round on the morning of 27 February 1991, President Bush gave it to him. Bush always intended the war with Iraq to be a "limited" war fought at the lowest possible cost in American and coalition lives. Pressing the ground offensive to "finish the job" doubtlessly raised the specter of protracted conflict, which Bush was deter-mined to avoid.[98]

Bush also seems to have reasoned that extending the war beyond the one-hundred-hour mark might also jeopardize the regional and international political support for U.S.-led military action he worked so hard to build. Though Bush's public appeal to the Iraqi people on 1 March 1991 to over-throw Saddam Hussein's regime suggested he sought much more than just the withdrawal of Iraqi forces from Kuwait, Colin Powell denied this was the case. Powell later said, "Our practical intention was to leave Baghdad enough power to survive as a threat to Iran that remained bitterly hostile toward the United States."[99]

Desert Storm ended as it began—with an air strike, this time with a two-thousand-pound GBU-28 bomb designed to penetrate thousands of tons of reinforced concrete. The target was a command bunker twenty feet under-ground northwest of Baghdad at al-Taji Airfield. Intelligence officers were convinced that Saddam Hussein was lurking in the bunker. He was not.[100] Since killing Saddam was not a publicly stated war aim, to the national lead-ership in Washington, DC, the failure was irritating but not yet deeply trou-bling.[101] That would come later.

CONCLUSION

In 1990, Israeli defense minister Moshe Ahrens was asked what he hoped American military power would achieve in Iraq. After pausing to consider the matter, Ahrens answered, "If Mr. Hussein stays in power and retains the weapons, there will be grounds for concern here, in this region and, I think, throughout the world. I hope this will not be the way the crisis ends."[102]

Ahrens' comments were prescient. Bush's decision to suspend the ground offensive after only one hundred hours was ill considered. Regardless of the pressure exerted by Bush's thirty-nine coalition members to end the war (not to mention the Chinese and Russian governments), once the decision was made to intervene with American military power on behalf of Kuwait against Iraq, the goal should have been to induce Iraq's military leaders to either expel or liquidate Saddam Hussein together with his supporting clique. Because Bush failed to do this, in the space of just a few years, the United States ended up dealing yet again with a recalcitrant and unrepentant Saddam (see table 2).[103]

In the immediate afterglow of victory over Iraq, Saddam's survival in power was forgotten. Back in Washington there were obligatory nods to

TABLE 2. The Road to War with Iraq in 2003

1 March–April 1991: Postwar Iraqi uprising encouraged by the George H. W. Bush administration is crushed by loyalist forces spearheaded by the *Iraqi Republican Guard*.
27 August 1992: *Operation Southern Watch* is established to contain Iraq.
7 October 1994: 80,000 Iraqi troops including two veteran *Republican Guard divisions* move south toward the Kuwaiti Border. Ambassador Madeleine K. Albright tells the UN Security Council, "Iraq might soon have some 60,000 troops and 1,000 tanks poised to attack Kuwait." The United States responds, putting 36,000 troops in planes and setting another 160,000 in motion.
1 January 1997: *Operation Northern Watch* is established.
31 October 1998: President Clinton signs the **Iraqi Liberation Act** into law.
December 1998: Iraq accepts UN-sponsored *"oil-for-food"* program.
16 December 1998: *Operation Desert Fox*, a four-day bombing campaign against Iraq, begins. Stated goal: Disrupt Saddam's grip on power. Air strikes by U.S. and U.K. forces continue weekly into 2001 (seven to fourteen tons of bombs and missiles per month on average).
June 2002–March 2003: *Operation Southern Focus* (54.6 tons dropped on Iraq in September 2002)
16 October 2002: Authorization for *Use of Military Force Against Iraq Resolution* enacted.
20 March 2003: *Operation Iraqi Freedom* begins.

jointness, but each service learned the lessons it wanted to learn, lessons that served its bureaucratic interests.[104] To the Army, jointness was interpreted to mean that additional artillery in the form of close air support or global strategic lift was on call in the Army's role as the permanently "supported service" in American warfare.[105] The Marine Corps that deployed and fought like the Army's XVIII Airborne Corps returned to its mission of reenacting World War II–style amphibious landings despite the absence of any demonstrated strategic need to do so. General Ronald Fogleman, who succeeded McPeak as the Air Force chief of staff, told airmen that "conventional air operations . . . could directly achieve operational and strategic level objectives—independent of ground forces, or even with ground forces in support."[106] Only the leadership of the Navy attempted to explore its future role in an ocean devoid of challengers.[107]

No one with stars on their shoulders saw value in disclosing the truth: that Desert Storm was really a modern version of Alexander's victory over the Persians at Gaugamela in 331 BCE, or even a replay of Kitchener's victory over Sudanese tribesmen at Omdurman in 1899.[108] There was no incentive to admit that Desert Storm could have been over in a week had anyone in the senior ranks of the Air Force and the Army wanted to speedily end it with the use of tightly integrated air and ground forces instead of fighting the weak Iraqi opponent on terms that favored the parochial interests of the services.[109]

What makes Desert Storm and its microcosm, the Battle of 73 Easting, landmark events that changed the twentieth century? The answer is three-fold. First, after Desert Storm, the United States held sway in the world like Rome did after the fall of Carthage. Its demonstrated superiority in military organization, technology, and human capital meant the U.S. military had no peer.[110] With the collapse of the Soviet state system, America's capacity to project power over vast distances and attack decisively in the Persian Gulf meant that American military power at sea, in the air, and on land was unchallenged and unmatched at the end of the twentieth century.[111]

Second, the 1991 Gulf War confirmed the wisdom of America's Cold War investment in training and high technology, particularly space-based assets that facilitated precision guidance. Not every precision guided munition struck its target, but the investment paid off handsomely and pointed to a bright future for precision strike. Some additional points for consideration that confirmed this investment:

> JSTARS—initially the persistent, long-standoff ground moving target indicator radar combined with near-real-time on-board battle management—also incorporated near-real-time high-resolution single-aperture radar imagery of specific targets once they stopped moving.

> Space-based capabilities altered warfare beyond recognition. Global positioning systems guided hundreds of thousands of troops, aircraft, and ships over vast distances. Near-precision guided weapons relying upon GPS time and navigation data provided a true standoff fire-and-forget capability that approached the accuracy of semi-active homing lasers and radar systems. This technology also enabled the highly accurate and lethal fire-on-the-move capabilities of the M1A1 Abrams tank.

> The first use of strike aircraft with stealth features to penetrate a dense, nearly state-of-the-art integrated air defense system (admittedly one operated by less than top-notch personnel) was successful. Strikes also included the first known use of "soft-kill" network attack capabilities that disrupted the Iraqi electric power grid without totally destroying it.

> Beyond-visual-range air-to-air missile capability combining advanced radars and semi-autonomous radar-guided missiles was implemented for the first time using the Patriot air defense system to create the foundation for tactical ballistic missile defense. The field-expedient modifications to its software gave the Patriot a rudimentary capability

to intercept Soviet ballistic missiles (primitive SS-1 SCUDs). After Desert Storm, U.S. missile technology developed rapidly to counter short-range ballistic missiles.

› America's mobile armored firepower was revolutionary both in its striking power and protection. At the same time, lacking attacking mobility and protection, American light infantry in the 82nd Airborne Division and the Marines were compelled to follow advancing armor into Iraq—the 82nd on Saudi school buses, the Marines on trucks.

› Real-time, integrated battle management tools designed for situational awareness were deployed down to the tactical level. These capabilities were already comparatively advanced for air combat, but it would take another decade for these technologies to mature inside the Army and Marines.

› The Navy was unchallenged at sea, but no technology in 1991 (or even today) could neutralize over a thousand enemy sea mines in the Persian Gulf. Even the best mine countermeasures could do little to penetrate the density of mines that made an amphibious assault extremely dangerous, if not impossible. As it was in the Battle of Mons and Battle of Shanghai, naval power was again a supporting player in a war with a continental opponent.

Finally, although the twentieth century closed on a note of unrivaled American superiority in military affairs, the failure of policymakers and military leaders in Washington to define the purpose, method, and end state of military operations robbed the United States and its coalition partners of a decisive strategic victory in 1991. Battlefield success offered strategic opportunities that America's national political and military leaders did not anticipate.[112]

When hostilities ended, Schwarzkopf was completely unprepared for his role as peacemaker.[113] The terms of the armistice he signed not only left Saddam Hussein in power, they also allowed him to reequip at least 50,000 Republican Guard troops and brutally suppress the rebellion inside Iraq that Bush had publicly encouraged. Years later, Lt. Gen. Buster Glosson, USAF (Ret.), observed, "Without a clear idea of the outcome the U.S. military forces wanted to achieve (beyond the liberation of Kuwait), is it any surprise then that the resulting peace was so unsatisfactory to the long-term interests of the United States?"[114]

Though the Bush administration and the press did much to conceal it, American generalship was far less impressive than the performance of America's Soldiers, Sailors, Airmen, and Marines. On the one hand, Schwarzkopf wisely scrapped plans for airborne and amphibious assault operations that made little sense given Iraqi military capabilities.[115] On the other, Schwarzkopf and his generals were too ready to believe such commentators as retired Army Chief of Staff Gen. Edward Meyer, who said that the war with Iraq would produce 10,000 to 30,000 U.S. casualties.[116]

In view of these concerns, Schwarzkopf and Powell pushed for and won approval from Bush for the overwhelming numbers of troops they wanted, but the Army generals confused the concentration of numbers on the ground with the application of firepower, willpower, and effective leadership at the critical point, the ingredients that deliver decisive victory in battle.[117] Stonewall Jackson's enduring lesson was ignored: "There is a power in war more potent than mere numbers."[118]

In the end, Franks failed to exploit the breakthrough that airpower created. Though allegedly infuriated with Franks' excessive caution, Schwarzkopf initially did little to goad him into action. When Schwarzkopf finally pushed Franks to act decisively to exploit the collapse of Iraqi forces, his intervention was too late to make a difference.[119] As a result, Franks' rigidity of mind, obsession with control, and lingering fear of casualties crushed initiative and rescued Iraq's Republican Guard from wholesale destruction or surrender.

In the euphoria that spread through the media and the American public, none of these points influenced the popular narrative. The myth of the bloodless victory was born, and with it, the seductive promise of silver bullet technology that encourages arrogance and fosters the illusion of victory with zero casualties was made.[120]

The idea of moving the Army, Air Force, Navy, and Marine Corps out of the industrial-age structure based on single-service self-sufficiency into an organizational design based on service interdependency was ignored. Any suggestion that it might be useful to reexamine service roles and missions in light of the more obvious changes wrought by new technologies and their proliferation at the end of the twentieth century was rejected. The acute need for an effective national defense staff to assist the president and the secretary of defense with the task of commanding the armed forces and imposing unity of effort across service lines was overlooked.

Instead, the numbers of Soldiers, Airmen, Sailors, and Marines who could actually deploy and fight fell while the numbers of admirals, generals, and headquarters grew. Nine years later, the armed forces entered the twenty-first century with a World War II force structure intact and institutions enshrined in the 1947 National Security Act—albeit with new, but increasingly expensive, single-service modernization programs that were not necessarily what the nation needed.[121]

CONCLUSION

America's Margin of Victory in the Twenty-First Century

This book began with the goal of developing an appreciation for the decisive margin of victory that emerges when national political, military, and economic forces work hand in hand. To examine the process of finding and keeping the margin of victory, five decisive battles were subject to an impartial review against the backdrop of national military strategy and the operational forces designed to execute it.

Whenever possible, the book tried to identify blind alleys and dead ends in the form of misguided strategic thinking and flawed force designs with the hope of avoiding them in the future. In doing so, we come to the understanding that whenever new military concepts and technologies appear, the complex interaction of national culture, bureaucratic interests, and economic power does not automatically work to support them.

In good times, when the opposing force is feeble or inept, large military establishments with a recent record of success can still prevail despite flaws in their organizations and command arrangements—as the British, Japanese, German, Soviet, and Israeli armed forces did before the events discussed in these chapters occurred. But when conditions change, and the margin of victory suddenly narrows, those frailties and vulnerabilities concealed from view inside the armed forces, features that normally make no difference to military performance, suddenly produce catastrophic failure.

When the tables turn as they did for the Soviets in 1941, the Germans in 1943, and the Israelis in 1973, bad policies, failed tactics, and dysfunctional command structures have to be abandoned. Policymakers and commanders whose ideas are wrong must be discarded and replaced with new policymakers and new commanders, as well as new strategic and operational concepts. The first-order questions in national military strategy have to be posed anew within the strategic and operational framework of purpose, method, and end state.

If culture and leadership obstruct this process of adaptation and change in war, the margin of victory is permanently lost. Then, the cost of indulging failure in action, of clinging to the carcass of wrong-headed strategy, tactics, and organizations, leads inexorably to defeat.[1]

Sir Richard Haldane stands out as a leader on the world stage who recognized the danger of clinging to military solutions rooted in comfortable interpretations of the past, solutions that would obstruct progressive development instead of conquering the future. However, in an island nation that favored the Royal Navy, Haldane's BEF was unavoidably a product of austere defense budgets, a force designed to "do more with less."

Nonetheless, Haldane's package of reform and reorganization was a far better solution than the Boer War status quo preferred by the British army's generals. Most important, Haldane's reform was influential enough to ensure the BEF would punch above its weight in August 1914, first slowing the German advance and then supporting the French counterattack at the Marne. When war broke out, Haldane's BEF bought time for Britain to assemble the industrial-age armies it needed to win the war. Today, Haldane's achievements are underappreciated in the United States and Great Britain.

Japan's decision to seize Shanghai and invade China in 1937 was taken "in the fever of a fanatical urge to act."[2] Early victories over weaker Chinese forces masked serious deficiencies in the IJA. Competition between the Japanese naval and ground forces undermined strategic unity of effort. The Japanese generals' failure to embrace the reform, reorganization, and modernization of the IJA proposed by the far-sighted general Ugaki Kazushige after World War I condemned Japanese soldiers to death in World War II on a horrific scale.[3] Superior Japanese airpower and naval power were never enough to compensate for the IJA's weakness in mobility, armor, and firepower in its wars with U.S. and Soviet forces.[4]

In 1941, Hitler could have avoided war with the Soviet Union. The Soviets supplied Nazi Germany with the raw materials it needed to sustain the Wehrmacht's fuel and modernization needs. In June 1941, half of the Luftwaffe was still committed in the West against British forces in the North Atlantic and the Mediterranean, and German army mechanization was incomplete.

Instead, Hitler invaded the Soviet Union knowing that unless the Wehrmacht could reach Moscow and knock the Soviet Union out of the war before January 1942, an Anglo-American-Soviet military coalition was likely to materialize with ominous consequences for Germany in a two-front war.[5] He decided to risk everything on one throw of the strategic dice despite the fact that his judgment of Russia was not informed by experience. Hitler spent

World War I in France, living and fighting in the trenches for yards of useless ground. He knew nothing about Russia's vastness and wide open spaces.[6]

Those in and out of uniform who told Hitler what he wanted to hear were rewarded with promotion and advancement. Lieutenant General Friedrich Paulus, Hitler's strategic planner for Operation Barbarossa, was a fine example. He echoed Hitler's words without hesitation: "It may be that in 3 to 4 weeks, the campaign [in Russia] is over. Perhaps, the whole house of cards will collapse after the first blow."[7]

When the Wehrmacht could advance no further, Hitler switched it from an enemy force–oriented strategy to a ground-holding strategy. "Holding ground" robbed the German soldier of his culturally ingrained ability to exercise operational discretion, to think, to adapt, and, most of all, outmaneuver his Soviet opponent.[8] Defending vast, irrelevant stretches of Russian territory pushed German ground forces, air power, and logistics to the breaking point and sentenced the Wehrmacht to destruction.[9]

The German approach of lashing up hundreds of single-service headquarters—air, land, and sea—each of which fought its war on its own terms, failed miserably. Colonel Claus Graf von Stauffenberg, the highly decorated general staff officer who organized the plot to kill Hitler in July 1944, described the German command structure with these words: "Our high command organization in the Second World War is more idiotic than the most capable General Staff Officer could invent, if he received the task to create the most senseless wartime high command structure he could."[10]

As the Wehrmacht declined in striking power, the Soviet high command learned to marshal and employ enormous strike and maneuver forces in close coordination. In contrast to German and Anglo-American command arrangements, the Soviet high command and its subordinate fronts controlled all of the military assets, resources, and capabilities—air, land, and sea—in their respective areas of operation. As a result, the Soviet high command could commit resources when and where they were needed to overwhelm the Wehrmacht. Soviet commanders could employ capabilities across service lines in minutes, whereas the Germans and their Anglo-American opponents required days or even months of negotiation between services and commanders to do so. Hundreds of thousands of German soldiers died in one major Soviet offensive after another because the Wehrmacht's infantry divisions, unchanged from their World War I posture, lacked mobility, armored protection, and firepower.[11]

When the leaders of Carthage congratulated Hannibal on crushing the Romans at Cannae in 216 BC, Hannibal reminded them that he had not broken the Roman will to fight—that no one in the Roman senate had appealed for peace or concessions to Carthage.[12] Had Israel's political leaders viewed Egypt in a similar light after 1967, they might have acted differently and launched an attack on Egypt's assembling ground forces in October 1973.

As it turned out, the judgment of Israel's national leadership yielded to wishful thinking that had no basis in fact. Israel's leaders thus provided Egypt's national leadership with a chance for military success Egypt would have otherwise missed. Surprised by the magnitude and effectiveness of Egyptian air defenses and anti-tank tactics, Israeli tank, artillery, and infantry formations were forced to fight without the advantage of local air superiority.

Israeli ground forces improvised, adapted, and counterattacked. In the final analysis, no sacrifice on the part of Egypt's valiant soldiers could rescue Egypt's army from defeat. Whereas Israeli culture rewarded thinking and independent action, Egyptian culture did not. Like most of the armies in the Middle East, Egyptian soldiers lacked the "knowledge, understanding and training to fully exploit the technology at their disposal."[13]

Operation Desert Storm involved a long, sophisticated, and destructive air campaign followed by the invasion of massive U.S. ground forces equipped with firepower, mobility, and armor on a scale undreamed of in all previous twentieth-century wars.[14] Yet one of the most complete military victories of the twentieth century exemplified by the attack to the 73 Easting failed to remove the essential cause of the Gulf War: Saddam Hussein.

Without a coherent warfighting doctrine or integrated, unified command structure to guide the application of American military power, each service— Army, Air Force, Navy, and Marine Corps—fought its own war largely independently of the others. When added to Washington's determination to hold its awkwardly large "coalition of the willing" together, the combination of the two allowed the Republican Guard to escape and Saddam Hussein to survive in power. This is a historic feature of American culture in the twentieth century: the calamitous "habit of not thinking much beyond the hour of victory."[15] It is another reminder that without effective strategic direction, battles such as 73 Easting can be won, but wars can still be lost.

These points aside, the enormous economic power, creative research, and technological innovation that combined to produce the American military establishment that launched Desert Storm halfway around the world testified to the extraordinary impact of America's own unique English-speaking culture.[16] American society climbed to the pinnacle of world power on the foundation of English-speaking values that Americans adopted and implemented. These values exalted the dignity of work, nurtured a competitive spirit, and stressed self-reliance.

However, these same English-speaking values also included the disinclination to maintain standing professional armies. This cultural attitude left the United States without a consistent policy that cultivated and sustained superior military expertise and strength in the years leading up to the two world wars. In 1991, Americans narrowly evaded this historic trap when they ended up as the beneficiaries of Cold War investments. Today there is no similar strategic focus like the Cold War to guide American investment in military organization, technology, and human capital.[17]

Only war itself can provide the aforementioned insights.[18] Only war reaffirms the enduring truth that to be effective in battle, armed forces must be cohesive, inspired, undemocratic, and coercive in character; that Western armed forces in particular must be separate and distinct from the individualistic, ultra-democratic, and materialistic societies they defend.[19] Making the most of the human capital that a free society provides to its armed forces requires professional military institutions to balance the aforementioned needs against nurturing the creativity and initiative of its Soldiers, Sailors, Airmen, and Marines. With this point in mind, it is now possible to discern the implications of these insights and to state a few general conclusions about twentieth-century warfare that are relevant to the United States strategic military thinking and force design in the twenty-first century:

> Political and military leaders who start wars always hope the fighting will be purposeful and short, but an accurate and sobering self-assessment of one's own strengths and weaknesses is absent from the strategic calculus. The ability to employ military power, rather than the valid strategic requirement to use force, tends to dominate national security decisionmaking. Realistic answers to the questions of strategic purpose, method, and end state before and during wartime operations are frequently missing.[20] Grand strategy, if it exists at all, consists of avoiding unnecessary conflict, not starting it.

> National culture is responsible for the pool of high-quality soldiers, sailors, and airmen that populate the armed forces and for the emergence of tens of thousands of exceptional leaders at the tactical and operational levels who can analyze, synthesize, and inspire. Culture

determines whether forces can operate in degraded environments where the first technology to fail is inevitably communications with higher headquarters. Cultural factors determine whether the civilian or military leaders that press for change and innovation are able to create superior combinations of leadership, technology, and organization. Culture is the foundation for human capital.[21] The state that is rich in human capital will normally prevail in battle or, as seen in Germany and Japan, recover strongly from defeat in war.

> Without unity of command, there is no unity of effort. Regardless of how powerful the nation-state or alliance of states may be, it is impossible to be strong everywhere at once. The only solution to the problem is the effective organization of military power from the strategic to the tactical level where fighting occurs together with the means to integrate and command the diversity of military capabilities. The combination of the two is the foundation for unity of effort in war—the essential ingredient for victory in battle and war. Armed forces that integrate capabilities across service lines within a streamlined and responsive command structure achieve unity of effort.

> Regardless of how well new technologies are networked, intelligence, surveillance, and reconnaissance (ISR) will never provide perfect situational awareness or perfect information. Countermeasures in many forms (including cyber warfare) ensure the fog of war will persist into the twenty-first century. Knowledge of the opponent will arise in the future as it has in the past from the employment of human understanding with technical means. Surprise in warfare will persist, which is why a more accurate and timely picture of the opposing forces' intentions and capabilities always confers a winning advantage. Field Marshal Arthur Wellesley, the First Duke of Wellington, said it best: "The whole art of war consists in getting at what is on the other side of the hill."[22] Wayne Gretzky put it differently: "A good hockey player plays where the puck is. A great hockey player plays where the puck is going to be."[23]

> By the end of the twentieth century, the application of massive firepower from standoff attack weapons in all domains altered warfare. This capability, referred to as "strike," has its roots in both world wars. Its effectiveness depends heavily on the contemporary marriage of space-based and terrestrial ISR capabilities with the timely

dissemination of analyzed intelligence through networks. It is the basis for an enduring paradigm shift in the conduct of warfare.

> Despite the enormous growth in the accuracy and lethality of strike along with the growing persistence of ISR, maneuver forces on the ground are still necessary to exploit the profound but temporary paralysis that precision strikes induce. Ground maneuver forces must always be capable of closing with and surviving contact with the enemy. No amount of precision strike will rescue ground maneuver forces from destruction if they cannot close with the enemy, sustain losses, keep fighting, and attack decisively.

> "Athleticism in uniform" does not equal fighting power in modern war. Regardless of how courageous, well trained, and physically fit individual soldiers may be, they cannot survive contact with the modern enemy's firepower if they are unprotected. In conflict with a peer or near-peer opponent, the exponential increase in the lethality of modern weapons makes light infantry—whether airborne, airmobile, or amphibious—a niche capability, not the foundation for a twenty-first-century ground maneuver force.[24]

> To survive and prevail in twenty-first-century close combat, soldiers must be protected; ideally, the vast majority should be mounted in tracked armored platforms equipped with accurate, devastating firepower.[25] Fortunately, when tightly integrated with ISR and strike, a smaller number of more highly trained mobile armored combat formations manned by professional soldiers can accomplish more in the future than the mass armies of the past.[26]

Margin of Victory threw all of these points into sharp relief. The question now is: Did the late twentieth century signal the beginning of a new, revolutionary epoch in the American way of war or the apogee of American national military power?

The answer is unclear. What can be said is that without a rational strategic framework in place, the service chiefs will shrink existing forces until money and people are provided to restore them to their former size.[27] History teaches that this is a dangerous practice. The last major war's technologies, force designs, and human capital strategies are seldom, if ever, the right solutions for the next major war.[28] Compared with the last war, "the next war is always virgin territory."[29]

Unless the U.S. Army and Air Force also move rapidly away from the last two decades' focus on "permissive non-contested operations" in counterinsurgency to higher-end operations in more contested, nonpermissive environments they are courting future defeat.[30] If today's four-stars have not figured it out, at least the American people have concluded that there is no point in trying to breathe new life into the comatose body of the perpetually failed states that litter the Eastern hemisphere with American military power.[31]

In the new century, the United States also needs the means to comprehensively plan and direct joint, integrated strike and maneuver operations. If national defense is to be affordable and effective, less overhead and more fighting power at the lowest level must become the organizing imperative.[32] These are the subjects to which the conclusions now turn.

CHANGE IN U.S. NATIONAL MILITARY STRATEGY

Like Haldane in 1905, Americans do not have the luxury of knowing precisely which great power or constellation of powers might threaten the United States in ten, fifteen, or twenty years. Time will solve this mystery, but until it does, the United States must prepare its forces to prevail wherever American national interests dictate. To do so, the United States must first devise and declare a new national military strategy, one that provides greater clarity regarding what actions constitute red lines or a casus belli in national security interests than it has in the past.[33]

World War I began, in part, because the participants thought they could anticipate the responses of the others when, in fact, all of the belligerents were predisposed to play dangerous wild cards.[34] By the war's end, British national power was exhausted, and Britain permanently lost its ability to maintain the international balance of power, shape the international system to its advantage, and ensure that no one power dominated Europe or Asia.[35] The United States must avoid Britain's fate. And, like the warring states presented in this volume, the United States must act now to build the means to command its armed forces and impose unity of effort across service lines.

The alliance structures that emerged in the aftermath of World War II are crumbling because the original interests and threats that gave them meaning and purpose either do not exist or are transforming. No nation-state or collection of nation-states should be consigned to the category of permanent enemy. In the future, Americans should be ready to cooperate with all nation-states whenever and wherever it is possible to do so. The U.S. government should adopt a broader policy of "limited liability partnerships" in lieu of binding alliances.

In his book *The Post-American World*, Fareed Zakaria made a similar point, urging Washington to adopt Prince Otto von Bismarck's thinking about foreign and defense policy: "Bismarck chose to engage with all of the great powers. His goal was to have better relations with all of them than any of them had with each other—to be the pivot of Europe's international system."[36] For the United States, East Asia is a good place to start implementing Bismarck's thinking.

American military and economic power in the western Pacific is a football in the regional power game between China and its neighbors, especially Japan.[37] This game involves oil, gas, and mineral deposits that overlap with centuries of cultural hostility and economic competition.[38] It is a power game the United States does not fully comprehend and cannot possibly control. This is bad news because U.S. military intervention in a small, seemingly minor dispute off the coast of Vietnam or Taiwan could present Americans with a war they do not want to fight.

Very few Americans appreciate the degree to which a historic mix of fear and envy of Chinese economic power induced many of the country's neighbors to repeatedly invade and conquer it. In fact, ethnic (Han) Chinese have ruled China for fewer than 350 of the last 1,000 years of Chinese history. The last dynasty, the Qing dynasty (1644–1912), was established by Jurchen nomads, a Mongol-Turkic people known to history as the Manchu. The Qing dynasty created the modern borders of contemporary China by gradually conquering the surrounding Mongol and Turkic peoples and asserting nominal suzerainty over Tibet.[39] A prominent Japanese statesman made essentially the same point 100 years ago when he noted that under the Manchus, the Chinese were nothing more than a conquered people alongside others: "The expansion of China is an important subject in history, but its limit was reached long ago. . . . The area of the original center of China was very limited, but its sphere of influence and activity gradually spread, generation after generation, as its civilization developed and extended to the surrounding regions. . . . The one peculiarity of this extension is that, roughly speaking, it has not been the result of aggressive conquest. China has always been on the defensive, and it is the surrounding peoples who have always assumed the offensive against her."[40]

China is a great continental power and must be treated as one, but it is foolish to think that China is a new version of the Soviet military state.[41] China's military power lags far behind the capabilities of the United States.

With each succeeding attempt to extend its military defenses in East Asia, China nurtures new and more powerful opposing forces from Vietnam to Korea.[42] China's leaders are also far more concerned with maintaining internal stability and control than with launching wars to extend Chinese dominion over the world.[43]

China is naturally interested in securing its own access to the sea lanes connecting its economy to its Mideast oil suppliers, African resources, and Arctic opportunities.[44] The South China Sea is also rich in undersea oil, but China does not own all of it.[45] Provided China does not interfere with other states' access to the same sea lanes and resources, China's interests in access to the global commons should be treated as legitimate.[46]

On the other hand, military ties with Japan in response to China's regional military strategy should not be unconditional. China's dreadful twentieth-century war with Japan explains why ordinary Chinese speak quite openly about the potential for future war with Japan.[47] Japan's use of Taiwan and Korea as platforms for the projection of its military forces against China in 1937 remains a guiding influence in the development of China's anti-access/ area denial (A2AD) strategy.[48]

In the evolving strategic environment, China's unrelenting hostility to Japan means the red lines in East Asia should be drawn in ways that protect and enhance U.S. strategic interests, not just Japan's interests.[49] Those interests in disputes over islands in the North or South China Seas, islands hundreds of miles from mainland China and Japan, should not be treated as matters of vital strategic interest to the United States.[50] America's interest in good relations with Tokyo should not entail unconditional American support for all of its goals in Northeast Asia.

Americans, like all of the English-speaking peoples, want naval and aerospace power to play the prominent role in most national security matters, but in wars with continental opponents, the two together are not enough. In a war with a continental power such as Germany, Russia, China, Turkey, or Iran, American military advantages at sea and, increasingly, in the air are negated, relegating air and naval power to a supporting role.

For example, the hypothetical seizure of southern Iran by U.S. forces would be a relatively straightforward operation, but U.S. action in southern Iran would likely precipitate Russian military intervention in northern Iran on the model of Chinese intervention in North Korea in 1950. The outcome would be a war with Russia on strategic terms that do not favor the United States. Both Russia and the United States possess nuclear weapons, but their use is very unlikely, meaning that the military outcome would depend primarily on the quality and composition of U.S. Army ground forces.

Americans experienced these conditions on the Korean Peninsula after China intervened, but apparently the lesson has not taken hold. In June 1950, the U.S. Army did not confront a truly formidable enemy in the North Korean army, but the United States lost the "first fight" with the North Koreans. The Army's understrength, poorly equipped, and inadequately trained infantry formations could not stop three hundred North Korean tanks, infantry, and artillery forces. Within a few months, the U.S. Army's capability to sustain its forces with fresh manpower was exhausted, and the U.S. Eighth Army was nearly driven into the sea.[51] A long war ensued that might have been avoided had the U.S. Army maintained standing, professional combat forces equipped with mobile armored firepower.

More to the point, wars with continental powers, large or small, demand the persistent employment of powerful aerospace and ground forces in tandem with allied forces. Maintaining the core capabilities to fight such wars is a necessary strategic hedge, but keeping millions under arms in readiness to fight them is unaffordable. In a period of falling defense spending, the U.S. armed forces, especially a smaller Army, cannot preserve its vital warfighting forces and still maintain large paramilitary forces for counterinsurgency and nation building in the Eastern hemisphere.[52]

It is, therefore, essential that elected and appointed leaders in Washington redefine the nation's core, existential interests. For the American people, these are interests that are inextricably intertwined with national economic prosperity, a condition that depends on unobstructed access to the global commons resource domains that lie beyond the political authority of any one nation state.

Contemporary international law identifies four global commons: the high seas, the atmosphere, Antarctica, and outer space. Access to these areas is guided by the historic open access doctrine of the *mare liberum* (free sea for everyone). Today, American economic stability and prosperity depend on access to and unconstrained action in all four domains.[53]

Americans must defend their own liberty and property, but Americans should seek to avoid military involvement in purely local conflicts and restrict direct military intervention in foreign wars to a preeminent objective: preventing the emergence of a single bloc or empire from dominating the great Eurasian landmass. Domination of the Eurasian landmass by any one power or one alliance should be a permanent red line in U.S. foreign and defense policy—a red line that both the American people and America's allies on or near the Eurasian landmass can enthusiastically support.

Inside the Washington Beltway, American values are treated as universal. They are not. Respect for private property and minority rights are the exceptions beyond the borders of the United States and Western Europe.[54] However much Americans exalt their values, they are not exportable with military power to other societies, as demonstrated quite recently in Iraq and Afghanistan.[55]

The recommended departure from the policies of the past, of spreading democracy with military power, is also bound up with the understanding that a large Navy, Air Force, and Army presence in the Mediterranean and the Middle East could not prevent the Muslim Brotherhood from taking power in Egypt. Nor did forward-deployed American military power prevent Iran from dominating Iraq, Syria from imploding, or anarchy from breaking out in Libya. It is also an admission that the power of national culture and social media frequently exceeds the power of special operations forces and cruise missiles.

Another notion prevalent in many Washington circles is that the use of American military power must always conclude with the annihilation of the opponent's armed might and the forcible imposition of the U.S. political system. This thinking is a legacy of World War II, arguably the most destructive war in human history. The idea of imposing a Western-style social system on societies that are decidedly not Western is not simply counterproductive; it is disastrous. In most conflicts, damage limitation is a more realistic, attainable goal for U.S. national military strategy focused on access to the global commons. In this connection, the arrangements that ended the 1973 war between Egypt and Israel—rather than the unconditional surrender of Japan or Germany in 1945—point the way forward for U.S. defense and foreign policy in the twenty-first century.

CHANGING THE WAY U.S. FORCES FIGHT

Full-spectrum military dominance on a global basis is both unaffordable and unnecessary. The good news is that the aforementioned strategic thinking does not impose the tax burden on American citizens to fund global military hegemony or full-spectrum military dominance.[56]

Nevertheless, achieving this dominance when and where the United States needs it is another matter. To attain this kind of mobile strategic dominance, America's armed forces must be postured to integrate their warfighting capabilities into joint operations when and where they are needed. Even with constrained defense budgets, this capability is attainable now, but it requires the American people to maintain powerful forces-in-being—forces designed to win the first fight, because we may not get the chance to win a second.[57]

Forces-in-being—aerospace, maritime, and ground maneuver—exist to cope with strategic surprise, such as an emergency on the 1950 Korean model or a sudden shift in the strategic balance of power like the 1939 Nazi-Soviet Pact.[58] Their deterrent value rests on their potent, ready military capabilities and composition: mobile, modular, scalable, and focused on winning wars.

Most of the ingredients for full-spectrum dominance when and where Americans need it already exist. Its contemporary maritime and aerospace dominance gives the United States the opportunity to wage war on its own terms, at places of its own choosing. Whether the opposing forces are nuclear, conventional, or irregular, American aerospace and maritime forces are accustomed to act as first responders or enablers in operations beyond America's borders. These forces are postured to execute "all arms/all effects" warfare. This is an overarching joint operational concept designed to integrate all available capabilities when and where they are needed.[59] The challenge is to integrate the diverse military capabilities from the aerospace and maritime forces with the Army's ground maneuver forces as seamlessly as possible whenever Army forces are committed. The task is not an easy one. The American legacy of service-centric warfare looms over the entire defense establishment.

Today, Americans are witnessing the resurrection of the dysfunctional German high command of the 1940s with the organization of U.S. naval and aerospace power to conduct Air-Sea Battle (ASB). Air-Sea Battle was originally billed as the leading edge of U.S. military efforts to defeat China's growing A2AD capabilities in the form of long-range missiles, satellites, cyber attacks, submarines, and sea mines.[60] In 2015, ASB was renamed the Joint Concept for Access and Maneuver in the Global Commons (JAM-GC). Despite the official name change, ASB's original purpose persists: to develop the concept and supporting technologies to overcome future opponents' A2AD capabilities.[61]

What makes JAM-GC truly valuable is its conceptual and operational demand for unity of effort on every level—strategic, operational, and tactical. Unfortunately, JAM-GC is pursuing the complex lash-up of multiple Army, Air Force, Navy, and Marine Corps headquarters across the air, cyber, sea, land, and space domains.[62] However, each of the service-based headquarters participating in JAM-GC is structured to conduct operations in its respective domain (air, land, or sea), not to routinely execute missions involving the integration of capabilities across service lines. Consequently, connecting these numerous service headquarters and equipping them with the expertise and the technology to perform the tasks JAM-GC demands is not just time-consuming, it is also prohibitively expensive.

The good news is that the leadership of the Air Force and the Navy has figured out that in future conflicts and crises (whether they involve China, Russia, or an alliance of nation-state and nonstate actors), there will be no time for a pickup game. The opponents will be ready to fight in their respective geographical areas.

Our potential opponents already know that the disruption of ISR and communications, particularly space-based capabilities, is arguably the best method to gain parity in a military confrontation with expeditionary U.S. forces. A continental power such as China or Russia, or even a major regional power such as Turkey or Iran with modest electronic warfare and cyber capabilities, can neutralize or negate the effects of America's precision strike weapons, GPS-based navigation and guidance systems, as well as our radio frequency–based networking between tactical platforms and operational commands.

In this kind of environment, the lash-up of headquarters on the JAM-GC model will not work. Cobbling together single service headquarters at the last minute to conduct complex warfighting operations against capable opponents is fraught with danger. In fact, without the capability to integrate powerful ground maneuver forces with accurate, devastating strikes, China (for that matter, most continental opponents) will absorb precision guided munitions the way a sponge absorbs water. The likely outcome is the loss of the first battle and a long war with the potential to destroy U.S., Chinese, or Russian prosperity— a war like World War I.

ORGANIZING FOR FUTURE VICTORY

Twentieth-century warfare teaches the importance of combining new warfighting capabilities at progressively lower levels. Integration is also about innovation, not invention; the integration of existing technology saves money, time, and lives. Modern warfare rewards armed forces with integrated military command structures that can orchestrate military capabilities across service lines.

Despite Japan's absolute control of the air during the opening stages of its invasion of China, Japan's light infantry–based armies repeatedly failed to encircle and annihilate Chiang Kai-shek's ground forces. Until the Soviet high command learned late in World War II to attack the Wehrmacht simultaneously from multiple directions and in multiple dimensions, the Wehrmacht always recovered from the initial disruption that strikes caused. Israeli air superiority could also not overcome Soviet-supplied air defense technology and defeat Egypt's massive ground force without the penetration of Israeli ground maneuver forces into Egypt. And, in 1991, even Iraq's weak army in Kuwait could not be defeated without the use of American ground maneuver forces. In the twenty-first century, advances in air defense radar and missile technology will present manned and unmanned aircraft with nearly impenetrable air defenses.

To terminate conflicts on terms that favor the United States and avoid long, destructive wars of attrition, the U.S. armed forces must combine the concentration of massive firepower across service lines with the near-simultaneous attack of ground maneuver forces in time and space to achieve decisive effects against opposing forces. The question is how to do it.

The first step involves recognizing that in the twenty-first century, large ground combat forces that immobilize soldiers in prepared defenses or mass in small areas (such as Kuwait in 1991 and 2003) will be identified, targeted, and destroyed from a distance. "Holding ground" in the face of ubiquitous overhead military surveillance and reconnaissance linked to an array of precision guided weapons is extremely dangerous.[63] Today, even midsized powers are building a large, diverse, and reliable range of conventional ballistic missiles for deep precision strikes designed to operate within terrestrial and space-based sensor networks.[64] The requirement that results from the proliferating ISR-strike revolution is a warfighting environment that rewards dispersed, mobile warfare, a brand of warfare that elevates tactical dispersion to the operational level of war.

Coping with the demands of dispersed mobile warfare requires the United States to build a twenty-first-century scalable building-block–type force design with an integrative framework for operations based on the warfighting functions of ISR, strike, maneuver, and sustainment. As JAM-GC demonstrates, the ISR-strike framework is widely understood and employed in American aerospace and maritime forces. It is also the key to combining the nation's ground maneuver forces with ISR-strike and sustainment capabilities from all of the services.

Of course, strike or stand-off attack involves much more than air strikes. Conventional strike capabilities reside in all of the services as well as inside the continental United States. Strike can also involve the application of non-kinetic forces. An in-depth discussion of cyber war is beyond the scope of this work, but it is worth noting that cyber attacks can disarm opposing military capabilities such as air defenses.[65] Inside a weak, divided, and disgruntled society, cyber attacks can also undermine trust in government—even promote political violence—by remaining completely invisible.[66]

Adding maneuver and sustainment to the ISR-strike framework is a vital step in the evolution of warfare. It moves the defense establishment beyond the ad hoc coordination of individual federal agencies and service-based elements of integration. It is far more than combined arms, air-ground cooperation, and amphibious operations. Within the operational framework of ISR-strike-maneuver-sustainment, the planning and execution of operations are routinely integrated through multi-service command and control—common mission purposes.

Restrictive, hierarchical, single-service Cold War command systems are anachronisms. The command and control of geographically dispersed armed forces requires "brain to brain" as well as "box to box" connectivity. Shared battle space awareness is both technical and intellectual. The industrial-age systems suffer from information overload and too many single-service levels of command, all of which are designed to say *no*, not *yes*, in a crisis or conflict.

Unity of effort, speed of decision, and action demand integrated command structures midway between the strategic and tactical levels that create and maintain a coherent picture of operations. In essence, American political leaders must do what the Soviet leadership did during World War II, albeit with a profoundly American twist—build joint, integrated command structures on the operational level that will provide American political and military leaders with the means to comprehensively direct military power to detect, deter, disrupt, neutralize, or destroy opposing forces and threats decisively. Like most things in American military history, the demand is not new.

Disappointed with the muddled conduct of operations during the Korean conflict, Army Lt. Gen. James Gavin said in a 1958 *Time* magazine interview, "I think really what is needed now is a competent military staff of senior military people working directly for the Secretary of Defense. I would have them take over the functions of the Joint Chiefs of Staff. I would have the military staff organized to handle operations, plans, intelligence, and in fact, break up the Joint Chiefs of Staff. Such a career staff should be drawn from all services, but should be 'completely integrated across the board.'"[67]

Gavin was expressing frustration with the conduct of war by the Joint Chiefs of Staff, the American military equivalent of the Articles of Confederation.[68] The Goldwater-Nichols Act created unified commands on the strategic level but left the money and, ultimately, the power entirely in the hands of the service chiefs.[69] Goldwater-Nichols did not change the fact that the senior leaders of the armed services possess the authority and the funding to determine what they will buy and how they will fight with minimal interference from the president or Congress. The service bureaucracies continue to set the requirements multi-billion dollar programs, not the Office of Secretary of Defense which rarely challenges service budgets or priorities. Goldwater-Nichols mandated Jointness, but it did not create an executive military body on the national level with the authority to enforce unity of effort at the expense of the powerful service bureaucracies.

The missing link is the national machinery—an American military high command—to direct the strategic preparation and conduct of military operations, allocate strategic resources, and define strategic military needs. Similar proposals for a unified American military high command and staff organization with a supporting national general staff system on the German model were presented on 25 February 1943 by officers in the War Department. According to the study's authors, the recommendations "were based on the acknowledgment that all of our U.S. war experiences to date (from Pearl Harbor to the present date) point to the necessity for unity of command on all levels."[70]

The machinery that answers this requirement is a national defense staff with a defense chief. Together with his staff, the chief of defense would answer directly to the secretary of defense and the president for the day-to-day administration of the armed forces, as well as for the warfighting readiness and development of the capabilities residing in all of the services. The chief of defense would exercise operational control over the armed services and issue directives on behalf of the commander-in-chief, the president, for the strategic planning and development of the armed forces. The chief's directives would have the effect of binding law.

Voices in Washington opposed to a national defense staff will make the argument that no one in military or civilian authority can ever accurately forecast the costs of strategic choices, determine the variables and stakes in war, or adequately control for the "Clausewitzian friction" and fog of war.[71] This may be true, but if no attempt is made to fashion the national military means to more effectively develop, command, and employ American military power in the twenty-first century, this record of post–World War II military fiascos—Iraq and Afghanistan, along with Vietnam and Korea—will also persist.[72]

The time for establishing a national defense staff selected from all of the services on the basis of merit (competitive examination, experience, and demonstrated expertise) is long overdue. If the president and Congress are ever to devise a military strategy that focuses American military power on national, not service, priorities, they will need a national defense staff to direct the change.

Trade-offs across service lines are tough. Senior officers on loan to the Joint Staff whose careers depend on their demonstrated loyalty to their respective services cannot perform these tasks without risking their survival inside their service. A national general staff system that competitively selects and then educates and promotes individual officers with the goal of cultivating an expert cadre of key staff officers and commanders for service on the National Defense Staff is essential. The promotion of these national general staff officers to flag rank and service at the highest levels must rest with the National Defense Staff, not the services.[73]

Expecting any of the services to sacrifice for the others is ridiculous. No matter how vital the Navy's nuclear submarine fleet is to the security and prosperity of the American people, the Air Force, Army, and Marine Corps will argue their own contributions are no less important. The United States, like Israel, Great Britain, Russia, Germany, Japan, China, and France, needs a core group of trained and educated professionals in the armed forces who can assist the nation's political leaders to deal intelligently with these issues, as well as with the inevitable unexpected war.

Below the strategic level, the United States needs regional unified command structures to direct warfighting operations from an "all arms/all effects" perspective. The Department of Defense must reorganize American military command structures inside the regional unified commands on the operational level—numbered armies, air forces, fleets, and marine headquarters—into a smaller number of joint force headquarters (see figure 2). The resulting regionally focused, three-star-commanded joint force headquarters should be designed from top to bottom to command whatever forces and capabilities are required for the mission. However, the new command structure cannot be a paper tiger. The joint force headquarters must be truly integrated and responsive, not a collection of bureaucratic fiefdoms with the façade of jointness.

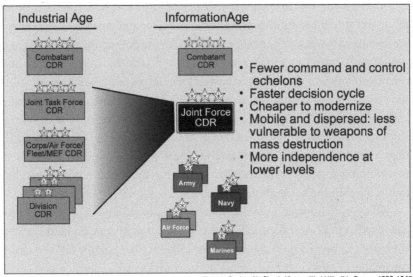

FIGURE 2. Joint Force Commands: The Path to Unity of Command in the Twenty-First Century

Once the joint force command headquarters inside the regional unified commands are established, tactical forces from the services organized around ISR, strike, maneuver, or sustainment can be packaged under one-star commanders to plug into these joint force headquarters depending on mission requirements. In this way, joint forces can be scaled up or down as needed. This action moves jointness at the strategic level as envisioned under Goldwater-Nichols to the operational level of war. It also addresses the need to flatten command structures and accelerate the decision cycle.

RESHAPING GROUND MANEUVER FORCES

The task for the U.S. Army in the twenty-first century is to reorganize the ground maneuver force into a mix of capability-based fighting formations that can deploy quickly and be strategically decisive in joint operations wherever and whenever they fight as well as effective for homeland defense. These forces must be capable of dispersed, decentralized operations to survive and fight in an ISR and strike-dominated battle space. The process of reorganization must embrace all of the U.S. Army's capabilities from theater air and missile defense to ground-based strike systems and logistical support structures.

To cope with the conditions that dispersed mobile warfare creates, ground maneuver forces must infiltrate a theater of war at points where the enemy's air defenses are weak or nonexistent. These are the points where manned and unmanned aircraft or missiles cannot easily attack them. The quality and quantity of maneuver, strike, and sustainment forces necessary to make a difference in a major theater war require that the force be brought ashore using conventional port facilities able to handle both roll-on/roll-off and container ships, complemented by conventional strategic airlift, and be able to self-deploy from the ports and airfields to where they are needed. From these points on land, Army maneuver forces must be capable of moving great distances to reach their operational objectives.

To execute infiltration tactics on the operational level of war, the Army needs self-contained independent battle groups that operate on land the way the Navy's ships operate at sea: within the range of their organic ISR and strike capabilities.[74] Moving brigade combat teams under Army division and corps headquarters to future joint warfighting operations is not the answer in a warfighting environment that rewards capability integration, maneuver, and dispersion. Army ground maneuver forces must fight as unreinforced, stand-alone formations that can operate inside a joint force. These formations should number between five thousand and six thousand personnel, small enough for agile maneuver but still large enough to sustain losses, keep fighting, and attack. They should also be commanded by young, energetic brigadier generals who should have the supporting staffs and authorities to make decisions without asking permission of unending numbers of superior flag officers.

To adapt to the new environment, ground maneuver forces will have to switch their operational orientation from a ground-holding strategy to a force-oriented strategy. This is not to suggest that there will never be times in the twenty-first century when the retention of key terrain affords a strategic or operational advantage to the holding force, but these advantages are likely to be fleeting. Again, the historical record is instructive.

From mid-January to mid-May 1944, a few hundred German paratroopers successfully held the mountaintop monastery of Monte Cassino, a linchpin in the German defense called the Gustav Line. The determined German defense over a five-month period cost the Allies thousands of lives at a relatively modest cost in lives and matériel to the German paratroopers holding the monastery.[75]

However, when the ground they held no longer afforded any strategic advantage, the German paratroopers rapidly withdrew to new positions a few miles further north. The point is that "holding ground" only makes sense when doing so confers an advantage on the holding force. Had the BEF held its ground in Mons in August 1914, it would most certainly have been destroyed.

Expectations of short-duration campaigns involving minimal, uncontested advances on the model of Operation Desert Storm or Operation Iraqi Freedom—operations that involve unchallenged U.S. air and naval supremacy—should be suppressed in favor of more challenging scenarios in contested environments. Such an approach should also diverge from the deliberate phasing of U.S. military operations beginning with a predictable buildup and a lengthy air campaign followed by a deliberate ground attack.[76]

STRATEGIC SUSTAINMENT

Full-spectrum military dominance when and where the United States needs it is unattainable without effective sustainment in joint operations. The U.S. capability to deliver military power and the matériel support it requires over vast distances is unsurpassed in the history of warfare, but this capability should not be taken for granted. Future conditions will not resemble Desert Storm. Operational movement varies tremendously from theater to theater.[77] For the present, U.S. military leaders can learn more about challenges to future force projection and logistical operations from Great Britain's Falkland Islands campaign than they can from Desert Storm.

The inevitable spread of precision strike capabilities presents new challenges to force projection. Many countries, not just China and Russia, are developing and will implement A2AD strategies. They will exploit sea mines, persistent surveillance, precision strike, cyber attacks, and electronic warfare to create "no-go" zones into which it will be difficult and costly for the United States to project military power using today's overseas bases and expeditionary forces.[78]

Future American warfighting operations will continue to involve influencing, moving to, and engaging opposing forces to confuse or disrupt the opponent's ability to sense, think, communicate, and prevail. To do this will require more speed and agility to get to the theater, as well as increased sea- and air-lifting capabilities for the needs of future forces. For decades, America has underinvested in strategic lift—a calculated choice to accept risk that shortages in lift could be accommodated by either taking more time to get forces to the theater or by prepositioning equipment in regions of foreseeable conflict. It is hard to see how prepositioning and sustaining equipment is a workable solution. The equipment ages whether it is used or not. It still costs money to acquire and store the equipment sets, even if they are never used and eventually scrapped. Prepositioned equipment sets are also easy to target and destroy.

A better solution is to invest in air- and sea-lift that fills gaps in lift capacity that can otherwise be acquired from the private sector. Such action would include the capability to lift hazardous cargos such as ammunition and explosives, as well as heavy outsized cargo that cannot easily be lifted using commercially available lift. Investment in transportation support systems to off-load military cargo in unimproved locations will also be important.

It is not enough to simply expect the private sector to step in and transport the bulk of the military to war on a moment's notice. Dedicated airlift and short-notice private sector support must be readily available, because long lead times to ramp up for war are becoming a luxury in the age of missiles with transcontinental ranges. Commercial sector transportation assets are also becoming a precious commodity. In Europe or northeast Asia, civilian traffic competes with military traffic over an extremely crowded transportation network. Regional host-nation support may also be insufficient to augment military transportation.[79]

Smart planning and better acquisition strategies can also help. Forces designed with intercontinental transportation in mind are essential. Vehicles sized to facilitate transportation rapidly to forward locations can avoid the need to devise newer airframes capable of lifting heavier vehicles. It also may preclude buying more airframes than needed, because larger vehicles consume more aircraft volume. Efficient power projection and force sustainment, with as lean a logistics tail as possible, can add combat capability to U.S. forces.

FINAL THOUGHTS

Friedrich Nietzsche said, "War makes the victor stupid."[80] The deceptively easy U.S. victory in 1991 turned Americans into global policemen with the mission of imposing a new liberal democratic order on a troubled world. In the haste to attack Afghanistan and Iraq, the United States' Cold War surplus of military power was squandered on interventions against weak insurgents, criminal networks, and tribal peoples.

Winston Churchill's observation that in great matters "very large errors are excused or even unperceived, but . . . small mistakes are punished out of all proportion" was confirmed again and again in American military operations.[81] Not a single civilian appointee or general officer was held accountable for the monumental failures of strategy, policy, or military command between 2001 and 2014.[82]

Meanwhile, the loss of its Cold War surplus put the American military—a defense establishment that spends hundreds of billions of dollars in any given year but cannot be audited, a system chasing dollars for big programs of questionable utility—on a very dangerous path.[83] In a rare admission of the truth, Vice Chief of Staff of the Army Gen. Richard Cody told an Army audience in June 2006 that before the September 11, 2001, attacks, the Army was really not prepared for modern warfare. He said it was undertrained and underequipped and in a generally poor state of maintenance.[84] Quite unintentionally, Cody highlighted a serious problem.

All too often, the service or services offering the best spending opportunities to Congress and industry are the ones that get the money. In the words of Charles Knight, co-director of the Project on Defense Alternatives, "What makes compelling political sense for the individual member of Congress often ends up distorting federal spending priorities."[85]

In Washington's chaotic scramble for dollars, the American people struggle with another difficult problem: collective military and civilian leadership. The Joint Chiefs, combatant commanders, the secretary of defense, and the president are all key players in a convoluted national security decisionmaking system. It is a conglomeration akin to Britain's grossly ineffective war cabinet in 1914, not a national defense staff capable of assisting the president and the defense secretary with the execution of their responsibilities.

Like Britain's political and military leaders in 1914, America's leaders are far too confident of their military superiority and contemptuous of the major advances in military technology, organization, and leadership occurring in other countries. Like the Japanese emperor in 1937, the president and the secretary of defense do not truly command the armed forces. Instead, they mediate and arbitrate interservice disputes.

Shrinking defense resources are causing destructive interservice fights inside a fragmented defense establishment.[86] Growing conceptual and organizational chaos means that shrinking defense funds are not always prudently invested. For instance, funds for the Navy are invested in amphibious carriers and unique aircraft (F-35B) for the Marine Corps, when naval experts widely fear that slow, diesel-powered mini-aircraft carriers will be sitting ducks in anything other than an extremely permissive environment.[87] It means the Navy is hard pressed to fund two separate air forces that operate variants of the same aircraft (F-35) for similar missions. This kind of redundancy comes at the expense of other vital needs, such as theater air and missile defense, new strike systems, and improved logistical operations.

In 2010, Secretary of Defense Robert Gates decided to address the problem by raising questions about the strategic value of amphibious forces: "We have to take a hard look at where it would be necessary or sensible to launch another major amphibious landing again—especially as advances in anti-ship systems keep pushing the potential launch point further from shore. On a more basic level, in the twenty-first century, what kind of amphibious capability do we really need to deal with the most likely scenarios, and, then, how much?"[88] In other words, it is time to fundamentally reexamine the Marine Corps, its mission, and its structure.[89]

A year later, Secretary Gates cancelled the Marine Corps' Expeditionary Fighting Vehicle (EFV), questioning its warfighting utility in future conflicts: "The most plausible scenarios requiring power projection from the sea could be handled through a mix of existing air and sea systems employed in new ways along with new vehicles—scenarios that do not require the exquisite features of the EFV."[90]

Robert Work, currently deputy secretary of defense, extended Gates' line of thinking, observing that "the Navy-Marine team will never contemplate littoral maneuver until an enemy's battle network, capable of firing dense salvos of guided weapons, is suppressed. Consequently, the initial phase of any joint theater–entry operation will require achieving air, sea, undersea, and overall battle-network superiority in the amphibious objective area. . . . Thus far we have only argued that some capability to conduct theater-entry operations and littoral maneuver must be retained. But it is fair to ask how much amphibious capacity is needed."[91]

To cope with mounting skepticism inside defense circles regarding the Marine Corps' utility in a war with a peer or near-peer opponent, the service's Expeditionary Force 21 future amphibious assault strategy set out to recast the Marines' amphibious assault tactics. In a departure from previous practices that entailed amphibious assaults against one large beach, the Marines argued they could still assemble a large naval task force offshore (supported by the Navy's carrier battle groups) to launch a Marine amphibious brigade sixty-five to one hundred miles from ship to shore. The Marines further insisted they would attack in small landing teams where they could exploit gaps in enemy defenses. These Marine expeditionary brigade operations would require four hundred Amphibious Assault Vehicles and seven hundred Amphibious

Combat Vehicles—which, predictably, is again the Marine's top acquisition priority.[92]

Yet the announced change in Marine amphibious tactics does not address the threat of persistent surveillance (commercial or military) in the sea lanes or the strategically important areas where the Marines argue they could be employed—the Persian Gulf, South China Sea, Sea of Japan, northern Norway, the Dardanelles/eastern Mediterranean, Baltic Sea, Arctic Ocean, and South China Sea. The tactical adjustment also does nothing to defeat or neutralize the vast array of long-range precision strike systems and air defense systems available to potential opponents. Even more troubling is that the change in tactics presupposes a detailed knowledge of a capable, future enemy. This kind of precise knowledge is something the Marines are unlikely to acquire.

Against the backdrop of air defense weapons from shoulder-fired missiles to missile systems capable of detecting and destroying stealth aircraft at very high altitudes, exclusive reliance on airmobile operations with V-22 Osprey aircraft from the sea is an equally vulnerable and dangerous scenario.[93] Based on these trends, the Marine Corps' military capabilities are more than sufficient for military interventions against weak opponents in Latin America, Africa, and the South Pacific Basin. However, these same capabilities are unusable in a fight with a peer or near-peer opponent in Europe, Russia, the greater Middle East, or northeast Asia.

This observation also applies to the Army's airborne and airmobile forces—light infantry–centric forces that are just as vulnerable as the Marine Corps in any contested nonpermissive environment. For Congress and the American people, the question is: How many versions of the light infantry–centric forces in the Marine Corps, Army Special Forces, Special Operations Forces, and Army airborne/airmobile forces does the nation really need?

Today, we can say with certainty that U.S. forces may well encounter the kind of contested environment Israeli forces confronted at the outset of the 1973 war—a battlespace in which manned and unmanned aircraft cannot operate. All U.S. forces will need larger strike weapons at sea, on land, and in the air with more penetration power in the future. All of the services have terrestrial platforms that were successful in the uncontested permissive environments of Iraq and Afghanistan but that will not survive modern air defenses, long-range strike, and electronic as well as cyber warfare capabilities.[94]

Hollowing out the Army's ground force by shrinking the service's mobile armored force is a politically expedient way of saving money, but it consigns future Army forces to defeat in any "first fight" with a peer or near-peer opponent. Unless the United States wants to relive the Japanese, Russian, German, and British experiences presented in this volume, Americans need armored forces that can take hits, keep fighting, and decisively counter-attack on land.

The Army's senior leaders, shaped as they are by recent experiences suppressing weak, tribal insurgent peoples, are partly to blame for neglecting the need for new, modern armored platforms.[95] Instead of fighting to preserve the nation's warfighting backbone, the Army is focused on maintaining the massive overhead of its superfluous two-, three-, and four-star headquarters (division, corps, and army).[96] The Army's resistance to a reorganization that would consolidate more combat power under fewer headquarters, and thus obtain more ready, deployable fighting forces from its remaining end strength, is another problem because it is eroding congressional support for new, more survivable combat platforms the Army needs. Operational maneuver in the form of mobile armored forces is a critical national warfighting capability.

Operational maneuver demands the capability for U.S. Army ground forces to operate in tandem with aerospace and maritime strike forces to encircle and destroy opposing forces, whether high-end conventional or irregular.[97] Unless Congress and the White House weigh in, the U.S. Army will end up with hundreds of generals, numerous installations, and expensive modernization programs of questionable value, but very few formations that can actually deploy and fight.

Americans must also focus their attention on force integration—the application of military capabilities across service lines—to achieve this result. As Field Marshal Erwin Rommel noted in 1942, "Anything which may deflect from unity of purpose, from the will to pull together, must be utterly eradicated."[98]

Wasteful spending, excessive redundancy in capability, and resistance to unity of effort are all symptomatic of the degree to which the service-centric American military structure sabotages unity of effort. These problems are part of the big defense-industrial complex game, one that will continue at great expense to the American taxpayer until Congress, the president, and the national security staff devise a coherent national military strategy to terminate excessive and unnecessary military commitments beyond the nation's borders.

Redundant manned and unmanned aviation organizations and platforms, as well as information technology and intelligence programs, must be reduced or phased out. Mandating joint, integrative command structures and passing laws that create a national defense staff to assist the president and secretary of defense with developing and commanding the U.S. armed forces are important actions that must be taken soon.

The president and Congress must reduce the number of combatant commands through amalgamation and place the four services under the authority of the proposed national defense staff. Congress must consolidate the numerous service headquarters inside the combatant commands into joint, integrated command structures.[99] The Department of Defense's capability requirements and operational testing and evaluation processes will have to become fully joint and integrated. These and additional actions must be folded into the future president's fiscal rear defense requests.

Americans want a national military strategy that diverges sharply from the ideologically driven interventionism of the past twenty years and a return to the use of force within clearly defined constitutional parameters.[100] Washington can no longer ignore the influence of national geography, culture, economy, and military history on the use of American military power.[101] The reason is obvious. The age of abundant wealth and unconstrained defense spending is at an end.

Doing nothing is not an option. Given the proliferation of powerful new military technologies in both the physical world and cyberspace, America's margin of victory in future wars of decision is likely to be thinner than ever.[102] Yet it is a matter of historical record that the men and women that are charged with the duty and responsibility of creating and maintaining that margin of victory know too little about military affairs, let alone the history of modern warfare.[103]

It is no accident that Congress has been submissive and deferential toward ineffective, even failed, military commanders despite very serious problems with the conduct of operations in Iraq and Afghanistan.[104] Politicians know that American society's consciousness is shaped by the forces of hype and publicity. For most Americans, the truth in military affairs is either unknown or an afterthought. This condition should not afflict Congress, but politicians are extremely risk-averse. Urging change on an American military that frequently wallows in self-congratulation is something few politicians are willing to risk.

War in the absolute sense, a true war of decision, is coming. Precisely when and where it will break out is hard to predict. Clearly, Russian president Vladimir Putin is determined to reverse the course of history and restore control of peoples in the Baltic littoral and Ukraine—peoples who despise Russia—to Moscow's control.[105] New alignments along the Sunni-Shi'a divide in the Middle East and Southwest Asia suggest we are at the beginning of a long war with unknown consequences for Israel, Egypt, Jordan, and, ultimately, Europe.[106] Precisely how China will evolve and what kind of future role it will play in Asia is unknown.

Still, even in reduced economic circumstances, Americans must cultivate a new margin of victory lest they end up without good strategic options. A laser-like focus on military organization, technology, and human capital with one eye on today's needs and the other on tomorrow's challenges is indispensable.

An aphorism often attributed to Leon Trotsky should resonate strongly with Americans: "You may not be interested in war, but war is interested in you. If war is combat and commerce, calamity, and commodity, it cannot be left to our political leaders alone—and certainly not to our generals."[107]

Notes

INTRODUCTION

1. Jack Kenny, "Calvin Coolidge and the Greatness of a 'Not great President,'" *New American*, 18 February 2013, 1.
2. MacGregor Knox and Williamson Murray, *The Dynamics of Military Revolution, 1300–2050* (Cambridge: Cambridge University Press, 2001), 6. Also see Robert M. Epstein, *Napoleon's Last Victory and the Emergence of Modern War* (Lawrence: University Press of Kansas, 1994), 182.
3. Carl von Clausewitz, *On War*, ed. and trans. Michael Howard and Peter Paret (Princeton: Princeton University Press, 1976), 488–89.
4. Paul Kennedy, *The Rise and Fall of the Great Powers: Economic Change and Military Conflict from 1500 to 2000* (New York: Vintage Books, 1989), 365.
5. David Wise, "Blowback as National Policy," *WarontheRocks.com*, 6 April 2015.
6. Daniel Davis, "Seduced by Success," *Armed Forces Journal*, 10 February 2014. Davis points out that in 13 years of operations in Iraq and Afghanistan, the U.S. Armed Forces sustained on average 331 casualties per month (6,700 killed and more than 45,000 wounded) that were overwhelmingly the result of land mines or improvised explosive devices encountered during mounted and dismounted patrols, sniper fire, hit-and-run ambushes, accidents, and "friendly fire" from Afghan or Iraqi troops.
7. Michael Hirsh and Jamie Tarabay, "Washington Losing Patience with Counterinsurgency in Afghanistan," *National Journal*, 25 June 2011.
8. Ellen Knickmeyer, "Iraqis Say Civilians Killed in U.S. Raids. Military Asserts Fatalities in West Were Insurgents," *Washington Post*, 18 October 2005, 1.
9. James Rickards, *Currency Wars: The Making of the Next Global Crisis* (New York: Penguin/Portfolio, 2012), 204–5.
10. Quincy Wright, *A Study of War*, 2nd ed. (Chicago: The University of Chicago Press, 1971), 662–64.

11. John Nelson Rickard, *Advance and Destroy: Patton as Commander in the Bulge* (Lexington: University Press of Kentucky, 2011), 49. Five percent of the German army was tied down defending northern Italy.

12. John Nyaradi, "Across the Globe, Financial Markets Are Falling Like Dominos, One by One," *MarketWatch.com*, 12 June 2013. Also see Bryan Jordan, "Report: Israel Passes U.S. Military Technology to China," *DefenseTech.org*, 24 December 2013.

13. Stephen Meyer, "Carcass of Dead Policies: The Irrelevance of NATO," *Parameters* (Winter 2003–2004), 84–96. Also see Anna Nemtsova, "Russia Slides Back to the Middle Ages," *TheDailyBeast.com*, 7 August 2015.

14. Philip Stephens, "Yellen or Summers: The Best Obama Can Do Is Toss a Coin," *Financial Times*, 12 July 2013, 7; Jeong Young-Su, "China Tried Muscling South Korea in Yellow Sea," *Korea JoongAng Daily*, 30 November 2013, 1. Also see Vassily Mikheev's statement regarding Russia's fear of China and Japan in Zachary Keck, "Russia Holds Military Exercise Aimed at China and Japan," *The Diplomat*, 17 July 2013.

15. Michael Adler, "Iran Nuclear Deal Will Transform Region; Saudis, Israelis Watching Every Move," *BreakingDefense.com*, 29 November 2013. Also see Elizabeth Dickinson, "2013 in Review: Events Since the Arab Spring Shift Regional Order," *TheNational.ae*, 29 December 2013.

16. Williamson Murray and others have noted that it can only begin with an honest study of the past. Williamson Murray and Allan R. Millett, *Military Innovation in the Interwar Period* (Cambridge: Cambridge University Press, 1996), 313–14.

17. Peter D. Feaver, "How to Read the President's National Security Strategy," *ForeignPolicy.com*, 6 July 2015.

18. "Almaz-Antey Launches Next Generation Buk Missile into Development," *Sputnik News.com*, 15 August 2015, 1. Dramatic advances in computational power combined with integrated radar systems elevate this threat to the strategic level.

19. John Carlin, "Guru of Downsizing Admits He Got it All Wrong," *The Independent*, 12 May 1996.

20. "Interview with LTG Ben Hodges," *Defense News*, 31 March 2015.

21. Colonel Richard J. Dunn III, USA (Ret.), "The Impact of a Declining Defense Budget on Combat Readiness," Backgrounder no. 2828 on Defense and National Security, Heritage Foundation, 18 July 2003.

22. Joseph Schumpeter, *The Theory of Economic Development: An Inquiry into Profits, Capital, Credit, Interest, and the Business Cycle*, trans. Redvers Opie (Brunswick, NJ: Transaction Publishers, 1983), introduction.

23. Beatrice Heuser, *The Evolution of Strategy: Thinking War from Antiquity to the Present* (Cambridge: Cambridge University Press, 2010), 17.

24. Quoted by George F. Hofmann in *Through Mobility We Conquer: The Mechanization of the U.S. Cavalry* (Lexington: University Press of Kentucky, 2006), 459.

25. Ibid., 459–60.

26. The author is indebted to Mike Robel for suggesting the "first fight" idea and its importance to what happens subsequently in war.

27. Richard Gabriel, *Genghis Khan's Greatest General: Subotai the Valiant* (Norman: University of Oklahoma Press, 2006), 137.

28. Nancy A. Youssef, "Pentagon Fears It's Not Ready for a War with Putin," *TheDailyBeast.com*, 14 August 2015.

29. Spencer C. Tucker, *The Great War 1914–1918* (Bloomington: Indiana University Press, 1998), 133.

30. *Doctrine for the Armed Forces of the United States,* Joint Publication 1 (Washington, DC: U.S. Government Printing Office, 23 March 2013), 1–5.

CHAPTER 1. MISSION IMPOSSIBLE

1. Niall Ferguson, *The Pity of War: Explaining World War I* (New York: Basic Books, 1999), 160–61; Donald Kagan, *On the Origins of War and the Preservation of Peace* (New York: Doubleday Books, 1995), 202.

2. Robert Lloyd George, *David and Winston: How the Friendship Between Churchill and Lloyd George Changed the Course of History* (New York: The Overlook Press, 2005), 108.

3. Ferguson, *The Pity of War*, 165–66. Lord Morley put the notes he took during cabinet deliberations in the ten days leading up to 4 August into a memorandum. His subsequent "Memorandum on Resignation" reveals that Grey's plea for Belgium's welfare as the motive for embroiling Britain in war with Germany was a lie. The memorandum is available online at https://archive.org/stream/memorandumonresi030576mbp/memorandumonresi030576mbp_djvu.txt.

4. David Fromkin, *A Peace to End All Peace: The Fall of the Ottoman Empire and the Creation of the Modern Middle East* (New York: Henry Holt and Company, 1989), 83.

5. William R. Griffiths, *The Great War* (Wayne, NJ: Square One Publishers, 2003), 89.

6. Peter Hart, *Fire and Movement: The British Expeditionary Force and the Campaign of 1914* (New York: Oxford University Press, 2015), 68.

7. Tucker, *The Great War 1914–1918*, 20.

8. Edward Spiers, *Haldane: An Army Reformer* (Edinburgh: Edinburgh University Press, 1980), 27.

9. Hermann Jahnke, *Fuerst Bismarck: Sein Leben und Wirken* (Berlin: Paul Kitte Verlag, 1890), 569.

10. Kennedy, *The Rise and Fall of the Great Powers*, 231.

11. Robert K. Massie, *Dreadnought: Britain, Germany, and the Coming of the Great War* (New York: Random House, 1991), 90.

12. Ibid., 819.

13. Niall Ferguson, *Empire: The Rise and Demise of the British World Order and the Lessons for Global Power* (New York: Basic Books, 2002), 237.

14. Dudley Sommer, *Haldane of Cloan: His Life and Times, 1856–1928* (London: George Allen and Unwin Ltd., 1960), 214, 428.

15. The Elgin Commission had already advocated changes in British army administration. It was chaired by Lord Esher, who strongly supported Haldane's reform efforts. The Esher Report was published successively in February and March 1904. King Edward VII welcomed the report and urged the Balfour government to accept its recommendations, which it did. Lord Kitchener was against it. After Richard Haldane became secretary of state for war in the Liberal Campbell-Bannerman government in 1905, he implemented many of its recommendations between 1906 and 1909. Among his advisers was Colonel (later General) Sir Gerald Ellison, who was also secretary of the Esher Committee.

16. Stephen E. Koss, *Lord Haldane, Scapegoat for Liberalism* (New York: Columbia University Press, 1969), 47.

17. Ernest M. Teagarden, *Haldane at the War Office: A Study in Organization and Management* (New York: Gordon Press, 1976), 156–57.

18. Spiers, *Haldane: An Army Reformer,* 185.

19. Robert R. Leonard, *Fighting by Minutes: The Time and Art of War* (Westport, CT: Praeger, 1994), 85.

20. Teagarden, *Haldane at the War Office*, 158–69.

21. Ibid., 81.

22. Ibid., 154.

23. Koss, *Lord Haldane*, 47.

24. "Learning from Haldane," RUSI online analysis, August 2010. Also see Ian F. W. Beckett and John Gooch, eds., *Politicians and Defence: Studies*

in the Formulation of British Defence Policy 1845–1970 (Manchester: Manchester University Press, 1981).

25. Gordon Craig, *The Battle of Koeniggraetz: Prussia's Victory over Austria, 1866* (Westport, CT: Greenwood Press, 1975), 174–75.

26. Teagarden, *Haldane at the War Office*, 143–45.

27. J. F. C. Fuller, *The Army in My Time* (London: Rich and Cowan, 1935), 111.

28. Horace Wyatt, *Motor Transports in War, 1914* (London: Hodder and Stoughton, 1914), 126.

29. Tucker, *The Great War 1914–1918*, 15.

30. Robert B. Asprey, *The German High Command at War: Hindenburg and Ludendorff, Conduct of World War I* (New York: William Morrow, 1991), 44.

31. Shelford Bidwell and Dominick Graham, *Fire-Power: British Army Weapons and Theories of War, 1904–1945* (London: George Allen and Unwin, 1982), 49.

32. Fred Watson, *Stargazer: The Life and Times of the Telescope* (New York: Da Capo Press, 2005), prologue.

33. Sommer, *Haldane of Cloan*, 213.

34. Spiers, *Haldane: An Army Reformer*, 73.

35. John Terraine, *Mons: The Retreat to Victory* (Barnsley, UK: Pen and Sword Ltd., 1991), 27.

36. J. E. Edmonds, *History of the Great War, Military Operations: France and Belgium, 1914,* vol. 2 (London: MacMillan and Co., 1925), 465.

37. Hart, *Fire and Movement*, 31.

38. For more on French, see George H. Cassar, *The Tragedy of Sir John French* (Newark: University of Delaware Press, 1985).

39. For more on Haig, see J. P. Harris, *Sir Douglas Haig and the First World War* (Cambridge: Cambridge University Press, 2009).

40. J. F. C. Fuller, *A Military History of the Western World,* vol. 3 (New York: DaCapo Press, 1956), 200.

41. General instructions by the German High Command for the deployment into Belgium as recounted in Alexander von Kluck, *The March on Paris and the Battle of the Marne 1914* (London: Edward Arnold, 1920), 9–10.

42. Ibid., 38.

43. Sir Horace Smith-Dorrien, *Memories of Forty-Eight Years' Service*, Chapter 24b, "The Retreat from Mons: Le Cateau," *The War Times Journal* online version, available at http://www.richthofen.com/smith-dorrien/.

44. Hart, *Fire and Movement*, 105–6.

45. Smith-Dorrien, *Memories of Forty-Eight Years' Service*, Chapter 24b, "The Retreat from Mons: Le Cateau."

46. Terraine, *Mons: The Retreat to Victory*, 76.

47. Arthur Corbett-Smith, *The Retreat from Mons* (New York: Nabu Public Domain Imprints, 2013), 60–83. Similar anecdotes are repeated in Terraine, *Mons: Retreat to Victory*, 80–126.

48. Hart, *Fire and Movement*, 126–30.

49. Terraine, *Mons: Retreat to Victory*, 86. Having lived in Mons, the author does not share Terraine's readiness to dismiss the canal as indefensible or irrelevant.

50. Jerry Murland, *Retreat and Rearguard 1914: The BEF's Actions from Mons to the Marne* (Barnsley, UK: Pen and Sword, Ltd., 2011), 24.

51. Ibid., 88.

52. Paddy Griffith, *Battle Tactics of the Western Front: The British Army's Art of Attack 1916–1918* (New Haven: Yale University Press, 1994), 48–49.

53. Hart, *Fire and Movement*, 118.

54. British soldiers who achieved expert status were rewarded with a higher rate of pay, so it paid to be a good shot.

55. Hart, *Fire and Movement*, 111.

56. J. B. A. Bailey, *Field Artillery and Firepower* (Annapolis, MD: Naval Institute Press, 2004), 236–38.

57. Terraine, *Mons: Retreat to Victory*, 90–91.

58. Terence Zuber, *The Mons Myth: A Reassessment of the Battle* (Gloucestershire, UK: The History Press, 2010), 132–33.

59. Murland, *Retreat and Rearguard 1914*, 24–25.

60. Hart, *Fire and Movement*, 118.

61. Murland, *Retreat and Rearguard 1914*, 19.

62. Zuber, *The Mons Myth*, 136.

63. Murland, *Retreat and Rearguard 1914*, 18–19.

64. Hart, *Fire and Movement*, 109, 114, 116–17.

65. Smith-Dorrien, *Memories of Forty-Eight Years' Service*, chapter 24b, "The Retreat from Mons: Le Cateau."

66. Murland, *Retreat and Rearguard 1914*, 32.

67. Asprey, *The German High Command at War*, 99.

68. J. Koettgen, trans., *A German Deserter's War Experience* (New York: B. W. Huebsch, 1917), 51. The author declined to release his name when the book was published.

69. Haig seems to have gotten French's message almost immediately with the result that his lead elements reached their destinations at Feignies, La Longueville, and Bavai around 10 o'clock in the morning. Murland, *Retreat and Rearguard 1914*, 32.
70. Murland, *Retreat and Rearguard 1914*, 131.
71. Hart, *Fire and Movement*, 120.
72. von Kluck, *The March on Paris and the Battle of the Marne 1914*, 52.
73. Helmuth von Moltke, *Kriege und Siege* (Berlin: Vier Falken Verlag, 1891), 344.
74. Hart, *Fire and Movement*, 140.
75. Murland, *Retreat and Rearguard 1914*, 42.
76. Smith-Dorrien, *Memories of Forty-Eight Years' Service*, chapter 24b, "The Retreat from Mons: Le Cateau."
77. Ibid.
78. Hart, *Fire and Movement*, 132–33.
79. Ibid., 141.
80. Ibid., 149.
81. Smith-Dorrien, *Memories of Forty-Eight Years' Service*, chapter 24b, "The Retreat from Mons: Le Cateau."
82. Ibid.
83. Hart, *Fire and Movement*, 142.
84. Ibid., 142.
85. J. E. Edmonds, *History of the Great War, Military Operations: The Retreat to the Seine, the Marne, and the Aisne, August-October 1914*, vol. 1 (London: MacMillan and Co., 1922), 142–43. Also see Sir John French, *The Dispatches of Sir John French*, vol. 1 (London: Chapman and Hall Ltd., 1914), 13.
86. Nigel Hamilton, *Monty: The Making of a General 1877–1942*, vol. 1 (New York: McGraw Hill, 1981), 77.
87. Edmonds, *The Retreat to the Seine, the Marne, and the Aisne, August-October 1914*, 144.
88. Murland, *Retreat and Rearguard 1914*, 69.
89. Quoted by Hart in *Fire and Movement*, 160.
90. Ibid., 159.
91. Edmonds, *The Retreat to the Seine, the Marne, and the Aisne, August-October 1914*, 169.
92. Smith-Dorrien, *Memories of Forty-Eight Years' Service*, chapter 24b, "The Retreat from Mons: Le Cateau."

93. Hermann Balck, *Order in Chaos: The Memoirs of General of Panzer Troops Hermann Balck*, ed. and trans. David Zabecki and Dieter Biedekarken (Lexington: University Press of Kentucky, 2015), 17.

94. Hart, *Fire and Movement*, 177. Hart reports 7,812 casualties and 38 guns. Jerry Murland reports fewer casualties, perhaps 5,000. Smith-Dorrien reports 6,000.

95. von Kluck, *The March on Paris and the Battle of the Marne 1914*, 62–65, 67.

96. Robert Cowley, "The What Ifs of 1914: The World War that Should Never Have Been," in *What If? The World's Foremost Military Historians Imagine What Might Have Been*, ed. Robert Cowley (New York: G. P. Putnam's Sons, 1999), 280.

97. Hamilton, *Monty*, 81.

98. Cowley, *What If*, 282.

99. Tucker, *The Great War 1914–1918*, 29–30.

100. von Kluck, *The March on Paris and the Battle of the Marne 1914*, 78.

101. Edmonds, *Military Operations: France and Belgium, 1914*, 465.

102. Earl Wavell, *The Good Soldier* (London: MacMillan and Company, 1948), 53.

103. Kennedy, *The Rise and Fall of the Great Powers*, 257. When World War I began, the German army had 36,693 officers. Of this number, 625 officers were assigned to the General Staff. However, only 352 were full-fledged members of the German General Staff Corps.

104. Brian Bond, *The Victorian Army and the Staff College 1854–1914* (London: Eyre Methuen, 1972), 286.

105. Edmonds describes operations in Antwerp in *Military Operations, France and Belgium, 1914*, 32–48.

106. Michael Korda, *Hero: The Life and Legend of Lawrence of Arabia* (New York: Harper Collins, 2010), 111.

107. The British cavalry's performance in action lent credence to British brigadier general Henry de Beauvoir de Lisle's prewar assessment of British cavalry officers: "They read nothing, could not use a map or a compass efficiently, and ignored the manuals completely." See Bidwell and Graham, *Fire-Power: British Army Weapons and Theories of War, 1904–1945*, 33.

108. Bailey, *Field Artillery and Firepower*, 223.

109. Zuber, *The Mons Myth*, 265.

110. Williamson Murray, "Red Teaming: Its Contribution to Past Military Effectiveness," working paper, Hicks and Associates, McLean, VA, September 2002, 35.

111. Eitan Shamir, *Transforming Command: The Pursuit of Mission Command in the U.S., British, and Israeli Armies* (Stanford: Stanford University Press, 2011), 3.

112. J. F. C. Fuller, *The Conduct of War 1789–1961* (Brunswick, NJ: Rutgers University Press, 1968), 160.

113. Robin Prior and Trevor Wilson, *Passchendaele: The Untold Story* (New Haven: Yale University Press, 1996), introduction.

114. Elizabeth Kier, "Culture and Military Doctrine: France between the Wars," *International Security* 19, no. 4 (Spring 1995): 82, 84, 91–92.

115. Nikolas Gardner, *Trial by Fire: Command and the British Expeditionary Force in 1914* (Westport, CT: Praeger Productions, 2003), 21.

116. B. H. Liddell-Hart, *Strategy*, 2nd rev. ed. (New York: Meridian Press, 1967), 24.

117. Geoffrey Regan, *Great Military Disasters* (New York: Barnes and Noble Inc., 1997), 61.

118. von Kluck, *The March on Paris and the Battle of the Marne 1914*, 38.

119. Tim Travers, *The Killing Ground: The British Army, the Western Front and the Emergence of Modern Warfare, 1900–1918* (London: Unwin Hyman, 1987), 37–97.

120. Ferguson, *Empire*, 319.

121. Steven Hayward, *Churchill on Leadership: Executive Success in the Face of Adversity* (Rocklin, CA: Prima Publishing Forum, 1997), 34.

122. Griffith, *Battle Tactics of the Western Front*, 11, 52.

123. Haig's note to Haldane was reprinted in Richard Haldane, *Lord Haldane's Autobiography* (London: Hodder and Stoughton, Ltd., 1925), 288.

124. John K. Dunlop, *The Development of the British Army 1899–1914* (London: Methuen, 1938), concluding chapter.

CHAPTER 2. WAR WITHOUT END

1. Edward Behr, *Hirohito: Behind the Myth* (New York: Vantage Books, 1989), 6.

2. David S. Landes, *The Wealth and Poverty of Nations: Why Some Are So Rich and Some Are So Poor* (New York: W. W. Norton and Company,

1999), 381. Even the Royal Navy relied primarily on signal flags in 1915 during the Battle of Jutland.

3. John J. Pershing, *My Life Before the World War, 1860–1917*, ed. John T. Greenwood (Lexington: University Press of Kentucky, 2013), 211.

4. The alliance was renewed and extended in scope twice, in 1905 and 1911. The Four Powers Treaty at the Washington Conference made the Anglo-Japanese alliance irrelevant in December 1921; however, it would not officially terminate until all parties ratified the treaty on 17 August 1923.

5. In some publications, his surname is anglicized as Ishihara. Ishihara and Ishiwara both use the same Japanese kanji.

6. Watanabe Tsuneo and James E. Auer, eds., *From Marco Polo to Pearl Harbor: Who Was Responsible?* (Tokyo: Yomiuri Shimbun, 2006), 74.

7. Herbert P. Bix, *Hirohito and the Making of Modern Japan* (New York: HarperCollins Publishers, 2000), 320.

8. Mark Peattie, *Ishiwara Kanji and Japan's Confrontation with the West* (Princeton: Princeton University Press, 1975), 301.

9. J. Bruce Jacobs, "Shanghai: An Alternative Centre?" in *China's Provinces in Reform: Class, Community and Political Culture*, ed. David Goodman (New York: Routledge, 1997), 164.

10. Hannah Pakula, *The Last Empress: Madame Chiang Kai-shek and the Birth of Modern China* (New York: Simon and Schuster, 2009), 276.

11. Masakazu Iwata, *Okubo Toshimichi: The Bismarck of Japan* (London: Cambridge University Press, 1964), 158–59.

12. Clive Sinclair, *Samurai: The Weapons and Spirit of the Japanese Warrior* (Guilford, CT: The Lyons Press, 2001), 135–37.

13. Landes, *The Wealth and Poverty of Nations*, 383.

14. Ibid., 367.

15. Iwata, *Okubo Toshimichi*, 158–59.

16. This debate had deep roots in Japanese history. See Min Daekkee in "The Muromachi Bakufu's Request to Joseon for the Facilitation of Tribute Trade with Ming China," in *The Foreseen and the Unforeseen in Historical Relations between Korea and Japan* (Seoul: Northeast Asia History Foundation, 2009), 253–66. Pages 264–65 show a chart that lists nearly all rejections of Japanese requests for access to trade with Ming China.

17. Alvin Coox, "Continental Expansion 1905–1941," in *The Cambridge History of Japan*, vol. 6, ed. Peter Duus, trans. Hata Ikuhiko (Cambridge: Cambridge University Press, 1988), 271–75.

18. Marius B. Jansen, *The Making of Modern Japan* (Cambridge: Harvard University Press, 2000), 5–6.

19. His name is also written in some publications as Kazunari Ugaki. Both pronunciations Kazushige and Kazunari use the same Japanese kanji.

20. Sven Saaler, "The Imperial Japanese Army and Germany," in *Japanese-German Relations, 1895–1945: War, Diplomacy, and Public Opinion,* ed. Christian W. Spang and Rolf-Harald Wippich (London: Routledge, 2006), 22.

21. Dennis Warner and Peggy Warner, *The Tide at Sunrise: A History of the Russo-Japanese War, 1904–1905* (London: Frank Cass, 1974), 364.

22. Ibid.

23. Leonard A. Humphreys, *The Way of the Heavenly Sword: The Japanese Army in the 1920s* (Stanford: Stanford University Press, 1995), 33–37, 83–84.

24. Warner and Warner, *The Tide at Sunrise,* 474.

25. Humphreys, *The Way of the Heavenly Sword,* 26.

26. Paul E. Dunscomb, *Japan's Siberian Intervention, 1918–1922: "A Great Disobedience Against the People"* (Plymouth, UK: Lexington Books, 2011), 76.

27. Ibid., 89, 90.

28. Edward J. Drea, *Japan's Imperial Army: Its Rise and Fall, 1853–1945* (Lawrence: University of Kansas Press, 2009), 151–53. Drea lists the differences between the IJA traditionalists' and Ugaki's strategies in this chart:

TRADITIONALISTS	UGAKI
Large army	Small army
Low-tech	High-tech
Morale	Matériel
Short war	Long war
Bayonet	Firepower
Infantry	Combined arms
Win first battle	Endure protracted war
Military mobilization	National mobilization
Limited war	Total war
Square division	Triangular division

29. Ibid., 147–48.

30. Humphreys, *The Way of the Heavenly Sword,* 102.

31. Dunscomb, *Japan's Siberian Intervention, 1918–1922,* 191.

32. Drea, *Japan's Imperial Army,* 149, 153–54.

33. Humphreys, *The Way of the Heavenly Sword,* 91–92.

34. Quote by Humphreys of Ito Masanori in *The Way of the Heavenly Sword*, 60.

35. Ibid., 78, 94. Ugaki retired eleven generals and several senior lieutenant generals who were opposed to his reforms. However, he could not retire two field marshals who resisted him.

36. Drea, *Japan's Imperial Army*, 175.

37. Dunscomb, *Japan's Siberian Intervention, 1918–1922*, 191; Humphreys, *The Way of the Heavenly Sword*, 90, 92, 94.

38. Humphreys, *The Way of the Heavenly Sword*, 126.

39. Gordon L. Rottman and Takizawa Akira, *World War II Japanese Tank Tactics* (Westminster, UK: Osprey Publishing, 2008), 16.

40. Humphreys, *The Way of the Heavenly Sword*, 79.

41. Drea, *Japan's Imperial Army*, 149, 185–86; Rottman and Akira, *World War II Japanese Tank Tactics*, 16.

42. Walter A. McDougall, *Let the Sea Make a Noise . . . : A History of the North Pacific from Magellan to MacArthur* (New York: HarperCollins, 1993), 587.

43. Hattori Satoshi with Edward J. Drea, "Japanese Operations from July to December 1937," in *The Battle for China: Essays on the Military History of the Sino-Japanese War of 1937–1945*, ed. Mark Peattie, Edward J. Drea, and Hans van de Ven (Stanford: Stanford University Press, 2011), 160.

44. Hsu Long-hsuen and Chang Ming-kai, *History of the Sino-Japanese War (1937–1945)*, trans. Wen Ha-hsiung (Taipei: Chung Wu Publishing Co., 1971),174.

45. William C. Kirby, *Germany and Republican China* (Stanford: Stanford University Press, 1984), 77–78. Despite Chiang's early military studies in Moscow, in 1933, Chiang invited Colonel General Hans von Seeckt, the towering intellect who launched the German army on the path to reform cooperation with the Soviets in the 1920s. From 1934 to 1935, Chiang did his best to implement the German reforms, assigning German military advisers to every Chinese division. He even sent his son to serve in the Wehrmacht. But Chiang's reform efforts met with much less success than Ugaki's. Chiang served in the Imperial Japanese Army from 1909 to 1911 and knew his enemy well.

46. The Chinese public was enraged, but there was little the Chinese could do about the Japanese in Manchuria. In addition, Manchuria was no more a historic or ethnic component of the Chinese nation than Mongolia or Korea.

47. Bruce A. Elleman, *Modern Chinese Warfare, 1795–1989* (London: Routledge Books, 2001), 162. Chiang's name in the Mandarin dialect would be Jiang Jieshi.

48. Manchus formed a minority in Manchukuo, whose largest ethnic group was Han Chinese. The population of Koreans increased during the Manchukuo period, and there were also Japanese, Mongols, White Russians, and other minorities. The Mongol regions of western Manchukuo were ruled under a system suited to the Mongolian traditions there. The southern part of the Liaodong Peninsula was ruled by Japan as the Kwantung Leased Territory.

49. Peter Harmsen, *Shanghai 1937: Stalingrad on the Yangtze* (Oxford, UK: Casemate Publishers Haverton, 2013), 14–16. Harmsen indicates that the events took place in the early hours of August 10. Other sources state that the events took place on the night of August 9.

50. Humphreys, *The Way of the Heavenly Sword*, 104.

51. Edward J. Drea, "The Japanese Army on the Eve of War," in Peattie, Drea, and van de Ven, *The Battle for China*, 107–11.

52. Spencer C. Tucker, ed., *World War II at Sea: An Encyclopedia,* vol. 1 (Santa Barbara, CA: ABC-CLIO, 2012), 342–43.

53. Military History Section, Headquarters, Army Forces Far East, "Political Strategy Prior to Outbreak of War, Part I," Japanese Monograph 144 (Washington, DC: Office of the Chief of Military History, Department of the Army, 1957), 30.

54. Long-hsuen and Ming-kai, *History of the Sino-Japanese War (1937–1945),* 202, 253. The Imperial Japanese Naval Forces that operated against the Chinese during the Shanghai campaign were:

> Fleet Headquarters Izumo and Notoro
>> 1st Task Force: *Shake* (flagship), ten battleships, five destroyers
>> 3rd Squadron: *Naka* (flagship), *Yura*
>> 1st Torpedo Squadron: *Yubari* (flagship), twelve destroyers
>> 1st Aviation Squadron: *Kaga* (carrier/flagship), *Hosho* (carrier), four destroyers.

55. "Political Strategy Prior to Outbreak of War, Part I," 23. "Rear Admiral [Tanimoto] Umataro, Commander of the 11th Gunboat Division. This division was composed of the flagship *Yaeyama, Hozu, Futami,* and *Kotaka* in Hankow, *Katada, Sumida,* and *Kuri* in Shanghai, *Tsuga* in Nanking, *Hasu* in Wuhu, *Atami* in Kiukiang, *Seta* in Changsha, *Toba*

in Ichang, *Hira* in Chungking, and detachment of 292 persons of the Shanghai Special Naval Landing Unit in Hankow."

56. Long-hsuen and Ming-kai, *History of the Sino-Japanese War (1937–1945)*, 253.

57. Liquidation Department of the Second Mobilization Bureau, "China Incident Naval Air Operations (July–November 1937)," Japanese Monograph 166, 13, 14.

58. Ibid., 10, 11.

59. Kirby, *Germany and Republican China*, 114.

60. Long-hsuen and Ming-kai, *History of the Sino-Japanese War (1937–1945)*, 203–4.

61. Ibid., 174. Both Japanese and Chinese infantry divisions consisted of two brigades (four regiments) of infantry, but Japanese formations also included one regiment each of artillery, cavalry, engineer, and quartermaster formations, in addition to a tank company. Chinese infantry divisions included only a single battalion of artillery, cavalry, and engineering units, respectively. In terms of total force disposition, this amounted to nearly 22,000 soldiers in a Japanese division and just short of 11,000 in a Chinese division. When factoring in nearly a 3:1 advantage in small arms and 2:1 advantage in machine guns of all types (not to mention artillery and tanks possessed by the Japanese divisions and not the Chinese divisions), this meant Japanese infantry divisions were much stronger than similar Chinese formations.

62. Harmsen, *Shanghai 1937*, 73–75.

63. "China Incident Naval Air Operations," 30.

64. Long-hsuen and Ming-kai, *History of the Sino-Japanese War (1937–1945)*, 254.

65. Colonel Claire Chennault led the failed bombing effort. Undeterred, Chennault would go on to lead the famous Flying Tigers. Earle Rice, *Claire Chennault: Flying Tiger* (New York: Chelsea House Publishers, 2003), 11–15.

66. "China Incident Naval Air Operations," 25–28.

67. Harmsen, *Shanghai 1937*, 160–62.

68. Headquarters, USAFFE and Eight U.S. Army (Rear), "Central China Area Operations Record, 1937–1941," Japanese Monograph 179 (Washington, DC: Office of the Chief of Military History, Department of the Army, 1955), 14–15.

69. Military History Section, Headquarters Army Forces Far East, "Air Operations in the China Area, July 1937–August 1945," Japanese Monograph 76 (Washington, DC: Office of the Chief of Military History, Department of the Army, n.d.), 7. It is stated as a squadron but is listed in Japanese Monograph 179 as the 6th Independent Air Company; it is more likely to have been a squadron.

70. "China Incident Naval Air Operations," 34. The 1st Air Attack Unit supported the 3rd Infantry Division, the 2nd Air Attack Unit supported the 11th Infantry Division, and the 4th Air Attack Unit patrolled Pudong where the Nationalist Chinese 8th Army Group defended the city.

71. Tucker, *World War II at Sea*, 530–31.

72. Satoshi with Drea, "Japanese Operations from July to December 1937," in Peattie, Drea, and van de Ven, *The Battle for China*, 169.

73. "China Incident Naval Air Operations," 46–47.

74. Ibid., 48–49.

75. Long-hsuen and Ming-kai, *History of the Sino-Japanese War (1937–1945)*, 201.

76. Yang Tianshi, "Chiang Kai-shek and the Battles of Shanghai and Nanjing" in Peattie, Drea, and van de Ven, *The Battle for China*, 147.

77. Satoshi with Drea, "Japanese Operations from July to December 1937," in Peattie, Drea, and van de Ven, *The Battle for China*, 170.

78. Harmsen, *Shanghai 1937*, 109.

79. Long-hsuen and Ming-kai, *History of the Sino-Japanese War (1937–1945)*, 208.

80. "China Incident Naval Air Operations," 73–74.

81. Satoshi with Drea, "Japanese Operations from July to December 1937," in Peattie, Drea, and van de Ven, *The Battle for China*, 171.

82. Long-hsuen and Ming-kai, *History of the Sino-Japanese War (1937–1945)*, 208.

83. Harmsen, *Shanghai 1937*, 134.

84. Long-Hsuen and Ming-kai, *History of the Sino-Japanese War (1937–1945)*, 201, 203–5, 208.

85. Harmsen, *Shanghai 1937*, 148.

86. Aleksandr Akovlevich Kaliagin, *Along Alien Roads*, Occasional Papers of the East Asian Institute (New York: Columbia University Press, October 1983), 228.

87. Herbert Ekins and Theon Wright, *China Fights for Her Life* (New York: McGraw-Hill, 1938), 232.

88. "China Incident Naval Air Operations," 118, 124, 125, 126.

89. Ibid., 128–41, lists the daily missions and which IJA divisions were being directly supported.

90. Harmsen, *Shanghai 1937*, 158, 160.

91. Long-Hsuen and Ming-kai, *History of the Sino-Japanese War (1937–1945)*, 208.

92. Ibid., 203–4.

93. Kazuo Yagami, *Konoe Fumimaro and the Failure of Peace in Japan, 1937–1941: A Critical Appraisal of the Three-time Prime Minister* (Jefferson, NC: McFarland and Company, 2006), 55–56.

94. Tianshi, "Chiang Kai-shek and the Battles of Shanghai and Nanjing," in Peattie, Drea, and van de Ven, *The Battle for China*, 172–74.

95. Harmsen, *Shanghai 1937*, 192–93.

96. The brigade commander, Colonel Sakai Kouji, protested, and Tojo promptly relieved him for insubordination, putting an end to the brigade's usefulness as an offensive weapon on the operational level. Rottman and Akira, *World War II Japanese Tank Tactics*, 4–5.

97. Satoshi with Drea, "Japanese Operations from July to December 1937," in Peattie, Drea, and van de Ven, *The Battle for China*, 172, 175.

98. Tianshi, "Chiang Kai-shek and the Battles of Shanghai and Nanjing," in Peattie, Drea, and van de Ven, *The Battle for China*, 152.

99. "China Incident Naval Air Operations," 154.

100. "Central China Area Operations Record," 16, 18.

101. Ibid., 17.

102. Frederic E. Wakeman, *The Shanghai Badlands: Wartime Terrorism and Urban Crime, 1937–1941* (New York: Cambridge University Press, 1996), 6, 7.

103. Zhaojin Ji, *A History of Modern Shanghai Banking: The Rise and Decline of China's Finance Capitol* (Armonk, NY: M. E. Sharpe, Inc., 2003), 205–7.

104. Sven Saaler and Christopher W. A. Szpilman, eds., *Pan-Asianism: A Documentary History, 1920–Present* (Plymouth, UK: Rowman and Littlefield Publishers, 2011), 140–41.

105. Saburo Ienaga, *Pacific War, 1931–1945* (New York: Random House, Inc., 1968), 86.

106. H. P. Willmott and Michael B. Barrett, *Clausewitz Reconsidered* (Santa Barbara: Praeger Security International, 2010), 99.

107. Emily Hahn, *Chiang Kai-shek: An Unauthorized Biography* (Garden City, NY: Doubleday and Co., 1955), 217.

108. Spencer C. Tucker, *Battles That Changed History: An Encyclopedia of World Conflict* (Santa Barbara, CA: ABC-CLIO, 2011), 455.

109. Victor Madej, *Japanese Armed Forces Order of Battle, 1937–1945* (Allentown, PA: Game Publishing Company, 1981), 118–22. There were actually four tank divisions by the end of 1945, but only three were ever used in combat. The Chinese learned that the Japanese army could only advance for about ten days before it ran out of bullets and food. The Chinese discovered that all they had to do was hold on for ten days against a Japanese offensive; then they could counterattack. This would happen especially in the battles around Changsha later in the war.

110. Martin Blumenson and James L. Stokesbury, *Masters of the Art of Command* (New York: Da Capo Press, 1975), 224.

111. Tsuji Masanobu, *Japan's Greatest Victory, Britain's Greatest Defeat: From the Japanese Perspective: The Capture of Singapore, 1942* (Gloucestershire, UK: Spellmount, 1997), 26–29, 86. This book is Colonel Masanobu's personal account of the campaign, its operations, and tactics. He served as the chief of staff for Lieutenant General Yamashita Tomoyuki, known in Japan and to the world as the Tiger of Malaya, but makes no mention of his involvement in the Sook Ching Massacre in Singapore.

112. Alvin Coox, *Nomonhan: Japan Against Russia, 1939* (Stanford: Stanford University Press, 1985), 84. The battle, also known as the Battle of Khalkha River, took place between the cities of Nuren Obo and Nomonhan. The total area was no more than one hundred kilometers wide and a little less than thirty kilometers at the deepest. In this small area would be the largest and most costly defeat for the Kwantung Army by the Soviets until August 1945. Japan was simply outmatched with about half the troops, almost a fifth of the aircraft, and one-tenth of the tanks as the Soviets.

113. Dimitar Nedialkov, *In the Skies of Nomonhan: Japan versus Russia May–September 1939* (Manchester, UK: Crecy Publishing Limited, 2011), 140–41.

114. Kennedy, *The Rise and Fall of the Great Powers*, 350–51; Peattie, Drea, and van de Ven, *The Battle for China*, 235. Also see Douglas A. MacArthur, *Reports of General MacArthur: The Campaigns of MacArthur in the Pacific*, vol. 1, plate no. 134, "Japanese Strength Overseas," August 1945 (Washington, D.C.: U.S. Army Center of Military History, 1994), 463.

115. David M. Glantz, *The Soviet Strategic Offensive in Manchuria, 1945: "August Storm"* (Portland, OR: Frank Cass Publishing, 2003), 95.

116. Stephen Large, *Emperor Hirohito and Showa Japan: A Political Biography* (New York: Routledge, 1992), 132.

117. Sato Hiroaki, "The Self-Defense Forces: Living with a Lie," *The Japan Times*, 24 September 2007.

118. Song Sang-ho, "China Bolstering Defense Strategy: Observers Say China's Moves on Air Defense Zone Aim to Fend Off Unfriendly Approaches," *The Korea Herald*, 1 December 2013, 1.

119. "Navy Official: China Training for Short, Sharp War with Japan," *USNI .org*, 18 February 2014.

CHAPTER 3. REVERSAL OF FORTUNE

1. Matthew Cooper, *The German Army, 1933–1945* (Lanham, MD: Scarborough House, 1978), 325.

2. Karl-Heinz Frieser, ed., "II. Der Zusammenbruch der Heeresgruppe Mitte im Sommer 1944," *Die Ostfront 1943/44: Der Krieg im Osten und an den Nebenfronten, Das Deutsche Reich und der Zweite Weltkrieg*, vol. 8 (Munich: Deutsche Verlags-Anstalt, 2007), 556; Andreas Kunz, *Wehrmacht und Niederlage: Die bewaffnete Macht in der Endphase der Nationalsozialistischen Herrschaft* (Munich: Oldenbourg Verlag, 2005), 68.

3. John Erickson, *The Road to Berlin: Stalin's War with Germany* (New Haven: Yale University Press, 1983), 228–29.

4. Lord Moran, *Churchill at War 1940–45* (New York: Carroll and Graf Publishers, 2002), 197.

5. Rickard, *Advance and Destroy: Patton as Commander in the Bulge*, 310.

6. David Eisenhower, *Eisenhower at War 1943–1945* (New York: Random House, 1986), 599–600.

7. Norman Davies, *No Simple Victory: World War II in Europe, 1939–1945* (New York: Viking Penguin, 2007), 90, 325. By the end of 1919, the Soviet government established 21 camps in addition to the regular network of work camps already operated by the Soviet Ministry of Justice. The Gulag (Main Administration of Collective Labor Camps) was created in 1920. At the end of 1920, the Gulag had 107 concentration camps, many inside the Arctic Circle. From that point forward, the Gulag operated continuously until 1989.

8. Walter S. Dunn Jr., *Hitler's Nemesis: The Red Army, 1930–1945* (Westport, CT: Praeger, 1994), 7.

9. William J. Bossenbrook, *The German Mind* (Detroit: Wayne State University Press, 1961), 337.

10. Robert Citino, *The German Way of War: From the Thirty Years' War to the Third Reich* (Lawrence: University Press of Kansas, 2005), 305.

11. Heinz Guderian, *Erinnerungen eines Soldaten* (Stuttgart: Motorbuch Verlag, 1994), 414–15.

12. David T. Zabecki, *Steel Wind: Colonel Georg Bruchmueller and the Birth of Modern Artillery* (Westport, CT: Praeger, 1994), 23. For example, in a little more than 5 hours, the German Eighth Army struck the Russian Twelfth Army in September 1917 with 560,000 rounds or 10,500 tons of explosives, the equivalent of 500 B-52 bombers.

13. Why these offensives created conditions inside Germany for social chaos and political upheaval and how to avoid this outcome in the future were also major themes in all of the studies.

14. Citino, *The German Way of War*, xiv–xv.

15. Guderian, *Erinnerungen eines Soldaten*, 26.

16. For more on the topic, see Jonathan Wright, *Gustav Stresemann: Weimar's Greatest Statesman* (Oxford: Oxford University Press, 2002).

17. James S. Corum, "A Comprehensive Approach to Change: Reform in the German Army in the Interwar Period," in *The Challenge of Change: Military Institutions and New Realities, 1918–1941*, ed. Harold Winton and David Mets (Lincoln: University of Nebraska Press, 2000), 60–61.

18. John Erickson, *The Soviet High Command: A Military-Political History, 1918–1941* (New York: St. Martin's Press Inc., 1962), 303–6.

19. Cooper, *The German Army, 1933–1945*, 136.

20. Balck, *Order in Chaos*, 220.

21. Albert Seaton, *The German Army, 1933–1945* (New York: St. Martin's Press, 1982), 93.

22. Cooper, *The German Army, 1933–1945*, 146.

23. James S. Corum, *The Roots of Blitzkrieg: Hans von Seeckt and German Military Reform* (Lawrence: University Press of Kansas, 1992), 45–46, 190.

24. On the Luftwaffe army/air liaison system in the early years of World War II, see James S. Corum, *The Luftwaffe: Creating the Operational Air War* (Lawrence: University Press of Kansas, 1997), 247–49.

25. Seaton, *The German Army, 1933–1945*, 141.

26. Ernst Koestring and Hermann Teske, *General Ernst Koestring: Der Militaerische Mittler zwischen dem Deutschen Reich und der Sowjetunion,*

1921–1941 (Frankfurt am Main: Verlag E. S. Mittler and Sohn, 1966), 145–47.

27. James S. Corum, "The Luftwaffe and Its Allied Air Forces in World War II: Parallel War and the Failure of Strategic and Economic Cooperation," *Airpower History* 51, no. 2 (Summer 2004): 4.

28. James S. Corum, "First Air Fleet Operations in the Baltic Region, June-December 1941" (unpublished manuscript, 2013), later published in *The Second World War and the Baltic States*, eds. James S. Corum, Olaf Mertelsmann, and Kaarel Piiramae (New York: Peter Lang Publishers, 2014).

29. Michael H. Kater, *The Nazi Party: A Social Profile of Members and Leaders, 1919–1945* (Cambridge: Harvard University Press, 1983), 236–37.

30. Geoffrey P. Megargee, *Inside Hitler's High Command* (Lawrence: University Press of Kansas, 2000), 62–64.

31. Benoit Lemay, *Erich von Manstein: Hitler's Master Strategist* (Philadelphia: Casemate, 2010), 163–64. When Hitler elevated 12 generals to the rank of field marshal, he rewarded each with 72,000 reichsmarks (RM). Field marshals and selected colonel generals enjoyed a tax-free stipend called an expense account in addition to their salaries. Field marshals received 4,000 RM per month, and colonel generals received 2,000 RM per month. Field Marshal von Manstein received a 48,000 RM tax-free supplement in addition to his 26,550 RM salary. In today's money, these gifts run into the hundreds of thousands of dollars. When the gifts included country estates, the amounts ran into the millions.

32. Kater, *The Nazi Party*, 225.

33. R. J. Overy, *War and the Economy in the Third Reich* (Oxford: Oxford University Press, 1994), 17.

34. Ibid., 29.

35. Albert Speer, *Inside the Third Reich, Memoirs* (New York: Simon and Schuster, 1997), 65–66.

36. Seaton, *The German Army, 1933–1945*, 238.

37. Kater, *The Nazi Party*, 211.

38. Hermann Balck, "Translation of Taped Conversation with General Herman Balck, 12 January 1979 and Brief Biographical Sketch" (Columbus, OH: Battelle Columbus Laboratories, Tactical Technology Center, January 1979), 36.

39. Overy, *War and the Economy in the Third Reich*, 254. On 8 February 1942, Minister of Armaments Fritz Todt, the prominent Nazi figure who

led "Organisation Todt," contributed to the plan, but he died in a plane crash shortly after taking off from Hitler's eastern headquarters at Rastenburg. Speer was his replacement.

40. Seaton, *The German Army, 1933–1945*, 239.
41. Suggested to the author by James S. Corum, PhD, dean of the Baltic Defense College.
42. See Corum, "The Luftwaffe and Its Allied Air Forces in World War II."
43. Robert M. Citino, *Death of the Wehrmacht: The German Campaigns of 1942* (Lawrence: University Press of Kansas, 2007), 271.
44. Torsten Diedrich, *Paulus: Das Trauma von Stalingrad: Eine Biographie* (Paderborn: Ferdinand Schoeningh, 2008), 242.
45. Richard J. Evans, *The Third Reich at War* (New York: The Penguin Press, 2009), 461.
46. Jacob W. Kipp, "Military Reform and the Red Army, 1918–1941," in Winton and Mets, *The Challenge of Change*, 141–42.
47. Erickson, *The Soviet High Command*, 297.
48. Jacob W. Kipp, "The Origins of Soviet Operational Art, 1917–1936," in *Historical Perspectives of the Operational Art*, ed. Michael D. Krause and R. Cody Phillips (Washington, D.C.: U.S. Army Center of Military History, 2005), 236.
49. Kipp, "Military Reform and the Red Army, 1918–1941," 143.
50. Charles Messenger, *The Blitzkrieg Story* (New York: Charles Scribner's Sons, 1976), 68.
51. Soviet academician Oleg Bogomolov stated in *Moscow News* in 1990: "For decades we lived . . . in conditions of a wartime economy." Russian presidential adviser Anatoly Rakitov corroborated this in the 26 March 1992 issue of *Izvestia*: "Over the last six decades, 80 to 90 percent of our national resources—raw material, technical, financial, and intellectual—have been used to create the military-industrial complex. Essentially, the military-industrial complex has absorbed everything that is good and dynamic that Russia has to offer, including its basic economic capacity and its best technology, materials, and specialists. Consequently, the military-industrial complex is virtually synonymous with our economy."
52. Robert Conquest, *The Harvest of Sorrow: Soviet Collectivization and the Terror-Famine* (Oxford: Oxford University Press, 1986). In 1929, the Soviet Union instituted collectivization in the Ukraine. Farmers were forced to give up their farms and surrender almost their entire harvest to the state; they lived off what little portion of their crops party officials

might allow them to keep. Dealing with deprivation, peasant protests ensued; in response, soldiers entered designated villages and burned them to the ground, killed the most outspoken protesters, arrested men, and deported women and children. In 1932, Stalin began an unyielding policy of submission through starvation.

53. Erickson, *The Soviet High Command*, 390.

54. Constantine Pleshkov, *Stalin's Folly: The Tragic First Ten Days of World War II on the Eastern Front* (Boston: Houghton Mifflin Company, 2005), 32.

55. Ibid., 66.

56. Ibid., 30.

57. John Yurechko, "Soviet Reinforcement and Mobilization," in *NATO-Warsaw Pact Force Mobilization*, ed. Jeffrey Simon (Washington, DC: National Defense University Press, 1988), 68.

58. Pleshkov, *Stalin's Folly*, 62–63.

59. Ibid., 63.

60. Yurechko, "Soviet Reinforcement and Mobilization," 69; Pleshkov, *Stalin's Folly*, 65.

61. Rudolf Lehmann, *The Leibstandarte II*, trans. Nick Olcott (Winnipeg: J. J. Fedorowicz Publishing, 1988), 192.

62. Yurechko, "Soviet Reinforcement and Mobilization," 69.

63. David M. Glantz, *Zhukov's Greatest Defeat: The Red Army's Epic Disaster in Operation Mars, 1942* (Lawrence: University Press of Kansas, 1999), 300–303.

64. Erickson, *The Soviet High Command*, 83.

65. Landes, *The Wealth and Poverty of Nations*, 240–41. "The Russian is passive and slow-moving, terribly slow-moving. . . . When facing the Russian you can't sit down and calculate that he has so and so many divisions or weapons or what not. That's all baloney. One must not be misled into tying down a division along such a long front. You have to attack him instantly and throw him out of his position. He is no match for that. . . . Instead, one must remain completely mobile and attack wherever it's necessary." Also see Balck, "Translation of Taped Conversation with General Herman Balck 13 April 1979," (Columbus, OH: Battelle Columbus Laboratories, Tactical Technology Center, July 1979), 15–16.

66. Isabel de Madariaga, *Russia in the Age of Catherine the Great* (New Haven: Yale University Press, 1981), 126–30.

67. David M. Glantz, *Colossus Reborn: The Red Army at War, 1941–1943* (Lawrence: University Press of Kansas, 2005), 123.

68. Catherine Merridale, *Ivan's War: Life and Death in the Red Army, 1939–1945* (New York: Picador, 2006), 125.

69. Williamson Murray, "Military Adaptation in War," Institute for Defense Analyses Paper P-4452, 18 September 2009, 1–30.

70. James Carroll, *House of War: The Pentagon and the Disastrous Rise of American Power* (New York: Houghton Mifflin Company, 2006), 493.

71. George H. Stein, *The Waffen SS: Hitler's Elite Guard at War* (Ithaca: Cornell University Press, 1966), 168–96.

72. Merridale, *Ivan's War*, 98. In August 1943, the rate of Soviet defections to the German army increased sharply whenever battle was joined: from 2,555 in June to 6,574 in July and 4,047 in August of that year.

73. From July 1941 onward, the 134th Infantry Division of the German army offered all of its Soviet prisoners of war the opportunity to become regular soldiers in the German army, a practice that was far more widespread than was appreciated. By the end of 1942, thanks to high casualties in the German infantry, roughly half the enlisted strength of this particular division consisted of former Soviet soldiers. See Julius Epstein, *Operation Keelhaul: The Story of Forced Repatriation from June 1946 to the Present* (Old Greenwich, CT: Devin-Adair, 1974), 61.

74. Antony Beevor provides several good snapshots in *Stalingrad* (New York: Penguin Books, 1999), 184. Also see 56, 88, 99, 168, 180, and 185.

75. Merridale, *Ivan's War*, 223. Colonel General Hermann Balck, a distinguished German commander with extensive experience against the Russians in both world wars, commented on this point in 1942 in an unpublished memoir: "One had to hand it to the Russians. Their leadership at the macro level was excellent. . . . *It would always remain an example of what a hard, brutal leadership under unfavorable conditions can wrest from even an unwilling people*" (emphasis added).

76. Kunz, *Wehrmacht und Niederlage*, 59–60.

77. Georgii K. Zhukov, *The Memoirs of Marshal Zhukov* (New York: Delacourt Press, 1971), 535.

78. Michael Orr, "Aleksey Innokentevich Antonov," in *Chief of Staff: The Principal Officers Behind History's Great Commanders*, vol. 2, ed. David Zabecki (Annapolis, MD: Naval Institute Press, 2008), 144.

79. Ibid., 148.

80. For an interesting snapshot of German military effectiveness before Kursk, see George M. Nipe Jr., *Last Victory in Russia: The SS-Panzer-korps and Manstein's Kharkov Counteroffensive, February–March 1943* (Atglen, PA: Schiffer Military History, 2000).

81. Orr, "Aleksey Innokentevich Antonov," 149.

82. Glantz, *Colossus Reborn*, 370.

83. Frieser, "II. Der Zusammenbruch der Heeresgruppe Mitte im Sommer 1944," 536–37.

84. S. M. Shtemenko, *The Soviet General Staff at War* (Moscow: Progress Publishers, 1970), 238.

85. Erickson, *The Soviet High Command*, 200–201.

86. Ibid., 222.

87. Kunz, *Wehrmacht und Niederlage*, 68.

88. 20,000 Bobruisk Jews were shot and buried in mass graves. After the German invasion, ghetto and labor camps were established with the assistance of the local population in the southwestern part of the town. The few Jews who escaped joined Soviet partisan forces in the surrounding forests.

89. Department of the Army, *Russian Combat Methods in World War II* (Washington, DC: U.S. Government Printing Office, 1950), 6. For a more contemporary view, see Paul Huard, "Maskirovka is Russian Secret War; Sneaky Tactics are an Old Russian Tradition," *WarisBoring.com*, 26 August 2014.

90. Erickson, *The Road to Berlin*, 212–14.

91. Robert Kirchhubel, *Hitler's Panzer Armies on the Eastern Front* (Barnsley, UK: Pen and Sword Books, Ltd., 2009), 119.

92. Walter S. Dunn Jr., *Stalin's Keys to Victory: The Rebirth of the Red Army* (Mechanicsburg, PA: Stackpole Books, 2006), 1.

93. Philip W. Blood, *Hitler's Bandit Hunters: The SS and the Nazi Occupation of Europe* (Washington, DC: Potomac Books, 2008), 229–31.

94. Alex Buchner, *The German Defensive Battles on the Russian Front, 1944*, trans. David Johnston (Atglen, PA: Schiffer Military/Aviation History, 1995), 145.

95. Frieser, "II. Der Zusammenbruch der Heeresgruppe Mitte im Sommer 1944," 548.

96. Earl F. Ziemke, *Stalingrad to Berlin: The German Defeat in the East* (Washington, DC: U.S. Army Historical Series, 1986), 205, 315–16.

97. Kirchhubel, *Hitler's Panzer Armies on the Eastern Front*, 118.

98. Steve Zaloga, *Bagration 1944: The Destruction of Army Group Center* (London: Reed Consumer Books, Ltd., 1996), 26.

99. Ibid., 22.

100. The shortfall in the number of actual German combat troops is attributed to everything from wounded on leave to commitments in rear areas against partisans. See Frieser, "II. Der Zusammenbruch der Heeresgruppe Mitte im Sommer 1944," 531.

101. Ibid., 534.

102. Zaloga, *Bagration 1944: The Destruction of Army Group Center*, 28–33.

103. Frieser, "II. Der Zusammenbruch der Heeresgruppe Mitte im Sommer 1944," 532.

104. Kirchhubel, *Hitler's Panzer Armies on the Eastern Front*, 119.

105. Buchner, *The German Defensive Battles on the Russian Front, 1944*, 144.

106. Zaloga, *Bagration 1944: The Destruction of Army Group Center*, 27.

107. Ibid., 44.

108. Frieser, "II. Der Zusammenbruch der Heeresgruppe Mitte im Sommer 1944," 539.

109. Zaloga, *Bagration 1944: The Destruction of Army Group Center*, 45.

110. Frieser, "II. Der Zusammenbruch der Heeresgruppe Mitte im Sommer 1944," 540.

111. Ibid., 540–41.

112. Ibid., 540.

113. Kirchhubel, *Hitler's Panzer Armies on the Eastern Front*, 118.

114. Ibid., 119.

115. Erickson, *The Road to Berlin*, 219.

116. Frieser, "II. Der Zusammenbruch der Heeresgruppe Mitte im Sommer 1944," 544.

117. Ibid., 543.

118. Keith Cumins, *Cataclysm: The War on the Eastern Front, 1941–45* (West Midlands, UK: Helion and Company, Ltd., 2001), 227.

119. Frieser, "II. Der Zusammenbruch der Heeresgruppe Mitte im Sommer 1944," 549.

120. Ibid., 549–51.

121. Zaloga, *Bagration 1944: The Destruction of Army Group Center*, 64.

122. Frieser, "II. Der Zusammenbruch der Heeresgruppe Mitte im Sommer 1944," 553.

123. Ibid., 553–54. Also see Zaloga, *Bagration 1944: The Destruction of Army Group Center,* 65–69.

124. Zaloga, *Bagration 1944: The Destruction of Army Group Center,* 68.

125. Shtemenko, *The Soviet General Staff at War,* 256.

126. Erickson, *The Road to Berlin,* 228.

127. Blood, *Hitler's Bandit Hunters,* 231.

128. Rolf Hinze, *To the Bitter End: The Final Battles of Army Groups North Ukraine, A, Center, Eastern Front 1944–45,* trans. Frederick Steinhardt (West Midlands, UK: Helion and Company Ltd., 2005), 23.

129. Frieser, "II. Der Zusammenbruch der Heeresgruppe Mitte im Sommer 1944," 556.

130. Williamson Murray and Allan R. Millett, *A War to Be Won: Fighting the Second World War* (Cambridge: The Belknap Press of Harvard University Press, 2000), 450.

131. Willmott and Barrett, *Clausewitz Reconsidered,* 57–58.

132. Clausewitz, *On War,* 579.

133. Michael Deane, Ilana Kass, and Andrew Porth, "The Soviet Command Structure in Force Design," *Strategic Review* (Spring 1984): 64–65. Notice, however, that fronts (equivalent in size to American armies) were also fully joint commands. When the Soviet Union's 40th Army deployed to Afghanistan in 1979, it did so as part of a joint task force structure that was fully joint. On the other hand, "jointness" stopped at the joint task force level, which caused serious problems on the tactical level.

134. Erickson, *The Soviet High Command,* 214.

135. Makhmut Akhmetovich Gareev, *If War Comes Tomorrow? The Contours of Future Armed Conflict,* trans. Yakov Vladimirovich Fomenko, ed. and with introduction by Jacob W. Kipp (London: Frank Cass, 1998), 3, 5. Gareev, who was a key member of Marshal Ogarkov's inner circle, notes Ogarkov's contribution.

136. Deane, Kass, and Porth, "The Soviet Command Structure in Force Design," 64–65.

137. Davies, *No Simple Victory,* 212.

138. This information is drawn from a discussion with a colonel general of the Russian General Staff in Moscow during the author's participation in an official U.S. military visit to the Russian General Staff Academy in November 2001. The colonel general who commanded the General Staff Academy told the author the NKVD archives indicated that losses in the Great Patriotic War were "39,900,000 dead and still counting." The

NKVD archives were subsequently closed to the public by the Vladimir Putin government.

139. "Russia Warns Foes in Soviet-style Show of Might," *DefenseNews.com*, 9 May 2009.

140. "Russia Targets NGOs: Conspiracy Theories," *Economist.com*, 15 April 2013.

CHAPTER 4. ENEMY AT THE GATE

1. Edward Luttwak and Daniel Horowitz, *The Israeli Army, 1948–1973* (Lanham, MD: University Press of America, 1983), 299.

2. Andrew Duncan and Michel Opatowski, *War in the Holy Land from Meggido to the West Bank* (Gloucestershire, UK: Sutton Publishers, Ltd., 1998), 170.

3. John R. Elting, *Swords Around a Throne: Napoleon's Grande Armee* (New York: The Free Press, 1988), 229.

4. At the Khartoum summit in August 1967, shortly after the Six-Day War, Arab leaders agreed that nothing less than the complete return of all the occupied territories would be acceptable. However, on 19 June, the Israeli government formally declared it was willing to return the Sinai and the Golan in exchange for a full peace treaty. At Khartoum, the Arab states formally responded that there would be "No peace, no negotiations and no recognition of the State of Israel." Meanwhile, even the post–Six-Day War cease-fire was not being kept; the first exchange of shots occurred on 1 July, just three weeks after the war officially ended, and then continued intermittently. The UN resolution was ambiguous: one version read that Israel had to relinquish "the territory" it had captured in the war—that is, all the territory—while another version read "territory."

5. That is the official date on which the Egyptians declared the war, but in fact fighting began just three weeks after the Six-Day War ended, on 1 July 1967, and continued on and off, waxing and waning in intensity until that official declaration.

6. Dani Asher, *The Egyptian Strategy for the Yom Kippur War* (Jefferson, NC: McFarland and Company, Inc., 2009), 42–43.

7. Luttwak and Horowitz, *The Israeli Army, 1948–1973*, 286.

8. Martin van Creveld, *The Sword and the Olive: A Critical History of the Israeli Defense Force* (New York: Public Affairs Press, 2002), 215.

9. Avraham Adan, *On the Banks of the Suez: An Israeli General's Personal Account of the Yom Kippur War* (London: Arms and Armour Press, 1980), 73.

10. Uri Bar-Joseph, *The Watchman Fell Asleep: The Surprise of Yom Kippur and Its Sources* (Albany: State University of New York Press, 2005), 18.

11. Chaim Herzog, *The War of Atonement, October 1973* (Boston: Little, Brown and Company, 1975), 271.

12. Adan, *On the Banks of the Suez,* 81–82.

13. O'Brien Brown, "Honor, Oil and Blood," *Military History Quarterly* (Autumn 2013): 35.

14. New figures for Israeli and Egyptian losses were provided to the author by Dr. Eado Hecht, lecturer in military history at the Israel Defense Forces General Staff College, during the author's trip to Israel in October 2013.

15. Anthony H. Cordesman and Abraham R. Wagner, *The Lessons of Modern War,* vol. 1: *The Arab-Israeli Conflicts, 1973–1989* (Boulder, CO: Westview Press, 1990), 47.

16. D. K. Palit, *Return to Sinai: The Arab Offensive 1973* (New Delhi: Palit and Palit Publishers, 1974), 30.

17. Asher, *The Egyptian Strategy for the Yom Kippur War,* 54.

18. Ibid., 60.

19. Ibid., 71.

20. Soviet military assistance teams consisted of two separate groups: the combat forces that were sent to fight in Egypt's defense during the War of Attrition, and the advisers and trainers who were already in Egypt instructing Egyptian forces before the 1967 war. Only Soviet combat forces and a fraction of the training teams were expelled.

21. U.S. decisionmakers (and likely those of all nations) were aware of the possibility of Israeli nuclear use as an implicit reality, but they judged that it was only plausible in extremis, and American leaders did not believe the situation, even in the dark hours of 7 October, had reached those depths. See Elbridge Colby et al., "The Israeli 'Nuclear Alert' of 1973: Deterrence and Signaling in Crisis," DRM-2013-U-004480-Final (Alexandria, VA: Center for Naval Analyses, April 2013.)

22. Avi Kober, "From Blitzkrieg to Attrition: Israel's Attrition Strategy and Staying Power," *Small Wars and Insurgencies* 16, no. 2 (June 2005): 219.

23. Ibid., 216.

24. Albert Hourani, *A History of the Arab Peoples* (New York: Warner Books, 1991), 387.

25. Sadat defeated a coup attempt in 1971 by Ali Sabry, who had served as Egypt's prime minister from September 1962 to October 1965. He was a Marxist of Turkish ancestry who commanded Egypt's air defense forces and enjoyed Soviet patronage.

26. Emil Ludwig, *The Nile: The Life-Story of a River*, trans. Mary Lindsay (New York: The Viking Press, 1937), 569.

27. Saad el-Shazly, *The Crossing of the Suez* (San Francisco: American Mideast Research, 1980), 47.

28. Norvell B. De Atkine, "Why Arabs Lose Wars," *Middle East Quarterly* 6, no. 4 (December 1999).

29. General Gamassy, the Egyptian army's deputy chief of staff, claims a three-phase plan: cross to shallow depth (10 to 12 kilometers), defeat IDF counterattacks, and advance to the mountain passes (40 to 50 kilometers) and halt there. Others, such as el Shazly, the chief of staff, claim the third phase did not exist.

30. Asher, *The Egyptian Strategy for the Yom Kippur War*, 95.

31. Palit, *Return to Sinai*, 31.

32. Quoted by Col. Drew A. Bennett, USMC, and Lt. Col. Michael W. Arnold, USAF, "Anwar Sadat's National Security Strategy in the October War: From Vision to Victory," National War College research paper, fall 2000, 4.

33. Anwar el Sadat, *In Search of Identity: An Autobiography* (New York: Harper and Row Publishers, Inc., 1978), 234.

34. Simon Dunstan, *The Yom Kippur War* (Oxford, UK: Osprey, 2007), 27.

35. Yousef H. Aboul-Enein, ed., *Reconstructing a Shattered Egyptian Army: War Minister General Mohammed Fawzi's Memoirs, 1967–1971* (Annapolis, MD: Naval Institute Press, 2014), 178.

36. Aryeh Shalev, *Israel's Intelligence Assessment before the Yom Kippur War: Disentangling Deception and Distraction* (Brighton, UK: Sussex Academic Press, 2010), 69.

37. Shazly, *The Crossing of the Suez*, 207.

38. Ibid.

39. Adan, *On the Banks of the Suez*, 86.

40. Hamilton, *Monty*, 682.

41. Ibid., 756.

42. Joseph Finklestone, *Anwar Sadat: Visionary Who Dared* (London: Frank Cass, 1996), 15–16. According to Finklestone, Sadat established a War Museum in El Alamein. Sadat was an admirer of Erwin Rommel's desert

tactics. Under the circumstances, Sadat would not have missed Montgomery's slow, methodical approach that rebuilt the Eighth Army.

43. Palit, *Return to Sinai*, 78.

44. Sadat, *In Search of Identity*, 240.

45. Adan, *On the Banks of the Suez*, 224.

46. Palit, *Return to Sinai*, 131.

47. Shazly, *The Crossing of the Suez*, 250.

48. Hashomer ("The Watchmen") preceded the Haganah and was established in 1909, itself a successor of Bar-Giora, founded in 1907. The Bar-Giora consisted of roughly one hundred Jewish immigrants who guarded Jewish settlements.

49. Palmach companies conducted reconnaissance and raiding operations for and with British forces against the Vichy French regime in Syria.

50. Doron Almog, *The Commitment: A Study of the Impact of American Jews on the Establishment of the State of Israel, 1945–1949* (Tel Aviv: Israeli Ministry of Defense Publishing House, 2012), 103.

51. Ibid., 102.

52. Luttwak and Horowitz, *The Israeli Army, 1948–1973*, 19.

53. Dov E. Glazer, "Conceptualizing Command and Operations in the Israeli Ground Forces, 1936–1966" (PhD diss., Bar Ilan University, Tel Aviv, February 2011), 114.

54. Shamir, *Transforming Command*, 87.

55. Luttwak and Horowitz, *The Israeli Army, 1948–1973*, 161.

56. Weizman received his training in the British army and served as a truck driver in the western desert campaigns in Egypt and Libya. In 1943, he joined the British Royal Air Force.

57. Reuven Gal, *A Portrait of the Israeli Soldier* (New York: Greenwood Press, 1986), 7.

58. Luttwak and Horowitz, *The Israeli Army, 1948–1973*, 194.

59. See chapter 7 in Elting, *Swords Around a Throne*.

60. van Creveld, *The Sword and the Olive*, 205.

61. Israel exploits its manpower to the fullest extent possible. For instance, even those who are physically or medically incapable of serving in the infantry are trained for jobs more suited to their capabilities in the artillery or support units. Standing professional combat units exist in the ground and naval forces, but professionals on long-term contracts were and are most numerous in the Israeli air force. Equally important, reserve units experience remarkably little personnel turbulence, and

the quality and duration of reserve training was and still is respectively higher and substantially longer than in most Western countries.

62. Luttwak and Horowitz, *The Israeli Army, 1948–1973*, 185–86. In 1973, the Israeli officer corps and senior leadership of the Israel Defense Forces were dominated by Jewish men descended from East European immigrants. This is still the case today. Oriental Jews from the Middle East and Africa are underrepresented in the senior ranks, yet there are very few Israelis who object. Affirmative action programs designed to alter the ethnic or sexual composition of the IDF leadership do not exist.

63. Born in Poland, Gonen immigrated to the British Mandate of Palestine with his family at the age of three. He served in the Haganah at fourteen and participated in the battles for Jerusalem in Israel's War of Independence. He was wounded five times in Israel's wars. He replaced General Ariel Sharon as commander of Southern Command on 15 July 1973.

64. Moshe Dayan, *Moshe Dayan: Story of My Life* (New York: William Morrow and Company, 1976), 510.

65. Shamir, *Transforming Command*, 91.

66. van Creveld, *The Sword and the Olive*, 232. Before the war broke out in October 1973, the IDF's planning branch under Brigadier General Avraham Tamir warned that the Egyptians and Syrians possessed thousands of new Soviet anti-tank missile systems, but this warning did not seem to have penetrated the minds of Israeli military commanders.

67. General Bar-Lev was born Haim Brotzlewsky in Vienna, Austria, in 1924. In 1946, Bar-Lev blew up the Allenby Bridge near Jericho to prevent Arab militiamen from entering Jewish towns west of the Jordan River. During the 1948 Arab-Israeli War, Bar-Lev was battalion commander in the Negev Brigade, which fought in the southern part of the country and the Sinai.

68. Herzog, *The War of Atonement, October 1973*, 192–93.

69. David "Dado" Elazar (27 August 1925–15 April 1976) was the ninth chief of staff of the Israel Defense Forces from 1972 to 1974. Lieutenant General Elazar was born in Sarajevo of Sephardic origin and came to Israel in 1940 as part of the Youth Aliyah program. He subsequently joined the Palmach and served in Israel's War of Independence. He resigned his office after the Yom Kippur War and is regarded as the scapegoat for the strategic missteps and failures at the outset of the conflict.

70. Adan, *On the Banks of the Suez*, 191. General Sharon wanted to leave the reconnaissance unit in place and attempt a hasty crossing of the canal

but was overruled. Sadly, the courageous and intelligent Major Brom was killed before dawn on 16 October during the canal crossing while leading Sharon's division through the breach his unit had detected on 8 October.

71. When General Magen crossed, he left half of his force in the Sinai under the command of his chief of staff, Colonel Granit.

72. Adan, *On the Banks of the Suez*, 253.

73. Ibid., 254.

74. Luttwak and Horowitz, *The Israeli Army, 1948–1973*, 219.

75. Trevor N. Dupuy, *Elusive Victory: The Arab Israeli Wars, 1947–1974* (New York: Harper and Row, 1974), 494–95. When Israeli forces seized the Sinai, Israeli soldiers mistook the characters on Japanese-made machinery in the area for Chinese characters, leading to the name "Chinese Farm" on Israeli military maps.

76. Ibid.

77. Cordesman and Wagner, *The Lessons of Modern War*, 101.

78. Dupuy, *Elusive Victory*, 497.

79. Ibid., 501.

80. Adan, *On the Banks of the Suez*, 270.

81. Herzog, *The War of Atonement, October 1973*, 221.

82. Shazly, *The Crossing of the Suez*, 197.

83. Ibid., 254.

84. Adan, *On the Banks of the Suez*, 271.

85. Herzog, *The War of Atonement, October 1973*, 221.

86. Ulysses S. Grant, *Memoirs of U. S. Grant* (New York: Konecky and Konecky, 1990, originally published in 1886), 204.

87. Dupuy, *Elusive Victory*, 503.

88. Adan, *On the Banks of the Suez*, 286–87.

89. Ibid., 287.

90. Dupuy, *Elusive Victory*, 506–7.

91. Ibid., 508.

92. Adan, *On the Banks of the Suez*, 297.

93. Ibid., 299.

94. Dupuy, *Elusive Victory*, 509.

95. Ibid., 510–11.

96. Adan, *On the Banks of the Suez*, 301–2.

97. General Sharon seems to have been an exception regarding the use of artillery.

98. On 8 October, Adan's reserve division had only one battery temporarily attached to it. All of its organic guns were still back at the storage depots or driving through the Sinai.

99. Dupuy, *Elusive Victory*, 527–29.

100. Cordesman and Wagner, *The Lessons of Modern War*, 93.

101. Robert Dallek, *Nixon and Kissinger: Partners in Power* (New York: Harper Collins Publishers, 2007), 526.

102. Adan, *On the Banks of the Suez*, 429.

103. Dupuy, *Elusive Victory*, 541.

104. Herzog, *The War of Atonement, October 1973*, 246–47.

105. Walter Isaacson, *Kissinger: A Biography* (New York: Touchstone Books, 1992), 526–28.

106. Dallek, *Nixon and Kissinger*, 529.

107. Ibid., 530.

108. Ibid., 531.

109. Victor Israelian, "Nuclear Showdown as Nixon Slept," *Christian Science Monitor* (Weekly Digital Edition), 3 November 1993.

110. Mohamed Abdel Ghani el Gamasy, *The October War: Memoirs of Field Marshal El-Gamasy of Egypt*, trans. Gillian Potter, Nadra Morcos, and Rosette Frances (Cairo: The American University in Cairo Press, 1993), 323.

111. George W. Gawrych, "The 1973 Arab-Israeli War: The Albatross of Decisive Victory," Leavenworth Paper no. 21 (Leavenworth, KS: Combat Studies Institute, 1996), 74.

112. Ibid., 79.

113. van Creveld, *The Sword and the Olive*, 245.

114. Shazly, *The Crossing of the Suez*, 213.

115. Shalev, *Israel's Intelligence Assessment before the Yom Kippur War*, 68.

116. Adan, *On the Banks of the Suez*, 73–86.

117. Gawrych, "The 1973 Arab-Israeli War: The Albatross of Decisive Victory," 75.

118. David Chandler, *Waterloo: The Hundred Days* (London: Osprey, 1997), 193.

119. Cordesman and Wagner, *The Lessons of Modern War*, 111.

120. Avigdor Kahalani, *The Heights of Courage: A Tank Leader's War on the Golan* (London: Greenwood Press, 1984), 37.

121. van Creveld, *The Sword and the Olive*, 255–69.

122. Cordesman and Wagner, *The Lessons of Modern War*, 103.

123. "The Israel Defence Force: Taking Wing. Israel's Armed Forces Are Shifting Emphasis from Mechanized Warfare Toward Air and Cyber Power," *The Economist*, 10 August 2013, 11.

124. Barbara Opall-Rome, "Israel Air Force Plan Shoots for 10-Fold Boost in Bombs on Target," *Defense News*, 28 October 2013, 3.

125. For an examination of Israel's operations in Lebanon and Gaza, see Benjamin S. Lambeth, "Israel's War in Gaza: A Paradigm of Effective Military Learning and Adaptation," *International Security* 37, no. 2 (Fall 2012): 81–118.

126. Eitan Shamir, "The 2014 Gaza War: Rethinking Operation Protective Edge," *Middle East Quarterly* (Spring 2015): 1–12.

127. Colum Lynch, "With Violence Surging in Israel, Washington Retreats from new Diplomatic Push at Turtle Bay," *Foreign Policy*, 23 October 2015.

128. Efraim Inbar, "Turkey's Changing Foreign Policy and Its International Ramifications," Foreign Policy Research Institute, Philadelphia, PA, 22 February 2011.

129. Landon Thomas Jr., "Turning East, Turkey Asserts New Economic Power," *New York Times*, 5 July 2010. The Turkish spokesman was quoted as saying, "Adding a defense industry dimension to their ties would augment the Turkish-Saudi alliance against Iran." The Turkish army has 720 German-made Leopard 1 and 2 tanks, 930 American M-60s, and 1,370 M-48s, most of which are Cold War–era tanks that need replacement. In a war, the Turks can field armies manned by disciplined and determined fighters, something the Arabs cannot do. The Sunni Arab Islamists would support the Turks in any confrontation with Israel.

130. Henri J. Barkey, "Erdogan's Great Losing Gamble," *The American Interest*, 11 September 2015.

131. Mustafa Akyol, "What Turned Erdogan Against the West?" *Al Monitor*, 2 February 2015, 1.

132. Wright, *A Study of War*, 1281.

133. De Atkine, "Why Arabs Lose Wars," 124.

CHAPTER 5. LOST VICTORY

1. In his book, *Ally to Adversary: An Eyewitness Account of Iraq's Fall from Grace* (Annapolis, MD: Naval Institute Press, 1999), intelligence officer Rick Francona suggests the Bush administration manipulated Saddam Hussein into believing that his invasion of Kuwait would provoke no more

than a public scolding from Washington, DC. After the Iran-Iraq war ended, Saddam Hussein's Iraq presented a serious threat to the peninsula Arabs and Israel. This is not implausible, but evidence to support the allegation in the form of documents and testimony has not come to light.

2. Michael Gordon, "1991 Victory over Iraq Was Swift, but Hardly Flawless," *New York Times*, 31 December 2012, A3.

3. Norman Schwarzkopf with Peter Petre, *It Doesn't Take a Hero* (New York: Bantam Books, 1993), 445.

4. Bernard E. Trainor and Michael Gordon, *The Generals' War: The Inside Story of the Conflict in the Gulf* (New York: Little, Brown and Company, 1995), 432.

5. Eighty-eight American soldiers and Marines were killed in action (KIA). Twenty-eight Americans were killed in Dhahran, Saudi Arabia, by Iraqi theater ballistic missiles. In addition, sixteen British soldiers, two French soldiers, and forty-one Egyptian, Saudi, and Kuwaiti soldiers were KIA. Michael Gordon and Eric Schmitt, "After the War, Much More Armor than U.S. Believed Fled Back to Iraq," *New York Times*, 25 March, 1991.

6. "Gulf War for Supremacy," *Christian Science Monitor*, 14 June 1984, 3.

7. Kevin M. Woods et al., *Saddam's War: An Iraqi Military Perspective of the Iran-Iraq War* (Alexandria, VA: Institute for Defense Analyses, 2009), 17.

8. Elisabeth Bumiller, "Was a Tyrant Prefigured by Baby Saddam?" *New York Times*, 15 May 2004, A5.

9. Olivier Guitta, "The Chirac Doctrine," *Middle East Quarterly* 22, no. 4 (Fall 2005): 43–53.

10. Landes, *The Wealth and Poverty of Nations*, 409. Landes quotes an Arab from the Emirates: "Without the knowledge, this understanding, we [Arabs] are nothing. We import everything. The bricks to make houses, we import. The men who build them, we import. You go to the market, what is there that is made by Arabs? Nothing. It is Chinese, French, American . . . it is not Arab. Is a country rich that cannot make a brick, or a motorcar, or a book? It is not rich, I think."

11. Woods et al., *Saddam's War*, 40.

12. George P. Shultz, *Triumph and Turmoil: My Years as Secretary of State* (New York: Charles Scribner's Sons, 1993). See chapter 1, "World in Turmoil."

13. For a thorough recapitulation of these U.S. policies and their impacts, see Douglas A. Borer, "Inverse Engagement: Lessons from U.S.-Iraq Relations, 1982–1990," *Parameters* 33, no. 2 (Summer 2003).

14. Iraqi forces employed chemical weapons during April 1987 in and around Basra with horrific results.

15. Woods et al., *Saddam's War*, 10.

16. Ibid., 20–21.

17. Ibid., 76.

18. Ibid., 53.

19. De Atkine, "Why Arabs Lose Wars," 124.

20. George W. Gawrych, "The Rock of Gallipoli," in *Studies in Battle Command* (Fort Leavenworth, KS: U.S. Army Command and General Staff College, 1996), 89.

21. Woods et al., *Saddam's War*, 76.

22. Alex Danchev and Dan Keohane, eds., *International Perspectives on the Gulf Conflict, 1990–91* (London: St. Martin's Press, 1994), 59–79.

23. John Mueller, "The Perfect Enemy: Assessing the Gulf War," *Security Studies* 55, no. 1 (Autumn 1995): 77–117, esp. 106.

24. Woods et al., *Saddam's War*, 59.

25. Trainor and Gordon, *The Generals' War*, 371.

26. Stephen A. Bourque, *Jayhawk! The VII Corps in the Persian Gulf* (Washington, DC: Department of the Army, 2002), 303.

27. Diane Putney, *Airpower Advantage: Planning the Gulf War Air Campaign, 1989–1991* (Washington, DC: U.S. Air Force History and Museums Program, 2004), 25–26.

28. President George H. W. Bush, address to the nation on the invasion of Iraq, 16 January 1991.

29. Michael T. Hayes, "The Republican Road Not Taken: The Foreign-Policy Vision of Robert Taft," *The Independent Review* 8, no. 4 (Spring 2004): 509–25.

30. George H. W. Bush and Brent Scowcroft, *A World Transformed* (New York: Vintage Books, 1999), 473.

31. Thomas A. Kearney and Eliot Cohen, *Gulf War Air Power Survey Summary Report* (Washington, DC: U.S. Department of the Air Force, 22 December 1993), 8.

32. Schwarzkopf with Petre, *It Doesn't Take a Hero*, 427.

33. Trainor and Gordon, *The Generals' War*, 300–2.

34. David E. Johnson, *Learning Large Lessons: The Evolving Roles of Ground Power and Air Power in the Post–Cold War Era* (Santa Monica, CA: RAND Project Air Force, 2007), 45.

35. Anne W. Chapman, "The Army's Training Revolution, 1973–1990, An Overview" (Fort Monroe, VA: Office of the Command Historian, Training and Doctrine Command, 1994).

36. John Sloan Brown, *Kevlar Legions: The Transformation of the U.S. Army, 1989–2005* (Washington, DC: U.S. Army Center for Military History, 2011), 38.

37. TRADOC Pamphlet 525-5, "U.S. Army Operational Concepts for the AirLand Battle and Corps Operations 1986" (Fort Monroe, VA: Headquarters, U.S. Army Training and Doctrine Command, 25 March 1981).

38. Brown, *Kevlar Legions,* 37.

39. Trainor and Gordon, *The Generals' War,* 154. According to Robert M. Gates, then deputy national security adviser, President Bush made it impossible on 8 November 1990 for Schwarzkopf to refuse to fight: "The White House had been accustomed over the years to the military coming in with very large force requirements for contingency plans. This was clearly partly out of caution, but there was also the perception at times it was to dissuade the President from action."

40. Schwarzkopf with Petre, *It Doesn't Take a Hero,* 383.

41. Ibid., 381–82.

42. U.S. Central Command Operations Order 91–001, 17 January 1991.

43. Schwarzkopf with Petre, *It Doesn't Take a Hero,* 502.

44. Tom Clancy with Fred Franks Jr., *Into the Storm: A Study in Command* (New York: Berkley Books, 1998), ix–xii.

45. Schwarzkopf with Petre, *It Doesn't Take a Hero,* 383.

46. Richard Swain, *Lucky War: Third Army in Desert Storm* (Fort Leavenworth, KS: Combat Studies Institute, 2011), 205.

47. Trainor and Gordon, *The Generals' War,* 304–7.

48. Rick Atkinson, *Crusade: The Untold Story of the Persian Gulf War* (New York: Houghton Mifflin Company, 1993), 212.

49. Ibid., 306.

50. To this number must be added the U.S. Navy's six carrier battle groups with four hundred additional fighters, fighter-bombers, and supporting aircraft. Norman Friedman, *Desert Victory: The War for Kuwait* (Annapolis, MD: Naval Institute Press, 1991), 300–303.

51. Atkinson, *Crusade,* 122–23.

52. Johnson, *Learning Large Lessons,* 35–37.

53. Richard Davis, *Decisive Force: Strategic Bombing in the Gulf War* (Washington, DC: Air Force History and Museums Program, 1996), 17; Heuser, *The Evolution of Strategy,* 343–44.

54. James Adams, *The Next World War: The Warriors and Weapons of the New Battlefields in Cyberspace* (London: Random House, 1998), 33–34.

55. Wild Weasel is a code name given in the U.S. Air Force to any type of aircraft that is equipped with radar-seeking missiles and is tasked with destroying the radars and surface-to-air missile installations of enemy air defense systems.

56. Johnson, *Learning Large Lessons*, 36.

57. Quoted in Heuser, *The Evolution of Strategy*, 343.

58. Richard T. Reynolds, *Heart of the Storm: The Genesis of the Air Campaign Against Iraq* (Maxwell Air Force Base, AL: Air University Press, 1995), 17–21.

59. Heuser, *The Evolution of Strategy*, 344.

60. General Accounting Office, "Operation Desert Storm: Evaluation of the Air Campaign," Report to the Ranking Minority Member, Commerce Committee, House of Representatives (Washington, DC: U.S. Government Printing Office, June 1997), 40, 46.

61. Kearney and Cohen, *Gulf War Air Power Survey Summary Report*, 12.

62. Described in detail to the author by Lt. Gen. David Deptula, USAF, Colonel Warden's deputy in Riyadh during the war. Also, see the Russian Academy of Military Sciences, "Lessons and Conclusions from the War in Iraq" (Moscow: Institute of Military History of the Russian Federation Armed Forces, Foreign Broadcast Information Service, 6 June 2003). On the last page of the translated study, the Russian Academy representatives identify the air forces as the dominant and most important branch of the armed forces.

63. Kearney and Cohen, *Gulf War Air Power Survey Summary Report*, 11.

64. Trainor and Gordon, *The Generals' War*, 283–84.

65. Ibid., 323.

66. Kearney and Cohen, *Gulf War Air Power Survey Summary Report*, 10.

67. Adam B. Siegel, "Scuds Against Al Jubayl?" U.S. Naval Institute *Proceedings* 128/12/1 (December 2002), 31.

68. The postwar Gulf War Air Power Survey concluded that roughly 84,000 Iraqi soldiers were either on leave or had deserted when the air war began. See Kearney and Cohen, *Gulf War Air Power Survey Summary Report*, 12–13.

69. Richard E. Matthews, "Defining the Operational End State: Operation Desert Storm" (master's thesis, School of Advanced Military Studies, Fort Leavenworth, KS, 1996), 23–24.

70. Patrick Sloyan, "U.S. Faced Fewer Iraqis; Casualty Estimates Also Being Lowered," *Newsday*, 24 January 1992. Lieutenant General Horner, who commanded U.S. and allied air forces during Desert Storm, was Sloyan's primary source.

71. Atkinson, *Crusade*, 228.

72. Paul Deichmann, *Spearhead for Blitzkrieg: Luftwaffe Operations in Support of the Army 1939–1945*, ed. Alfred Price (London: Greenhill Books, 1996), 15.

73. Scott W. Conrad, "Moving the Force: Desert Storm and Beyond," McNair Paper 32, Institute for National Strategic Studies, National Defense University, Washington, DC, December 1994.

74. Trainor and Gordon, *The Generals' War*, 362.

75. Bourque, *Jayhawk!*, 303. 73 Easting happened in spite of the regimental and corps commanders' intentions.

76. The 2nd ACR was also reinforced with a brigade of artillery. Even with this additional force, the 2nd ACR could still have easily reached the position it was in on 25 February by the evening of 24 February.

77. Atkinson, *Crusade*, 309; Schwarzkopf with Petre, *It Doesn't Take a Hero*, 527–29.

78. On the evening of 24 February, the courageous men of Cougar Squadron's forward reconnaissance element (6 Bradley fighting vehicles and a mortar section) operating 10 to 12 miles ahead of Cougar Squadron's 1,100-man battle group defeated an Iraqi infantry brigade of roughly 1,400 men in less than 30 minutes. See Douglas Macgregor, *Warrior's Rage: The Great Tank Battle of 73 Easting* (Annapolis, MD: Naval Institute Press, 2009), 77–81.

79. "Translation of Taped conversation with General Hermann Balck, 13 April 1979," 24.

80. Russell Holloway, former sergeant gunner on Cougar Forward, HHT, 2nd Squadron, 2nd Cavalry, as told to the author in an interview for his book *Warrior's Rage*.

81. Schwarzkopf with Petre, *It Doesn't Take a Hero*, 536.

82. From operations log, 2nd Squadron, 2nd Cavalry.

83. Bourque, *Jayhawk!*, 307.

84. George S. Patton Jr., *War as I Knew It* (New York: Bantam Books, Inc., 1979), 382.

85. Lieutenant Michael Hamilton, Scout Platoon leader, Eagle Troop, after the battle. Mine fields were also scattered across the desert from PT 698021 to PT 685000.

86. Vince Crawley, "Ghost Troop's Battle of the 73 Easting," *Armor Magazine*, May-June 1991, 8.

87. Supporting historical data for the paragraphs that follow can be found in Michael D. Krause, *The Battle of 73 Easting, 26 February 1991: A Historical Introduction to a Simulation* (Washington, DC: U.S. Army Center for Military History and the Defense Advanced Research Projects Agency, 27 August 1991); J. R. Crooks et al., *73 Easting Re-Creation Data Book*, IEI Report No. DA-MDA972-1-92 (Westlake, CA: Illusion Engineering, Inc., 1992), appendices, shooting history by vehicle for Eagle and Ghost Troops; "The Battle of 73 Easting," briefing slides prepared by Janus Gaming Division, TRADOC Analysis Command, White Sands, NM, 30 March 1992.

88. Krause, *The Battle of 73 Easting, 26 February 1991*, 32–57, which treats the key events described in this section in greater detail. The numbers of enemy tanks and fighting vehicles destroyed became the subject of a dispute after the battle when some of the Iraqi tanks and troops attacked and destroyed by Eagle Troop were subsequently credited to Iron Troop, which was part of 3rd Squadron, 2nd Armored Cavalry Regiment. Iron Troop moved forward in darkness 40 minutes after Cougar Squadron was already established along the 73 Easting. Subsequently, Iron Troop fell back behind the 70 Easting. Physical inspection of the destroyed Iraqi armor by the author and the Eagle Troop commander after the cease-fire was declared showed that the Iraqi tanks had been shot twice from different angles. Also see Bourque, *Jayhawk!*, 328. Iron Troop's actions, as well as its prewar training, had nothing to do with the action fought by Cougar Squadron. For this reason, Iron Troop's activities on 26 February 1991 are not a subject for discussion in this chapter.

89. Ibid., 16, 17.

90. Taken from 2nd Squadron's After Action Report.

91. The tank platoon's fight seems to have occurred from PT 690030 to PT 695001. Center of mass for the company-sized strong point of three tanks and thirteen BMPs plus one hundred or more infantry was PU 7380800. See Krause, *The Battle of 73 Easting, 26 February 1991*, 18, 21.

92. Vince Crawley, "Death by Death, Minute by Minute, Ghost Troop's Fight in the Battle of 73 Easting," *Stars and Stripes*, 9 March 1991.

93. Daniel Davis, "Artillerymen in Action—The 2nd ACR at the Battle of 73 Easting," *Artillery Journal*, February 1992.

94. As explained to the author on site by the Iraqi brigade commander, a veteran of the Iran-Iraq war and instructional courses at the U.S. Army Infantry School at Fort Benning, Georgia.

95. As it turned out, the Iraqi tank guns were oriented 10–20 degrees to Cougar Squadron's right on the road leading out of Kuwait northeast toward Iraq. This was the direction from which the captured Iraqi Republican Guard brigade commander said the American attack was expected. The Iraqi tanks' orientation on the road gave the cavalrymen attacking out of the desert time to shoot on the move before the Iraqi tank crews could swing their gun tubes toward Cougar Squadron.

96. Bourque, *Jayhawk!*, 329.

97. "Translation of Taped Conversation with General Hermann Balck, 13 April 1979," 30–31.

98. Eric Nordlinger, *Isolationism Reconfigured* (Princeton: Princeton University Press, 1995), 272.

99. Jason Embry, "Uprising in Iraq May Be Slow because of U.S. Inaction in 1991," *Seattle Intelligencer*, 4 April 2003, 2.

100. Thomas Houlahan, *Gulf War: The Complete History* (New London, NH: Schrenker Military Publishing, 1999), 423.

101. Atkinson, *Crusade*, 274.

102. Moshe Arens quoted in the *International Herald Tribune*, 29 August 1990.

103. Angelo Codevilla, *Advice to War Presidents* (New York: Basic Books, 2009), 107.

104. Johnson, *Learning Large Lessons*, 42–44.

105. Grant T. Hammond, "Paths to Extinction: The U.S. Air Force in 2025," in *Air Force 2025* (Maxwell Air Force Base, AL: Air University, August 1996), 13–14.

106. Johnson, *Learning Large Lessons*, 46.

107. William A. Owens, "The Emerging U.S. System-of-Systems," Strategic Forum 63, Institute for National Strategic Studies, National Defense University, Washington, DC, February 1996.

108. Victor Davis Hanson, *Carnage and Culture: Landmark Battles in the Rise to Western Power* (New York: First Anchor Books, 2001). Hanson recreates nine "landmark" battles fought between the West and the non-European world.

109. Mueller, "The Perfect Enemy," 106.

110. James Blackwell, *Thunder in the Desert: The Strategy and Tactics of the Persian Gulf War* (New York: Bantam, 1991), 220–23.

111. Although 95 percent of U.S. military equipment, ammunition, and supplies were moved by ship, U.S. aircraft moved more than 500,000 troops and 543,548 tons of cargo to the Persian Gulf. See *Gulf War Air Power Survey*, vol. 5 (Washington, DC: U.S. Government Printing Office, 1993), 76.

112. Peter Turnley, "Special Report: The Day We Stopped the War," *Newsweek*, 20 January 1992, 18.

113. Schwarzkopf with Petre, *It Doesn't Take a Hero*, 556.

114. Buster Glosson, *New Perspectives on Effects-Based Operations: Annotated Briefing* (Alexandria, VA: The Joint Advanced Warfighting Program of the Institute for Defense Analyses, 2001).

115. Peter Wilson and Jon Grossman, "Whither Airborne and Air Assault Capabilities?" RAND Annotated Briefing, AB-445-A (Santa Monica, CA: RAND Arroyo Center, November 2000), 15.

116. Patrick Coffey, *American Arsenal: A Century of Waging War* (New York: Oxford University Press, 2014), 273.

117. Wavell, *The Good Soldier*, 155.

118. G. F. R. Henderson, *Stonewall Jackson and the American Civil War* (New York: Da Capo Press, 1988), 689.

119. Trainor and Gordon, *The Generals' War*, 432.

120. David Adams, "We Are Not Invincible," U.S. Naval Institute *Proceedings* 123/5/1 (May 1997).

121. Bill Sweetman, "Contractors Dispute F-35 Cost Report," *AviationWeek.com*, 30 December 2013. Also see Colin Clark, "F-35's ALIS 'Way Behind,' Bogdan Says; One Step Forward Last Week," *BreakingDefense.com*, 25 February 2014.

CONCLUSION

1. David Steele, *Lord Salisbury—A Political Biography* (New York: Routledge, 1999), 121.

2. This phrase is from Peter Paret's translation of Gerhard Ritter's *Frederick the Great* (Berkeley: University of California Press, 1968), 73. Ritter challenges Friedrich Nietzsche's assertion that rationality subverts decisive action.

3. Nedialkov, *In the Skies of Nomonhan*, 140–41.

4. Coox, *Nomonhan: Japan Against Russia, 1939*, 84. The battle, also known as the Battle of Khalkha River, took place between the cities of Nuren Obo and Nomonhan. In a small area of one hundred kilometers by thirty kilometers, the largest and most costly defeat for the Kwantung Army by the Soviets until August 1945 occurred. Japan was outmatched, having about half the troops, almost one-fifth of the aircraft, and one-tenth of the tanks as the Soviets.

5. Barry A. Leach, "Halder," in *Hitler's Generals: Authoritative Portraits of the Men Who Waged Hitler's War*, ed. Correlli Barnett (New York: Quill/William Morrow, 1989), 114–15.

6. Balck, *Order in Chaos*, 221–22.

7. Diedrich, *Paulus*, 162.

8. For a thorough examination of German culture as it applies to combat effectiveness, see Martin van Creveld, *Fighting Power: A Comparative Study of the German and American Armies in World War II* (Westport, CT: Greenwood Press, 1982). Also see Joerg Muth, *Command Culture: Officer Education in the U.S. Army and the German Armed Forces, 1901–1940, and the Consequences for World War II* (Denton: University of North Texas Press, 2011).

9. Speer, *Inside the Third Reich, Memoirs*, 465.

10. Megargee, *Inside Hitler's High Command*, xiii.

11. Guderian, *Erinnerungen eines Soldaten*, 270–71.

12. Codevilla, *Advice to War Presidents*, 230.

13. Greg Grant, "Iran, Through Iraqi Eyes," *DoDBuzz.com*, 8 June 2009.

14. Heuser, *The Evolution of Strategy*, 478.

15. Alfred Vagts, *A History of Militarism: Civilian and Military*, rev. ed. (Toronto: Meridian Books, 1937), 474.

16. Kevin Phillips, *1775: A Good Year for Revolution* (New York: Penguin Books, 2012), 58–59.

17. For more on the impact of English-speaking culture and institutions on American thinking about national defense, see Richard Kohn, *Eagle and Sword: The Federalists and the Creation of the Military Establishment in America, 1783–1802* (New York: Free Press, 1975); Garry Wills, *A Necessary Evil: A History of American Distrust of Government* (New York: Simon and Schuster, 1999); and Jane A. Mills, ed., *Cromwell's Legacy* (Manchester, UK: Manchester University Press, 2012).

18. W. F. Kiernan, *Defense Will Not Win the War* (Boston: Little, Brown and Company, 1942), 7.

19. "Dempsey's Message on Women in Combat: Trust Transcends Gender," *Defense One*, 28 January 2014.

20. Heuser, *The Evolution of Strategy*, 499.

21. Peter F. Drucker, *The New Realities in Government and Politics/In Economics and Business/In Society and World View* (New York: Harper Business, 1994), 173–74.

22. Chandler, *Waterloo*, 43.

23. Robert L. Cantrell, *Outpacing the Competition: Patent-Based Business Strategy* (New York: John Wiley and Sons, Inc., 2009), 260–61.

24. Karl Heinz Golla, *The German Fallschirmtruppe 1936–1941: Its Genesis and Employment in the First Campaigns of the Wehrmacht* (Lexington: University Press of Kentucky, 2012). Because of the heavy casualties German airborne forces suffered on Crete, Adolf Hitler refused to consider any more large-scale airborne operations for the duration of the war.

25. Robert S. Cameron, *Mobility, Shock, and Firepower: The Emergence of the U.S. Army's Armor Branch, 1917–1945* (Washington, DC: U.S. Army Center for Military History, 2008). Cameron provides hundreds of pages of detailed research validating this point.

26. Alvin Toffler and Heidi Toffler, *War and Anti-War: Survival at the Dawn of the Twenty-First Century* (Boston: Little, Brown and Company, 1993), 77.

27. Walter Pincus, "Pentagon Officials: Spending Is Bloated. Senate Panel Is Told About Need to Reduce Costs," *Washington Post*, 29 September 2010, 1.

28. Lou Pritchett, *Stop Paddling and Start Rocking the Boat: Business Lessons from the School of Hard Knocks* (New York: HarperCollins, 1995), 160.

29. Balck, *Order in Chaos*, 448.

30. Barry Rosenberg, "Command Conversation: Maj. Gen. John N. T. Shanahan, Air Force ISR Agency," *C4ISRNet.com*, 2 December 2013.

31. Sydney Freedberg, "Three Truths, Four Fallacies," *BreakingDefense.com*, 24 February 2014. Lt. Gen. H. R. McMaster (director, Army Capabilities Integration Center) argues for continued entanglement in these tragic regions on the grounds that what happens there actually matters to the American people, when there is no evidence it does. For a different perspective, see Coleen Rowley, "Calls for U.S. Military Intervention in Syria Resurfacing," *Original.AntiWar.com*, 25 February 2014.

32. John J. McGrath, "The Other End of the Spear: The Tooth to Tail Ratio (T3R) in Modern Military Operations," The Long War Series Occasional Paper 23, Combat Studies Institute, Fort Leavenworth, KS, June 2012.

33. Phillip Karber, "Net Assessment for SecDef: Future Implications from Early Formulations," *Potomac Papers* 13, no. 2 (February 5, 2014), 8.

34. David Stevenson, *Cataclysm: The First World War as Political Tragedy* (New York: Basic Books, 2004), 485.

35. Ferguson, *The Pity of War*, 395–432.

36. Fareed Zakaria, *The Post-American World* (New York: W. W. Norton and Co., 2008), 241.

37. Steve Clemons, "Japan Knew that Biden Would Go Soft on China," *The Atlantic*, 5 December 2013.

38. Linda Jakobson, "How Involved Is Xi Jinping in the Diaoyu Crisis?" *The Diplomat*, 9 February 2013. Japanese financial institutions and interests in Southeast Asia are beginning to rival China's, especially as wages rise and Chinese products become less competitive with higher quality Japanese products.

39. Edward Luttwak, *The Rise of China Versus the Logic of Strategy* (Cambridge: Harvard University Press, 2012), 89.

40. Kenchō Suematsu, *The Risen Sun* (London: Archibald Constable and Co., 1905), 269–70.

41. Gopal Ratnam, "Obama's 'Paper Tiger' Pentagon Budget Spends Five Times China," *Bloomberg.com*, 22 May 2012. Also see, "Bank of America advises China default contracts to hedge debt storm: Chinese bond yields have already risen to the highest in a decade yet markets remain 'complacent' about the implications," *The Telegraph*, 16 December 2013, 1.

42. "Japan-ASEAN Draft Implies China's New ADIZ Is a Security Threat," *Japan Times*, 6 December 2013.

43. Salvatore Babones, "Why China's Massive Military Buildup Is Doomed," *NationalInterest.org*, 5 August 2015.

44. Nanae Kurashige, "Ex-Producer Accuses Chinese State-Run TV of Hiding 'Truths'," *The Asahi Shimbun*, 4 December 2013.

45. Jon Harper, "Chinese Warship Nearly Collided with USS Cowpens," *Stars and Stripes*, 13 December 2013, 1.

46. Heather Timmons, "U.S. Calls China's New South China Sea Defense Zone Potentially Dangerous," *DefenseNews.com*, 13 January 2013.

47. Bradley Perrett, "China Uses ADIZ as Part of Buffer-Building Strategy," *AviationWeek.com*, 9 December 2013.

48. Kenneth B. Pyle, *Japan Rising: The Resurgence of Japanese Power and Purpose* (New York: Public Affairs, 2007), 15.

49. Nanae Kurashige and Yoshihiro Makino, "Japan Baffled by U.S. Telling Airlines to Respect New Chinese Air Zone," *The Asahi Shimbun*, 1 December 2013.

50. Americans forget that much of the tension at sea began when Japan nationalized the Senkakus, a matter that was shelved in 1972 by then–prime minister Tanaka Kakuei.

51. William T. Bowers, *Combat in Korea: Striking Back March-April, 1951* (Lexington: University Press of Kentucky, 2010), 3–5.

52. The threat to pro-U.S. governments in the United States' "near abroad" countries is more likely to be from narco-trafficking insurgents than from a conventional power. However, such forces should not be committed to Eurasia, Africa, or the western Pacific.

53. Mark E. Redden and Michael P. Hughes, "Global Commons and Domain Interrelationships: Time for a New Conceptual Framework?" *Strategic Forum* 259 (Washington, DC: Institute of Strategic Studies, National Defense University, October 2010), 2.

54. Walter A. McDougall, *Promised Land, Crusader State: The American Encounter with the World Since 1776* (New York: Houghton Mifflin Company, 1997), 37.

55. Samuel Abrams, "States, Societies, Resistance and COIN," *Military Review* (January-February 2014), 37–41.

56. Michael Brenner, "Afghanistan—Parting Is Such Sweet Sorrow," *Huffington Post*, 25 November 2013.

57. Scott Gebicke and Samuel Magid, "Lessons from Around the World: Benchmarking Performance in Defense," in *McKinsey on Government* (Pittsburgh, PA: McKinsey and Co., Spring 2010), 12–13. In addition, national militaries that centralize formerly duplicative, single-service support functions including human resources, information technology, finance, media and communications, health services, and facilities management achieve substantial monetary savings.

58. Wright, *A Study of War*, 1281.

59. Wayne P. Hughes Jr., *Fleet Tactics: Theory and Practice* (Annapolis, MD: Naval Institute Press, 1986), 87–89.

60. J. Randy Forbes, "America's Pacific Air-Sea Battle Vision," *The Diplomat–Blogs*, 8 March 2012.

61. David Goldfein, "Document: Air Sea Battle Name Change Memo," *U.S. Naval Institute News*, 8 January 2015.

62. Christopher J. Castelli, "War Game Identifies Potential Need for Senior Cyberwar Commanders," *InsideDefense.com*, 22 November 2013.

63. The term "overhead" as used here is synonymous with orbital space, and most space collectors perform reconnaissance because they are in low Earth orbits that severely limit dwell time or because of aiming or bandwidth limitations. Most surveillance "from above" is airborne rather than orbital.

64. Burak Ege Bekdil, "For Turkey, Precision is Maximum Lethality, Minimum Cost," *Defense News*, 21 January 2014, 1. For another example, see how the Chinese counter U.S. military strength in "asymmetric" ways. Instead of trying to match the Air Force's deep strike capabilities, they built a very large, diverse, and reliable range of conventional ballistic missiles for deep precision strike. Instead of trying to match the U.S. ability to develop and operate advanced aircraft, they invest in technologies or entire aircraft and adapt them to their own needs and complement them with similarly obtained advanced surface-to-air missiles. Instead of trying to match Navy aircraft carriers, they are building long-range conventionally armed ballistic missile systems designed to attack those carriers and are deploying a network of sensor systems to target them.

65. Thomas Rid, *Cyber War Will Not Take Place* (New York: Oxford University Press, 2013), 10–13.

66. Brendan Sasso, "NSA Director to Retain Cyber War Powers," *The Hill*, 13 December 2013.

67. "Interview with U.S. Retired Generals Gavin and Doolittle," *TIME*, 23 December 1957, 28.

68. Pete Chiarelli, "Beyond Goldwater-Nichols," *Joint Force Quarterly* 2 (Autumn 1993): 71.

69. James R. Locher III, "The Goldwater Nichols Reorganization Act. Has It Worked?" *Naval War College Review* 54, no. 4 (Autumn 2001): 110–14.

70. Ray S. Cline and Maurice Matloff, "Development of War Department Views on Unification," *Military Affairs* 13, no. 2 (1949), 67.

71. Walter A. McDougall, "Can the United States Do Grand Strategy?" *The Telegram*, no. 3 (April 2010). McDougall provides a characteristically brilliant review of the challenges and intricacies inherent in formulating national strategy.

72. Robert Scheer, "The Super Bowl of War: Three Decades of Failure in Afghanistan," *TruthDig.com*, 3 February 2014.

73. Bill Eisel, "An American General Staff: An Idea Whose Time Has Come?" monograph, U.S. Army School for Advanced Military Studies, 14 May 1993.

74. The Russians have recently disbanded their division-based structure and embraced the structure outlined in the author's 1997 book. See Macgregor, *Breaking the Phalanx: A New Design for Landpower* (Westport, CT: Praeger, 1997); Mikhail Barabanov, "Military Reform: Toward the New Look of the Russian Army," *Valdaiclub.com*, July 2012.

75. Kenneth Macksey, *Kesselring: German Master Strategist of the Second World War* (London: Greenhill Books, 1996), 201.

76. Meir Finkel, *On Flexibility: Recovery from Technological and Doctrinal Surprise on the Battlefield*, trans. Moshe Tlamim (Stanford: Stanford University Press, 2011), 185.

77. The entire premise of Air-Sea Battle rests upon the maintenance of secure lines of communications stretching from the United States to the western Pacific.

78. Barry Watts, "Precision Strike: An Evolution," *NationalInterest.org*, 2 November 2013.

79. Conrad, "Moving the Force: Desert Storm and Beyond."

80. Quoted by van Creveld in *The Sword and the Olive*, 199.

81. Winston Churchill, quoted by Hayward in *Churchill on Leadership*, 28.

82. Thomas A. Schweich, "The Pentagon is Muscling in Everywhere. It's Time to Stop the Mission Creep," *Washington Post*, 21 December 2008, B1.

83. Scot J. Paltrow, "Why the Pentagon's Many Campaigns to Clean Up Its Accounts Are Failing," Reuters, 23 December 2014. Also see Tom Vanden Brook, "4 Stars for Hire: Pentagon to Give Info on Mentors," *USA Today*, 13 August 2010, 5; Nathan Hodge, "How the Afghan Surge Was Sold," *Wired.com*, 3 December 2009.

84. Quoted by Haninah Levine in "The Army Still Needs Tanks," *Military .com*, 6 June 2006.

85. Quoted by Leigh Munsil and Austin Wright in "Is Lockheed Martin Too Big to Fail?" *Politico.com*, 12 August 2015.

86. J. Phillip London, "Navy Will Always Be Vital to U.S. Global Strategy," *U-T San Diego*, 8 December 2013, OpEd page.

87. Lara Seligman, "DOD Testers Have Doubts about LHA-6 Survivability, Self-Defense System," *Inside the Navy*, 10 February 2014.

88. Quoted by Richard Fernandez in "Is Amphibious Warfare Obsolete?" *PJMedia.com*, 18 June 2010.

89. Tony Perry and Julian Barnes, "U.S. Rethinks a Marine Corps Specialty: Storming Beaches," *Los Angeles Times*, 21 June 2010, 1.

90. Robert M. Gates, Department of Defense, 6 January 2011.

91. Robert Work and F. C. Hoffman, "Hitting the Beach in the 21st Century," U.S. Naval Institute *Proceedings* 136/11/1 (2010): 293.

92. "ACV 1.1 Clears Joint Requirements Oversight Council, OSD Review," *Inside the Navy*, 23 March 2015.

93. David Axe, "China, Russia Could Make U.S. Stealth Technology Obsolete," *Wired*, 7 June 2011.

94. Sydney Freedberg Jr., "McCain Hammers Navy Nominee on LCS, Audits," *Breaking Defense*, 10 October 2013.

95. "Service Begins Tipping Its Hand on Combat Vehicle Modernization Strategy," *Inside the Army*, 17 August 2015, 1.

96. "Campbell Discusses 3,000 Man BCTs," *Army Times*, 14 January 2013, 14. General John Campbell was vice chief of staff of the U.S. Army. Tony Perry and Julian Barnes, "U.S. Rethinks a Marine Corps Specialty: Storming Beaches. During an Amphibious Assault Exercise at Camp Pendleton, Marines Appear Rusty. They haven't made such a landing since the Korean War—and some leaders wonder whether they will ever do it again," *Los Angeles Times*, 21 June 2010, 1.

97. "A Marine tank struck an improvised explosive device today in Fallujah. The tank was severely damaged and caught fire, but no coalition casualties were reported." "Coalition Forces Attacked in Fallujah," release no. 20070106–03, Multi-National Corps Iraq Public Affairs Office, Camp Victory, Iraq.

98. Erwin Rommel, *The Rommel Papers*, ed. B. H. Liddell-Hart (New York: Da Capo, 1953), 519.

99. "The Pentagon is dismissing proposals to merge some regional warfighting commands and will instead push forward with efforts to shrink the sizes of these headquarters, sources said." See Marcus Weisberger, "U.S. Shelves Combatant Command Proposals," *DefenseNews.com*, 9 February 2014.

100. Megan Eckstein, "Hagel Announces Arctic Strategy to Begin Shaping Investment, Collaboration," *Defense Daily*, 25 November 2013, 1. Former secretary of defense Chuck Hagel's Arctic Strategy provides a more recent example of the problem. Is the strategy designed to secure maritime access, to exploit energy resources, or to compete with Russia for energy resources? The Arctic adds yet another region of interest with

no budget line and no explanation for the military purpose, ways, and means the United States will pursue.

101. Oswald Spengler, *Der Untergang des Abendlandes: Umrisse einer Morphologie der Weltgeschichte*, vol. 1: *Gestalt und Wirklichkeit* (Munich: C. H. Beck'sche Verlagsbuchhandlung, 1923), 29.

102. Chung Min-uck, "Japan's Nuclear Capability Matches U.S.: Chinese Daily," *Korea Times*, 1 January 2014. Also see Colin Freeman, "Saudi Arabia Targeting Iran and Israel with Ballistic Missiles," *The Telegraph*, 10 July 2013; "Ballistic and Cruise Missile Threat," National Air and Space Intelligence Center Report 1031–0985–13 (July 2013).

103. Alex Strick van Linschoten, "Five Things David Petraeus Wants You to Believe," *Current Intelligence*, 22 November 2010.

104. Charles A. Stevenson, *Congress at War: The Politics of Conflict Since 1789* (Washington, DC: Potomac Books, 2007), 79.

105. Matthew Bodner, "Despite Sanctions, Russian Defense Revenues Soaring," *Defense News*, 27 July 2015. 1.

106. Desmond Butler, "Turkish Bombing of Kurds Carries Risk of Instability," Associated Press, 27 July 2015, 1.

107. Leon Trotsky may have borrowed this statement from Lenin. Historians are unsure. It is probable that both men made similar statements. See Robert C. Tucker, ed., *The Lenin Anthology* (New York: W. W. Norton and Co., 1975), liii, note 4.

Selected Bibliography

Adams, James. *The Next World War: The Warriors and Weapons of the New Battlefields in Cyberspace.* London: Random House, 1998.

Adan, Avraham. *On the Banks of the Suez: An Israeli General's Personal Account of the Yom Kippur War.* London: Arms and Armour Press, 1980.

Asher, Dani. *The Egyptian Strategy for the Yom Kippur War.* Jefferson, NC: McFarland and Company, Inc., 2009.

Atkinson, Rick. *Crusade: The Untold Story of the Persian Gulf War.* New York: Houghton Mifflin Company, 1993.

Bailey, J. B. A. *Field Artillery and Firepower.* Annapolis, MD: Naval Institute Press, 2004.

Balck, Hermann. *Order in Chaos: The Memoirs of General of Panzer Troops Hermann Balck.* Edited and translated by David Zabecki and Dieter Biedekarken. Lexington: University Press of Kentucky, 2015.

———. "Translation of Taped Conversation with General Hermann Balck, 12 January 1979." Columbus, OH: Battelle Columbus Laboratories, Tactical Technology Center, January 1979.

———. "Translation of Taped Conversation with General Hermann Balck, 13 April 1979." Columbus, OH: Battelle Columbus Laboratories, Tactical Technology Center, July 1979.

Barabanov, Mikhail. "Military Reform: Toward the New Look of the Russian Army." *Valdaiclub.com,* July 2012.

Bar-Joseph, Uri. *The Watchman Fell Asleep: The Surprise of Yom Kippur and Its Sources.* Albany: State University of New York Press, 2005.

Beevor, Antony. *Stalingrad.* New York: Penguin Books, 1999.

Bix, Herbert P. *Hirohito and the Making of Modern Japan.* New York: Harper-Collins Publishers, 2000.

Blood, Philip W. *Hitler's Bandit Hunters: The SS and the Nazi Occupation of Europe.* Washington, DC: Potomac Books, 2008.

Blumenson, Martin and James L. Stokesbury. *Masters of the Art of Command.* New York: Da Capo Press, 1975.

Bond, Brian. *The Victorian Army and the Staff College 1854–1914*. London: Eyre Methuen, 1972.

Bourque, Stephen A. *Jayhawk! The VII Corps in the Persian Gulf War*. Washington, DC: Department of the Army, 2002.

Brown, John Sloan. *Kevlar Legions: The Transformation of the U.S. Army, 1989–2005*. Washington, DC: U.S. Army Center for Military History, 2011.

Bush, George H. W. and Brent Scowcroft. *A World Transformed*. New York: Vintage Books, 1999.

Citino, Robert. *The German Way of War: From the Thirty Years' War to the Third Reich*. Lawrence: University Press of Kansas, 2005.

———. *Death of the Wehrmacht: The German Campaigns of 1942*. Lawrence: University Press of Kansas, 2007.

Clancy, Tom with Fred Franks Jr. *Into the Storm: A Study in Command*. New York: Berkley Books, 1998.

Clausewitz, Carl von. *On War*. Edited and translated by Michael Howard and Peter Paret. Princeton: Princeton University Press, 1976.

Codevilla, Angelo. *Advice to War Presidents*. New York: Basic Books, 2009.

Conquest, Robert. *The Harvest of Sorrow: Soviet Collectivization and the Terror-Famine*. Oxford: Oxford University Press, 1986.

Conrad, Scott. "Moving the Force: Desert Storm and Beyond." McNair Paper 32. Washington, DC: Institute for National Strategic Studies, National Defense University, December 1994.

Cooper, Matthew. *The German Army, 1933–1945*. Lanham, MD: Scarborough House, 1978.

Coox, Alvin. *Nomonhan: Japan Against Russia, 1939*. Stanford: Stanford University Press, 1985.

Corbett-Smith, Arthur. *The Retreat from Mons*. New York: Nabu Public Domain Imprints, 2013.

Corum, James S. *The Roots of Blitzkrieg: Hans von Seeckt and German Military Reform*. Lawrence: University Press of Kansas, 1992.

Craig, Gordon. *The Battle of Koeniggraetz: Prussia's Victory over Austria, 1866*. Westport, CT: Greenwood Press, 1975.

Creveld, Martin van. *The Sword and the Olive: A Critical History of the Israeli Defense Force*. New York: Public Affairs Press, 2002.

Dallek, Robert. *Nixon and Kissinger: Partners in Power*. New York: HarperCollins Publishers, 2007.

Danchev, Alex and Dan Keohane, eds. *International Perspectives on the Gulf Conflict, 1990–91*. London: St. Martin's Press, 1994.

Davies, Norman. *No Simple Victory: World War II in Europe, 1939–1945*. New York: Viking Penguin, 2007.

Davis, Daniel. "Artillerymen in Action—The 2nd ACR at the Battle of 73 Easting." *Artillery Journal*, February 1992.

Dayan, Moshe. *Moshe Dayan: Story of My Life*. New York: William Morrow and Company, 1976.

De Atkine, Norvell B. "Why Arabs Lose Wars." *Middle East Quarterly* 6, no. 4 (December 1999).

Deichmann, Paul. *Spearhead for Blitzkrieg: Luftwaffe Operations in Support of the Army 1939–1945*. Edited by Alfred Price. London: Greenhill Books, 1996.

Diedrich, Torsten. *Paulus: Das Trauma von Stalingrad: Eine Biographie*. Paderborn: Ferdinand Schoeningh, 2008.

Drea, Edward J. *Japan's Imperial Army: Its Rise and Fall, 1853–1945*. Lawrence: University Press of Kansas, 2009.

Dunlop, John K. *The Development of the British Army 1899–1914*. London: Methuen, 1938.

Dunscomb, Paul E. *Japan's Siberian Intervention, 1918–1922: "A Great Disobedience Against the People."* Plymouth, UK: Lexington Books, 2011.

Edmonds, J. E. *History of the Great War. Military Operations: The Retreat to the Seine, the Marne, and the Aisne, August–October 1914*. Vol. 1. London: MacMillan and Co., 1922.

———. *History of the Great War. Military Operations: France and Belgium 1914*. Vol. 2. London: MacMillan and Co., 1925.

Elleman, Bruce A. *Modern Chinese Warfare, 1795–1989*. London: Routledge Books, 2001.

Elting, John R. *Swords Around a Throne: Napoleon's Grande Armee*. New York: The Free Press, 1988.

Epstein, Julius. *Operation Keelhaul: The Story of Forced Repatriation from June 1946 to the Present*. Old Greenwich, CT: Devin-Adair, 1974.

Epstein, Robert M. *Napoleon's Last Victory and the Emergence of Modern War*. Lawrence: University Press of Kansas, 1994.

Erickson, John. *The Soviet High Command: A Military-Political History, 1918–1941*. New York: St. Martin's Press Inc., 1962.

———. *The Road to Berlin: Stalin's War with Germany*. New Haven: Yale University Press, 1983.

Evans, Richard J. *The Third Reich at War*. New York: The Penguin Press, 2009.

Ferguson, Niall. *The Pity of War: Explaining World War I.* New York: Basic
    Books, 1999.
——. *Empire: The Rise and Demise of the British World Order and the Lessons
    for Global Power.* New York: Basic Books, 2002.
Forbes, J. Randy. "America's Pacific Air-Sea Battle Vision." *The Diplomat—
    Blogs,* 8 March 2012.
French, Sir John. *The Dispatches of Sir John French.* Vol. 1. London: Chapman
    and Hall, Ltd., 1914.
Frieser, Karl-Heinz, ed. "II. Der Zusammenbruch der Heeresgruppe Mitte im
    Sommer 1944." *Die Ostfront 1943/44: Der Krieg im Osten und an den
    Nebenfronten, Das Deutsche Reich und der Zweite Weltkrieg.* Vol. 8.
    Munich: Deutsche Verlags-Anstalt, 2007.
Fromkin, David. *A Peace to End All Peace: The Fall of the Ottoman Empire and
    the Creation of the Modern Middle East.* New York: Henry Holt and
    Company, 1989.
Fuller, J. F. C. *The Army in My Time.* London: Rich and Cowan, 1935.
Gal, Reuven. *A Portrait of the Israeli Soldier.* New York: Greenwood Press, 1986.
Gamasy, Mohamed Abdel Ghani el. *The October War: Memoirs of Field Mar-
    shal El-Gamasy of Egypt.* Translated by Gillian Potter, Nadra Morcos,
    and Rosette Frances. Cairo: The American University in Cairo Press,
    1993.
Gardner, Nikolas. *Trial by Fire: Command and the British Expeditionary Force
    in 1914.* Westport, CT: Praeger Productions, 2003.
Gawrych, George W. "The 1973 Arab-Israeli War: The Albatross of Decisive
    Victory." Leavenworth Paper no. 21. Leavenworth, KS: Combat Studies
    Institute, 1996.
Glantz, David M. *Zhukov's Greatest Defeat: The Red Army's Epic Disaster in
    Operation Mars, 1942.* Lawrence: University Press of Kansas, 1999.
——. *The Soviet Strategic Offensive in Manchuria, 1945: "August Storm."*
    Portland, OR: Frank Cass Publishing: 2003.
——. *Colossus Reborn: The Red Army at War, 1941–1943.* Lawrence: Univer-
    sity Press of Kansas, 2005.
Glazer, Dov E. "Conceptualizing Command and Operations in the Israeli
    Ground Forces, 1936–1966." PhD diss., Bar Ilan University, Tel Aviv,
    February 2011.
Glosson, Buster. *New Perspectives on Effects-Based Operations: Annotated
    Briefing.* Alexandria, VA: The Joint Advanced Warfighting Program of
    the Institute for Defense Analyses, 2001.

Golla, Karl Heinz. *The German Fallschirmtruppe 1936–1941: Its Genesis and Employment in the First Campaigns of the Wehrmacht*. Lexington: University Press of Kentucky, 2012.

Gordon, Michael and Eric Schmitt. "After the War, Much More Armor than U.S. Believed Fled Back to Iraq." *New York Times*, 25 March 1991.

Grant, Ulysses S. *Memoirs of U.S. Grant*. New York: Konecky and Konecky, 1990 (reprint).

Griffith, Paddy. *Battle Tactics of the Western Front: The British Army's Art of Attack 1916–1918*. New Haven, CT: Yale University Press, 1994.

Guderian, Heinz. *Achtung Panzer*. Translated by Christopher Duffy. London: Arms and Armour Press, 1992.

——. *Erinnerungen eines Soldaten*. Stuttgart: Motorbuch Verlag, 1994.

Haldane, Richard Burdon. *Lord Haldane's Autobiography*. London: Hodder and Stoughton, Ltd., 1925.

Hamilton, Nigel. *Monty: The Making of a General, 1877–1942*. Vol. 1. New York: McGraw Hill, 1981.

Harmsen, Peter. *Shanghai 1937: Stalingrad on the Yangtze*. Oxford: Casemate Publishers Haverton, 2013.

Harris, J. P. *Sir Douglas Haig and the First World War*. Cambridge: Cambridge University Press, 2009.

Hart, Peter. *The Great War: A Combat History of the First World War*. Oxford: Oxford University Press, 2013.

——. *Fire and Movement: The British Expeditionary Force and the Campaign of 1914*. New York: Oxford University Press, 2015.

Hayes, Michael T. "The Republican Road Not Taken: The Foreign-Policy Vision of Robert Taft." *The Independent Review* 8, no. 4 (Spring 2004).

Henderson, G. F. R. *Stonewall Jackson and the American Civil War*. New York: Da Capo Press, 1988.

Herzog, Chaim. *The War of Atonement, October 1973*. Boston: Little, Brown and Company, 1975.

Heuser, Beatrice. *The Evolution of Strategy: Thinking War from Antiquity to the Present*. Cambridge: Cambridge University Press, 2010.

Hofmann, George F. *Through Mobility We Conquer: The Mechanization of the U.S. Cavalry*. Lexington: University Press of Kentucky, 2006.

Humphreys, Leonard A. *The Way of the Heavenly Sword: The Japanese Army in the 1920s*. Stanford: Stanford University Press, 1995.

Iwata, Masakazu. *Okubo Toshimichi: The Bismarck of Japan*. London: Cambridge University Press, 1964.

Jahnke, Hermann. *Fuerst Bismarck: Sein Leben und Wirken*. Berlin: Paul Kitte Verlag, 1890.

Johnson, David E. *Learning Large Lessons: The Evolving Roles of Ground Power and Air Power in the Post–Cold War Era*. Santa Monica, CA: RAND Project Air Force, 2007.

Kagan, Donald. *On the Origins of War and the Preservation of Peace*. New York: Doubleday Books, 1995.

Kater, Michael H. *The Nazi Party: A Social Profile of Members and Leaders, 1919–1945*. Cambridge: Harvard University Press, 1983.

Kearney, Thomas A. and Eliot Cohen. *Gulf War Air Power Survey Summary Report*. Washington, DC: U.S. Department of the Air Force, 22 December 1993.

Kennedy, Paul. *The Rise and Fall of the Great Powers: Economic Change and Military Conflict from 1500 to 2000*. New York: Vintage Books, 1989.

Kier, Elizabeth. "Culture and Military Doctrine: France Between the Wars." *International Security* 19, no. 4 (Spring 1995).

Kiernan, W. F. *Defense Will Not Win the War*. Boston: Little, Brown and Company, 1942.

Kirchhubel, Robert. *Hitler's Panzer Armies on the Eastern Front*. Barnsley, UK: Pen and Sword, Ltd., 2009.

Kluck, Alexander von. *The March on Paris and the Battle of the Marne, 1914*. London: Edward Arnold, 1920.

Knox, MacGregor, and Williamson Murray. *The Dynamics of Military Revolution, 1300–2050*. Cambridge: Cambridge University Press, 2001.

Kober, Avi. "From Blitzkrieg To Attrition: Israel's Attrition Strategy and Staying Power." *Small Wars and Insurgencies* 16, no. 2 (June 2005).

Koestring, Ernst, and Hermann Teske. *General Ernst Koestring: Der Militaerische Mittler zwischen dem Deutschen Reich und der Sowjetunion, 1921–1941*. Frankfurt am Main: Verlag E. S. Mittler und Sohn, 1966.

Koettgen, J., trans. *A German Deserter's War Experience*. New York: B. W. Huebsch, 1917.

Koss, Stephen E. *Lord Haldane, Scapegoat for Liberalism*. New York: Columbia University Press, 1969.

Krause, Michael. *The Battle of 73 Easting, 26 February 1991: A Historical Introduction to a Simulation*. Washington, DC: U.S. Army Center for Military History and the Defense Advanced Research Projects Agency, August 1991.

Kunz, Andreas. *Wehrmacht und Niederlage: Die bewaffnete Macht in der End-phase der Nationalsozialistischen Herrschaft.* Munich: Oldenbourg Verlag, 2005.

Landes, David S. *The Wealth and Poverty of Nations: Why Some Are So Rich and Some Are So Poor.* New York: W. W. Norton and Company, 1999.

Large, Stephen. *Emperor Hirohito and Showa Japan: A Political Biography.* New York: Routledge, 1992.

Leonard, Robert R. *Fighting by Minutes: The Time and Art of War.* Westport, CT: Praeger, 1994.

Liddell-Hart, B. H. *Strategy.* 2nd rev. ed. New York: Meridian Press, 1967.

Lloyd George, Robert. *David and Winston: How the Friendship Between Chur-chill and Lloyd George Changed the Course of History.* New York: The Overlook Press, 2005.

Long-hsuen, Hsu and Chang Ming-kai. *History of the Sino-Japanese War (1937–1945).* 2nd ed. Taipei: Chung Wu Publishing Company, 1972.

Luttwak, Edward and Daniel Horowitz. *The Israeli Army, 1948–1973.* Lan-ham, MD: University Press of America, 1983.

Masanobu, Tsuji. *Japan's Greatest Victory, Britain's Greatest Defeat: From the Japanese Perspective: The Capture of Singapore, 1942.* Gloucestershire, UK: Spellmount, 1997.

Massie, Robert K. *Dreadnought: Britain, Germany, and the Coming of the Great War.* New York: Random House, 1991.

McDougall, Walter A. "Can the United States Do Grand Strategy?" *The Tele-gram* no. 3, April 2010.

Megargee, Geoffrey P. *Inside Hitler's High Command.* Lawrence: University Press of Kansas, 2000.

Merridale, Catherine. *Ivan's War: Life and Death in the Red Army, 1939–1945.* New York: Picador, 2006.

Moltke, Helmuth von. *Kriege und Siege.* Berlin: Vier Falken Verlag, 1891.

Moran, Lord. *Churchill at War 1940–1945.* New York: Carroll and Graf Pub-lishers, 2002.

Mueller, John. "The Perfect Enemy: Assessing the Gulf War." *Security Studies* 5, no. 1 (Autumn 1995).

Murland, Jerry. *Retreat and Rearguard 1914: The BEF's Actions from Mons to the Marne.* Barnsley, UK: Pen and Sword, Ltd., 2011.

Murray, Williamson, and Allan R. Millett. *Military Innovation in the Interwar Period.* Cambridge: Cambridge University Press, 1996.

Muth, Joerg. *Command Culture: Officer Education in the U.S. Army and the German Armed Forces, 1901–1940, and the Consequences for World War II*. Denton: University of North Texas Press, 2011.

Nedialkov, Dimitar. *In the Skies of Nomonhan: Japan versus Russia May–September 1939*. Manchester, UK: Crecy Publishing Limited, 2011.

Nordlinger, Eric. *Isolationism Reconfigured*. Princeton: Princeton University Press, 1995.

Overy, R. J. *War and the Economy in the Third Reich*. Oxford: Oxford University Press, 1994.

Pakula, Hannah. *The Last Empress: Madame Chiang Kai-shek and the Birth of Modern China*. New York: Simon and Schuster, 2009.

Palit, D. K. *Return to Sinai: The Arab Offensive 1973*. New Delhi, India: Palit and Palit Publishers, 1974.

Peattie, Mark. *Ishiwara Kanji and Japan's Confrontation with the West*. Princeton: Princeton University Press, 1975.

Pershing, John J. *My Life Before the World War, 1860–1917*. Edited by John T. Greenwood. Lexington: University Press of Kentucky, 2013.

Pleshkov, Constantine. *Stalin's Folly: The Tragic First Ten Days of World War II on the Eastern Front*. Boston: Houghton Mifflin Company, 2005.

Prior, Robin and Trevor Wilson. *Passchendaele: The Untold Story*. New Haven: Yale University Press, 1996.

Rice, Earle. *Claire Chennault: Flying Tiger*. New York: Chelsea House Publishers, 2003.

Rickard, John Nelson. *Advance and Destroy: Patton as Commander in the Bulge*. Lexington: University Press of Kentucky, 2011.

Rid, Thomas. *Cyber War Will Not Take Place*. New York: Oxford University Press, 2013.

Rommel, Erwin. *The Rommel Papers*. Edited by B. H. Liddell-Hart. New York: Da Capo Paperback, 1953.

Rottman, Gordon L. and Takizawa Akira. *World War II Japanese Tank Tactics*. Westminster, UK: Osprey Publishing, 2008.

Sadat, Anwar el. *In Search of Identity: An Autobiography*. New York: Harper and Row Publishers, Inc. 1978.

Schwarzkopf, Norman with Peter Petre. *It Doesn't Take a Hero*. New York: Bantam Books, 1993.

Seaton, Albert. *The German Army, 1933–1945*. New York: St. Martin's Press, 1982.

Shalev, Aryeh. *Israel's Intelligence Assessment Before the Yom Kippur War: Disentangling Deception and Distraction*. Brighton, UK: Sussex Academic Press, 2010.

Shamir, Eitan. *Transforming Command: The Pursuit of Mission Command in the U.S., British, and Israeli Armies*. Stanford: Stanford University Press, 2011.

Shazly, Saad el. *The Crossing of the Suez*. San Francisco: American Mideast Research, 1980.

Shtemenko, S. M. *The Soviet General Staff at War*. Moscow: Progress Publishers, 1970.

Shultz, George P. *Triumph and Turmoil: My Years as Secretary of State*. New York: Charles Scribner's Sons, 1993.

Sinclaire, Clive. *Samurai: The Weapons and Spirit of the Japanese Warrior*. Guilford, CT: The Lyons Press, 2001.

Smith-Dorrien, Sir Horace. *Memories of Forty-Eight Years' Service, The War Times Journal*. Online version, available at www.richthofen.com /smith-dorrien/.

Sommer, Dudley. *Haldane of Cloan: His Life and Times, 1856–1928*. London: George Allen and Unwin Ltd., 1960.

Spang, Christian W. and Rolf-Harald Wippich, eds. *Japanese-German Relations, 1895–1945: War, Diplomacy, and Public Opinion*. London: Routledge, 2006.

Spengler, Oswald. *Der Untergang des Abendlandes: Umrisse einer Morphologie der Weltgeschichte*. Vol. 1, *Gestalt und Wirklichkeit*. Munich: C.H. Beck'sche Verlagsbuchhandlung, 1923.

Spiers, Edward. *Haldane: An Army Reformer*. Edinburgh: Edinburgh University Press, 1980.

Stein, George H. *The Waffen SS: Hitler's Elite Guard at War*. Ithaca: Cornell University Press, 1966.

Stevenson, David. *Cataclysm: The First World War as Political Tragedy*. New York: Basic Books, 2004.

Strick van Linschoten, Alex. "Five Things David Petraeus Wants You to Believe." *Current Intelligence*, 22 November 2010.

Swain, Richard. *Lucky War: Third Army in Desert Storm*. Fort Leavenworth, KS: Combat Studies Institute, 2011.

Teagarden, Ernest M. *Haldane at the War Office: A Study in Organization and Management*. New York: Gordon Press, 1976.

Terraine, John. *Mons: The Retreat to Victory*. Barnsley, England: Pen and Sword, Ltd., 1991.

Toffler, Alvin and Heidi Toffler. *War and Anti-War: Survival at the Dawn of the Twenty-First Century*. Boston: Little, Brown and Company, 1993.

Trainor, Bernard E. and Michael Gordon. *The Generals' War: The Inside Story of the Conflict in the Gulf*. New York: Little, Brown and Company, 1995.

Tsuneo, Watanabe and James E. Auer, eds. *From Marco Polo to Pearl Harbor: Who Was Responsible?* Tokyo: Yomiuri Shimbun, 2006.

Tucker, Spencer C. *The Great War 1914–1918*. Bloomington: Indiana University Press, 1998.

Vagts, Alfred. *A History of Militarism: Civilian and Military*. Rev. ed. Toronto: Meridian Books, 1937.

Warner, Dennis and Peggy Warner. *The Tide at Sunrise: A History of the Russo-Japanese War, 1904–1905*. London: Frank Cass, 1974.

Wilson, Peter and Jon Grossman. "Whither Airborne and Air Assault Capabilities?" RAND Annotated Briefing AB-445-A. Santa Monica, CA: RAND Arroyo Center, November 2000.

Woods, Kevin et al. *Saddam's War: An Iraqi Military Perspective of the Iran-Iraq War*. Alexandria, VA: Institute for Defense Analyses, 2009.

Wright, Quincy. *A Study of War*. 2nd ed. Chicago: University of Chicago Press, 1971.

Zabecki, David T. *Steel Wind: Colonel Georg Bruchmueller and the Birth of Modern Artillery*. Westport, CT: Praeger, 1994.

———, ed. *Chief of Staff: The Principal Officers Behind History's Great Commanders*. Vol. 2, *World War II to Korea and Vietnam*. Annapolis, MD: Naval Institute Press, 2008.

Zakaria, Fareed. *The Post-American World*. New York: W. W. Norton and Company, 2008.

Zaloga, Steve. *Bagration 1944: The Destruction of Army Group Center*. London: Reed Consumer Books, Ltd., 1996.

Zhukov, Georgii. *The Memoirs of Marshal Zhukov*. New York: Delacourt Press, 1971.

Ziemke, Earl F. *Stalingrad to Berlin: The German Defeat in the East*. Washington, DC: U.S. Army Historical Series, 1986.

Zuber, Terence. *The Mons Myth: A Reassessment of the Battle*. Gloucestershire, UK: The History Press, 2010.

Index

Adan, Avraham, 115–16, 119, 121–23, 124–25, 126–27, 129, 227n98

Afghanistan, 2, 195n6, 220n133

Air Force, U.S.: AirLand Battle doctrine, 142; airpower and air supremacy of, 135–36, 140, 145–49, 165, 231n50; Desert Storm fighting by, 136, 170; dominant and importance of air forces, 232n62; integrated, joint force structure, move toward, 165–66, 182–85; integrated communication system for, 146; jointness lessons from Desert Storm, 162; permissive non-contested operations, move from, 174, 191–92; Wild Weasel code name, 146, 232n55

aircraft and airpower: centralized control of airpower, concern about, 146; effectiveness of airpower, 146; German aircraft and colored smoke signal use during Mons battle, 22; German aircraft production, 77–79; German airpower, 75, 76, 81; IJA airpower, xii, 53, 54, 57–58, 66, 68, 209n69; Soviet airpower, 81; Soviet strike forces, 71; stealth aircraft, 163, 191; strategic air warfare, 146–47; U.S. airpower and air supremacy, 135–36, 140, 145–49, 165, 231n50

AirLand Battle doctrine, 142

air-lift capabilities, 187–88

Air-Sea Battle (ASB)/Joint Concept for Access and Maneuver in the Global Commons (JAM-GC), 179–80, 181, 242n77

Allenby, Edmund, 27, 29, 31, 36–37

amphibious operations, 190–91, 243n97

Antonov, Aleksei, 84–85, 87

Arctic Strategy, 243–44n100

Armed Forces, U.S.: AirLand Battle doctrine, 142; attitudes toward military power and capabilities of, 4–5; capabilities of, xiii, 4; Cold War investment in training, wisdom of, 163–64, 170; command structure and unity of effort, 170–71, 182–85; defense budget spending on, 177, 189–93, 243n96, 243–244n100; Defense Condition (DEF-CON) level and Yom Kippur War cease-

fire negotiations, 128; defense spending, decisions about, 189–93, 243–44n100, 243n96; downsizing of, 3–4; force structures and institutions to fight future wars of decision, 3–4, 196n16; forces-in-being, 4, 178–80, 240n57; industrial-age military, xiii; industrial-age military, move beyond, 136, 165–66; integrated, joint force structure, importance of, 5; integrated, joint force structure, move toward, 136, 165–66, 182–85, 192–93, 243n99; integrated communication system for, 146; interservice rivalry and competition, 5, 189–93; jointness lessons from Desert Storm, 162; military failure and encouragement of further aggression, 5; military power of, demonstration of superiority of, 163–64, 236n111; military-technology edge of U.S., 4; operational flexibility of, 4; organization of, xiii; permissive non-contested operations, move from, 174, 191–92; reform of and new thinking and organizations, 5–6; single-service modernization programs, 165–66; size of, xiii, 4; strategic military thinking and force design, 171–74; sustainment and strategic lift capabilities, 187–88, 242n77; unity of effort across service lines, 165–66, 170–71

Army, U.S.: airborne/airmobile forces, 191–92; AirLand Battle doctrine, 142; artillery equipment and capabilities, 142; capabilities of, 4–5; centralized control of airpower, concern about, 146; defense spending on, 177, 191–92; Desert Storm fighting by, 136, 170; force strength for Desert Storm, 142–46, 165, 231n39; ground forces, importance of, 5; ground maneuver forces, reshaping of, 185–87; importance of powerful, standing, professional, 5, 177; integrated, joint force structure, move toward, 165–66, 182–85; jointness lessons from Desert Storm, 162; light infantry-centric forces, 191–92; mission of, 177, 240n52; modern warfare,

Egyptian command structure and decision process, 119–20; Egyptian defensive positions on eastern bank, 101, 106; Egyptian losses and casualties, 101, 109, 114, 123–24, 125, 130, 222n14; Egyptian offensive from bridgeheads, 109; Egyptian pincer attack, 124–25; Egyptian plans for Badr operation, xii, 103–8, 223n29; Egyptian response to Israeli forces on west side of canal, 119–20; flammable liquid storage points along, remote ignition of, 104; force strength of Egyptian forces, 101, 108–9; helicopter use during, 117; holding ground operations of Israelis, 114, 115; Israeli attacks on Egyptian forces, 101, 113–14; Israeli barriers and defensive positions along canal, 104; Israeli breakout operations, 124–26; Israeli counterattack across canal (Operation Valiant), 101–2, 114–24; Israeli losses and casualties, 101, 109, 119, 123, 125, 127, 130, 222n14; Israeli occupation of right bank of, 100, 221n4; Israeli paratrooper operations, 115, 116, 117–19, 121–23, 127; Matzmed as crossing location, 116–17, 123; reconnaissance by Brom and information about Egyptian troops, 115, 225–26n70; success of and false sense of confidence of Israel, 106–7; success of plan, 108; surprise element of operation, 101, 104, 108; water cannons to blast openings in canal berms, xii–xiii, 106
Suez City, advance on and seizure of, 126–27
Sunni forces: Middle East conflicts, role in, 132–33, 228n129; potential for war of decision and, 193–94
Syria: Golan Heights, attack to seize, 105; Middle East conflicts, role in, 132–33; pressure on armed forces and Yom Kippur War, 109; Russian move into, 132; Six Day War, 100, 221nn4–5

tactics: battle management tools, 164; BEF tactical weaknesses, 36–37, 202n107; changes in Israeli military tactics, 101–2; decisions from distant rear of battle about what is going on in front, 121; firepower use instead of, 9; German tactical fighting power, xii, 72, 97; new facts and changes in, 38; written orders and decisions about, 21
Taiwan (Formosa), 69, 176
Tamari, Dovik, 123
Tanaka Giichi, 46

Tanggu truce, 48–49
tanks: Desert Storm ground offensive operations, 135–36, 147, 149–61, 233n78, 234n88, 234n91, 235n95; German tanks and armored vehicles, 72, 75, 77–78, 81, 88, 89–91, 95; IJA use of, xii, 63, 67, 210n96, 211n109; Iraqi tanks, 139; JGSDF use of, 69; Soviet use and strategy for use of, 81–82, 86, 95–96; U.S. use of, 142
technology: Cold War investment in, wisdom of, 163–64, 170; GPS (global positioning system), 153, 163, 180; Japanese margin of victory for future wars and, 69; military-technology edge of U.S., 4; space-based assets, 163, 181, 241n63; strategy, technology, military organization, and outcome of war, 4, 171
Tibet, 175
Trotsky, Leon, 80, 137, 194, 244n107
Truman, Harry S., 4
Turkey, 132–33, 228n129

Ugaki Kazushige, 44–48, 63, 68, 69, 168, 205n19, 205n28, 206n35, 206n45
Ukraine: collectivization system and starvation in, 80, 215–16n52; deception plan to keep German troops in, 87, 88; events in and potential for future war, 3; potential for war of decision in, 193; threat to from Russian forces, 5
United States (U.S.): casualties of wars and interventions, 2–3, 195n6; culture, values, and military power of, 170–71; defense budget decisions, 177, 189–93, 243n96, 243–44n100; global policemen role to impose democratic order, 177–78, 188; industrialization model of, 43; lend-lease program, 70–71, 83–84; local conflicts, avoidance of involvement in, 177–78; margin of victory of, 5–6, 193–94; military failure and encouragement of further aggression, 5; military power of, 135, 173–75, 238n31; military-technology edge of, 4; political and economic status of, 3; strategic interests of, defense of, 3; strategic partnerships and relationships of, 3; World War I entrance by, 2, 38; Yom Kippur War cease-fire proposal and negotiations, 126, 127–29, 133

V-22 Osprey aircraft, 191
Vasilevskiy, Aleksandr, 84, 86, 92
Victoria Cross, 23

About the Author

Col. Douglas Macgregor, USA (Ret.), is a decorated combat veteran and the author of five books. He holds a PhD and is the executive vice president of Burke-Macgregor Group LLC, a defense and foreign policy consulting firm in Northern Virginia.